GENDERING BORDER STUDIES

Gender Studies in Wales
Astudiaethau Rhywedd yng Nghymru

The aim of this series is to fill a current gap in knowledge. As a number of historians, sociologists and literary critics have for some time been pointing out, there is a dearth of published research on the characteristics and effects of gender difference in Wales, both as it affected lives in the past and as it continues to shape present-day experience. Socially constructed concepts of masculine and feminine difference influence every aspect of individuals' lives; experiences in employment, in education, in culture and politics, as well as in personal relationships, are all shaped by them. Ethnic identities are also gendered; a country's history affects its concepts of gender difference so that what is seen as appropriately 'masculine' or 'feminine' varies within different cultures. What is needed in the Welsh context is more detailed research on the ways in which gender difference has operated and continues to operate within Welsh societies. Accordingly, this interdisciplinary and bilingual series of volumes on Gender Studies in Wales, authored by academics who are leaders in their particular fields of study, is designed to explore the diverse aspects of male and female identities in Wales, past and present. The series is bilingual, in the sense that some of its intended volumes will be in Welsh and some in English.

GENDERING BORDER STUDIES

Edited by

Jane Aaron, Henrice Altink
and Chris Weedon

CARDIFF
UNIVERSITY OF WALES PRESS
2010

www.uwp.co.uk

British Library Cataloguing-in-Publication Data
A catalogue record for this book is available from the British Library.

ISBN 978-0-7083-2170-6
e-ISBN 978-0-7083-2311-3

Printed in Wales by Dinefwr Press, Llandybïe

Contents

Notes on Contributors

JANE AARON is a professor of English at the University of Glamorgan, where she teaches Welsh writing in English and research skills. Her recently published books include *Nineteenth-Century Women's Writing in Wales: Nation, Gender and Identity* (University of Wales Press, 2007), which was awarded the Roland Mathias Prize in 2009.

JOCELYN C. AHLERS is associate professor of linguistics in the Liberal Studies Department at California State University San Marcos. Her areas of research include gender and language, language socialization, cognitive linguistics and the documentation and revitalization of endangered Native California languages.

HENRICE ALTINK is a lecturer in modern history at the University of York. She has published on representations of slave women in discourses of slavery and abolition and is currently studying the ideologies of femininity in the African Jamaican community between 1865 and 1938.

JANET BAUER, former director of the Women, Gender, and Sexuality Program, teaches at Trinity College (Hartford, CT). Her research and publications focus on the consequences of migration and resettlement for women and families in Muslim communities. Her translation of a Persian memoir, *I am Raziye: The Life of an Iranian Woman Political Activist* is forthcoming.

DEBORAH COHEN has a position in history at the University of Missouri-Saint Louis. She has published in various journals, among them *Journal of American Ethnic History*, *Hispanic American Historical Review*, *Estudios Sociológicos and International Labor and Working*

Class History, and her co-edited volume, *Sex and Gender in 1968: Transformative Politics in the Cultural Imagination*, was recently published with Palgrave Macmillan. In addition, her book, *Braceros: Migrant Citizens and Transnational Subjects in Postwar United States and Mexico*, will be published by University of North Carolina Press in September 2010.

KATIE GRAMICH is a reader in English literature at Cardiff University. She has research interests in modern Welsh writing in English, Welsh women's writing, and postcolonial and travel literature. Her most recent publication is *Twentieth-Century Women's Writing in Wales: Land, Gender, Belonging* (University of Wales Press, 2007).

MARGARET JACOBS is a professor of history and the director of women's and gender studies at the University of Nebraska-Lincoln. Her book, *White Mother to a Dark Race: Settler Colonialism, Maternalism, and the Removal of Indigenous Children in the American West and Australia, 1880–1940*, was published by the University of Nebraska Press in 2009.

GLENN JORDAN, a reader in cultural studies at the University of Glamorgan and director of Butetown History & Arts Centre in Cardiff docklands, has published widely on visual culture, race, representation and immigrants and minorities in Wales. His books include *Cultural Politics* (with Chris Weedon, 1994) and *Somali Elders: Portraits from Wales* (2004). He is currently writing *Race* for Routledge's New Critical Idiom series.

KIM KNOWLES-YÁNEZ is associate professor of urban and regional planning in the Liberal Studies Department at California State University San Marcos. Her areas of research include land use and community planning, public participation, and children's issues.

SUZANA MAIA is Professor at Universidade Federal do Recôncavo da Bahia (UFRB), Brazil, investigating the role of anthropologists in the political organizing of indigenous people in Bahia. Her Ph.D., from the City University of New York, focused on Brazilian women immigrants who worked in the sex industry in that city, looking at issues such as transnationalism, postcolonialism, gender and sexuality.

SIÂN REYNOLDS is emerita professor of French at Stirling University, a co-editor of the *Biographical Dictionary of Scottish Women* (2006) and a founder member of Women's History Scotland. Her latest book is *Paris– Edinburgh: Cultural Connections in the Belle Epoque* (2007).

JOHAN SCHIMANSKI is associate professor of comparative literature at the Department of Culture and Literature, University of Tromsø, Norway. He has worked on literary forgeries, literature in Welsh, science fiction, genre theory, national identity in literature, post-colonialism and arctic discourses. Co-leader of the border poetics working group at the University of Tromsø, he co-edited (with Stephen Wolfe) the anthology *Border Poetics De-Limited* (Wehrhahn, 2007).

WILLIAM J. SPURLIN is Professor of English at the University of Sussex where he also directs the Centre for the Study of Sexual Dissidence and Cultural Change. His most recent books are *Imperialism within the Margins: Queer Representation and the Politics of Culture in Southern Africa* (2006) and *Lost Intimacies: Rethinking Homosexuality under National Socialism* (2008). He has published widely in queer and postcolonial studies and in twentieth-century comparative literature and culture.

CHRIS WEEDON is director of the Centre for Critical and Cultural Theory at Cardiff University. Her books include *Feminist Practice and Poststructuralist Theory* (1987); *Cultural Politics* (with Glenn Jordan, 1994); *Postwar Women's Writing in German* (ed., 1997); *Feminism, Theory and the Politics of Difference* (1999); *Identity and Culture: Narratives of Difference and Belonging* (2004); and *Gender, Feminism and Fiction in Germany 1840–1914* (2006).

SIAN RHIANNON WILLIAMS, senior lecturer in history education at the University of Wales Institute, Cardiff, is the author of a monograph on the Welsh language in nineteenth-century Monmouthshire (1992), and a number of articles on Welsh women's history. She also co-edited *Struggle or Starve: Women's lives in the South Wales Coalfield between the Two World Wars* (1998).

Introduction

HENRICE ALTINK AND CHRIS WEEDON

In the last two decades, universities located in areas with a past of border struggles or cross-border cooperation have set up research centres on borders, such as the Centre of International Border Research at Queen's University Belfast, the Center for Inter-American and Borders Studies at the University of Texas in El Paso, and the Centre for Border Research at the Radboudt University in Nijmegen in the Netherlands. Scholarly books and articles on borders, and even the publication of specialized journals, such as the *Journal of Borderland Studies*, have also increased. This outburst of interest in borders should be seen in light of worldwide processes of globalization and, in Europe, the fall of the Berlin Wall in 1989. Globalization, which gathered momentum from the 1970s onwards, has made some borders more permeable to accommodate specific interests in the flow of goods, people and money (for example, NAFTA, the North Atlantic Free Trade Agreement). Meanwhile, movement across borders that is perceived by states as negative or threatening, particularly from south to north and from developing to developed countries, has led to the strengthening of external borders. The fall of the Berlin Wall was followed by the dissolution of the USSR, which helped to reawaken nationalism in some parts of Europe, triggered conflict in others, and also led to more cooperation between western European states. These trends in turn resulted in the weakening of some state borders (for example, the borders between European Union (EU) member states), the creation of new or the revival of old borders (for example, the border between the Czech Republic and Slovakia), and the strengthening of existing borders (for example, the EU's external border).

Initially, border studies concentrated on borders between states and on borderlands, that is, the land immediately adjacent to state borders, and was particularly interested in issues of security and sovereignty. More recently, it has started to examine the symbolic, cultural and conceptual borders that separate and unite populations within and across state borders, such as language, ethnicity, class, race and gender (see Altink and Gemie, 2008). Conceptual borders, too, are being challenged in cultural theory and in feminist, gender, queer and race studies. Today, then, borders are not just studied as part of the international geopolitical landscape and the nation and nation-state system, but also as other forms of discursive practices that create and negotiate meanings, norms and values and thereby shape lived experience. This more interdisciplinary approach to border studies is based on four assumptions. First, that borders are not fixed but variable and constructed in concrete historical settings. Secondly, that borders are used to separate populations or groups of people into 'them' and 'us'. Thirdly, that borders are the products of interaction and negotiation between interest groups that try to use territorial, symbolic, cultural and conceptual borders to create power relations and hierarchies. And, fourthly, that innovative research on border studies should try to connect territorial and other types of borders (see, for example, Castillo and Cordoba, 2002).

The Centre for Border Studies that was established at the University of Glamorgan in 2003 brings together territorial, symbolic and cultural borders. Its research concentrates mainly on Wales but it also undertakes work that is European in scope and global in significance. In October 2005, it hosted a conference entitled Gendering Border Studies that moved beyond approaches that treat gender merely as a 'metaphorical' border, examining the materiality of gender in a range of areas. These included gendered representations of borders and borderlands, the ways in which gender ideologies shape people's experiences of living in a borderland or crossing territorial and metaphorical borders, the ability of real and metaphorical borderlands to contest dominant gender ideologies, and the role that territorial borders play in the construction of gender ideologies. This volume contains a selection of essays, most of which were initially delivered as papers at the conference, and brings together different global regions and disciplinary approaches. It aims to give an overview of some recent innovative approaches in the new interdisciplinary field of gendered border studies. The first part of this introductory chapter summarizes the ways in which different disciplines have approached the theme of gender and borders. The second part briefly introduces the essays, shows the possibilities of this new interdisciplinary field of gendered border studies and sets out some areas for future research.

Approaches to gender and borders

Most of the work on gender and borders thus far has come from the social sciences, especially sociology and anthropology, and has tended to concentrate on migration. Early work consisted mainly of adding women to the picture of migration within an assimilation framework. By the mid-1990s, however, the focus shifted to showing that the patterns, causes, experiences and effects of migration, as well as the ties that link migrants to their homeland and receiving country, are heavily gendered. Various studies have shown, for example, that being a woman can hinder access to regular employment in the receiving country so that female migrants often turn to jobs in the informal sector, such as domestic or care work, or engage in illegal sex work. Much of the recent work on gender and migration is based on qualitative sources. Many scholars, for instance, invoke oral testimonies of female migrants that not only give a voice to a group of migrants often marginalized in existing work on migration but also shed light on the role that gender plays in the lives of migrants (see, for example, Curran et al., 2006; Morokvasic-Muller et al., 2003).

In recent years, scholars working in the field of gender and migration have begun to shift their attention to transnational theory, that is, ideas about belonging to two or more countries. Many have presented transnationalism as a positive gendered phenomenon. Nira Yuval-Davis and Marcel Stoezler, for example, have argued that women 'often feel freer to cooperate with other women across ethnic and national conflict boundaries than men in a similar situation would' and that there is thus a 'growing salient place for women's peace political activism aimed at crossing and transcending ethnic and national boundaries and borders' (2002: 340; see also Tatsoglou and Dobrowolsky, 2006). Some scholars, however, have pointed out that while transnationalism can improve the lives of migrants by providing them with more material, psychological and emotional resources, it can have considerable social costs. In her study of gendered, short-term trans-border movements in post-1989 eastern Europe, Mirjana Morokvasic has shown, for instance, that women who crossed borders for work had to come up with new mothering practices and family arrangements (2004: 16; see also Mendez and Wolf, 2001).

The social sciences have also paid attention to the ways in which gender affects the lives of people living in borderlands, especially the land straddling the US–Mexican border (see Vila, 2005). In much of this work, borderlands are presented as places of empowerment and opportunity for women. Graciela Sánchez, for example, has examined the successful lawsuit of the women-founded and lesbian-led Esperanza Peace and Justice Center against the city of San Antonio for prohibiting expressions and activities that challenged dominant sexual and gender norms (2003; see also Ruiz and Tiano, 1987). Following the lead of Gloria Anzaldúa and other Chicana feminists, some of the recent work on gender and borderlands has begun to explore the extent to which gender intersects with other systems of domination. Maria Antonietta Berriozabal has shown, for instance, in her analysis of growing up in San Antonio that gender in this particular borderland is inextricably entwined with class and religion (2003).

Migration also features prominently in historical studies of gender and borders. Much of this work has borrowed concepts, theories and techniques from the social sciences, such as assimilation theory. In the early 1990s, the focus shifted from the lives of female migrants to the ways in which gender ideologies – both in sending and receiving countries – shaped the migration process for men and women. Hamilton Sipho Simelane has argued, for example, that men dominated labour migration from Swaziland from the 1930s until the 1950s because Swazi men, in collaboration with the colonial administration, employed various strategies to control the movement of women, informed by the ideology of male appropriation of the labour of women (2004). And Eithne Luibheid has shown in her *Entry Denied: Controlling Sexuality at the Border* (2002) that the reception of female migrants by the US immigration service between 1875 and the 1990s was shaped by assumptions about gender, class, race and sexuality and that the service's methods of deciding whether a female applicant was eligible for entry helped to reproduce 'patriarchal heterosexuality as the nation's official sexual and gender order' (xviii). Although most historians working on gender and migration use a qualitative approach like Simelane and Luibheid, there are also many who use demographic and other quantitative data to unravel gendered patterns and effects of migration. Their work has done much to illuminate gender imbalances in past migration and has pointed to both continuities and discontinuities. These scholars have shown not only marked differences in patterns of male and female migration over time, but also the power of gender to determine who migrates and how and to direct male and female migrants into varying occupations and family relationships (see Sinke, 2006).

Historians have paid less attention than social scientists to the role of gender in borderlands (for exceptions, see Menon, 2004; McManus, 2005; and Masson, 2000) but have looked more closely at the role of gender in the constitution of symbolic and cultural borders. Various studies have focused on women who have tried to move away from or transcend the constraints that gender exerted on their behaviour and opportunities and have presented this movement as an empowering experience. Scant attention, however, has been paid to the negative responses to women who rejected gender constraints, such as increased policing and disciplining. Historians have done considerable work in recent years on the use of women as 'symbolic border guards'. This work has shown that the duty to embody the line that distinguishes those who belong to the collectivity from the threat of external aggressors or other cultures exerted both positive and negative effects on women. Thus, because they were seen to represent the nation, many women in the past, as in the present, have, for example, been raped during war by aggressor soldiers (see Abrams and Hunt, 2000). Historians have also explored border-creating activities by women. Caitriona Beaumont, for example, has looked at religious and secular women's organizations in the interwar years and the ways in which they constructed an identity around the idea of citizenship while removing themselves from feminism and feminist groups (2000).

Since the 1970s, with the growth of cultural studies, the expansion of literary studies into new areas and the turn to theory, borders have come to play a major role in the study of culture. They have figured in cultural theories ranging from post-structuralism and deconstruction to psychoanalysis. They are central to postcolonial, race, feminist, queer and gender studies. The ways in which borders are constructed and their role in the production of meanings and values have been questioned in relation to a range of areas: crucially, the constitution of fields of knowledge, the establishment of meanings as truths, the composition of the human subject and the workings of power. A range of theories have suggested ways of understanding how borders function within discursive practices and have material effects in a wide range of areas that are central to work in cultural, media and literary studies. The expansion of work on gender and borders in these areas has also gained impetus from the growth of postcolonial studies, in particular theorizations of the relations between colonizers and colonized (see, for example, Mohanty, 2003, and Alexander and Mohanty, 1997).

Much recent feminist, queer, post-structuralist, psychoanalytic and postmodern cultural theory has focused on questioning binary oppositions and the borders that they seek to hold in place. At issue are questions of meaning and power. Borders function to fix meanings, at least temporarily, to create the illusion of given truth, to delineate 'us' from 'them', while actually necessarily including the trace of what Derrida calls the 'self-same' in the other. Much recent work in cultural history and cultural analysis has focused on the ways in which knowledge in the West has assumed, either explicitly or implicitly, a number of exclusive binary oppositions – nature and culture, men and women, heterosexual and homosexual, the conscious and the unconscious, and so on.

Often the borders between these binary oppositions have been presented as either god-given or natural. Thus, for example, the gendered and racialized borders that have defined women and men and white and non-white peoples have been discursively guaranteed by both religion and natural science. In drawing borders in the production of meanings and identities and constituting fields of knowledge, the two sides of the binary oppositions that are produced in the process are rarely given equal status and value.

Recent work in postcolonial studies has questioned a number of key binary oppositions and the borders that sustain them, including Europe and its others, the North versus the South, the Orient versus the Occident, the global and the local, the centre and the periphery and the 'First' and the 'Third' worlds. It has analysed their construction under colonialism, together with the effects of the colonial legacy and the degree to which such borders are permeable. The binary opposition of colonizer and colonized has become a major focus of feminist postcolonial studies, influenced by the work of Homi Bhabha (see Bhabha, 1994). Bhabha uses the concept of mimicry as a way of analysing how, in the production of colonized subjects, full control is eluded and communication never fully achieved. He argues that colonial practices produce moments of ambivalence, which open up spaces for the colonized to subvert the master discourse. These ideas have been important in feminist work where ideas of gender as masquerade were already widely used. Bhabha, for example, employs the concept of 'hybridity' to signify the new forms of subjectivity and culture that are produced by the mixing of colonizers with colonized. From a feminist perspective, what is particularly interesting is the degree to which patriarchal power structures cut across the colonizers/colonized divide and do not allow women the potentially subversive positions and modes of operation open to men.

Writing by black and Third World women in the West has argued for breaking down traditional binary categories and liberating difference. This is a perspective developed by lesbian Chicana writer and theorist Gloria Anzaldúa, who offers an interesting model for non-Eurocentric feminist cultural criticism. Anzaldúa locates her work both inside and outside western frames of reference. She argues that borderlands offer an in-between space that enables the development of new categorizations and modes of theorizing which both subvert and challenge hegemonic western models. In *Borderlands/La Frontera*, Anzaldúa shows how history has shaped the material conditions under which Chicanos and Chicanas live and problematizes a number of borders and binaries. She argues that when the present-day Texan–Mexican border passed from Native American to Spanish and finally to white control, the inhabitants became mixed, creating a new group of Chicanos and Chicanas, who are seen not just as a distinct ethnic group but also as a racialized other. As such, they are the constant victims of oppressive racist practices, while themselves often perpetuating patriarchal oppression. Chicana feminists thus have to be rooted in this broader history of ethnic and racist oppression while struggling to transform the patriarchal dimensions of Chicano culture from within. Gloria Anzaldúa draws on her own experience, history and place, to suggest that 'new *mestiza*' women who are racially and ethnically mixed are in a position to challenge and move beyond the binaries which structure racism, sexism, heterosexism and ethnocentrism because they have developed a 'tolerance for contradictions, a tolerance for ambiguity' (1987: 79):

> The work of *mestiza* consciousness is to break down the subject-object duality that keeps her a prisoner and to show in the flesh and through images in her work how duality is transcended. The answer to the problem between the white race and the colored, between males and females, lies in healing the split that originates in the very foundation of our lives, our culture, our languages, our thoughts. A massive uprooting

> of dualist thinking in the individual and collective consciousness is the beginning of a long struggle, but one that could, in our best hopes, bring us an end of rape, of violence, of war. (p. 80)

The *mestiza* consciousness, which mirrors Homi Bhabha's 'third space', opens up a utopian vision of a world in which difference is valued and respected, not produced and policed by hierarchical power relations which oppress (see Rutherford, 1990: 207–21).

If cultural theory, new social movements and geographical border locations come together in the influential work of Gloria Anzaldúa, much work in literary and cultural studies is not so geographically grounded but is concerned with the crossing of symbolic and cultural borders. Various studies, for instance, explore the ways in which female protagonists in novels probe dominant gender ideals, or examine the impact that the crossing of territorial boundaries has/had on female writers' ability to cross the boundaries of genre, style or content in their work (see Humm, 1991; George, 1996; Pearce, 2000; Kirkpatrick, 2001; and Schimanski and Wolfe, 2007). An excellent example of recent attempts to link metaphorical and territorial borders in literary studies on gender and borders is Debra A. Castillo and María-Socorro Tabuenca Córdoba's *Border Women: Writing from La Frontera* (2002). Contrary to much work on Chicana literature, this book does not focus on Mexican women writers who have moved to North America or who write about the border from within the Mexican heartland, but concentrates on Mexican women writers who live on the US–Mexico border. In doing so, it presents a rather different picture of the US–Mexico border than that given by Anzaldúa, for example, which is less negative. The book also represents a gradual shift away from viewing borderlands as spaces of both opportunities and limits.

Political science has only recently begun to explore the theme of gender and borders, largely because of reluctance on the part of political scientists to use qualitative sources. Its main concern is with the gendered nature of policies that shape migration processes, from the reasons for migrating and choice of destination to the various policies that relate to the assimilation of migrants. Most of the work is more concerned with policies in the receiving than in the sending country and ignores short-term, forced and return migration. In spite of these and other shortcomings, however, it has made some important observations about gender and migration. Its work on sex trafficking and the employment of recent female migrants in domestic work and health care, for instance, has pointed to the need to study migration within a framework of the international division of socially reproductive labour (see Piper, 2006).

Much of the existing scholarship on gender and borders, then, understands borders as territorial divisions between nations and tends to equal gender with women. It furthermore largely ignores gender's intersection with other markers of difference such as class, race and ethnicity. Finally, it presents border crossings – literal or metaphorical – predominantly as positive phenomena. The essays in this volume both mirror and differ from existing work on gender and borders. Thus, while they have adopted similar techniques and concepts to examine the theme of gender and borders, they have tried much more than existing work to study the interplay between territorial, symbolic and cultural borders and to provide a more complex understanding of border crossings, showing that the crossing of territorial and other borders can lead to both more and less freedom.

An agenda for the future

The essays are divided into four sections: I. Migration and Gender; II. Gendered Narratives of Border Crossing; III. Gender and the Drawing of Internal Borders; and IV. Teaching Gendered Borders. The first part provides an illustration of the ways in which gender ideologies in both the sending and receiving country shape the experiences of migrants. In her discussion of nearly two million Mexican men who crossed the US–Mexico border between 1942 and 1964 as part of the so-called 'Bracero Program', Deborah Cohen is particularly concerned to show that the views on masculinity in the US and Mexico which shaped the experiences of the 'Braceros' intersected in various and complicated ways with racial and to a lesser extent class ideologies. The essays by Janet Bauer and Suzana Maia deal with contemporary migration to North America. Bauer engages with a growing body of work in the social sciences on marriage migration (see, for example, Constable, 2005). She explores the lives of Iranian mail-order brides in Canada and Germany and illustrates that many women migrated because they hoped that their new homeland would offer them greater opportunities but that few saw their dreams realized because their husbands and members of the Iranian diasporic community expected them to be 'traditional' Iranian women and closely monitored their dress, mannerism and demeanour. Bauer, then, clearly conveys that border crossings can be far from liberating experiences. Maia, on the other hand, alerts us, in her chapter on the lives of Brazilian women who work as erotic dancers in New York City, to the fact that it is not just the gender ideologies in a receiving country that determine the extent to which migrants are incorporated in their new homeland but also the skewed visions that a receiving country has of the systems of gender and sexuality in the sending country. She shows that idealized and eroticized images of Brazilian women, which had their origin in the European colonisation of Brazil, limit the dancers' incorporation in the US nation. Sian Rhiannon Williams's chapter on Welsh men and women who crossed the border in order to work as teachers in England in the interwar years not only sheds light on the role that gender ideologies played in the decision of men and women to migrate and their experiences in their new places of abode but also illustrates what scholars of migration and gender can gain by combining qualitative and quantitative methods. By using the latter, she is able to set out the gendered nature of migration across the Welsh–English border, while employing the former, in particular in oral interviews, allows her to demonstrate the differing experiences of the Welsh men and women who became teachers in England.

The second part explores how gender intersects with fictionalized narratives of border crossings. Gender refers here not just to the 'sex' of authors but also to the gender ideologies that shaped their narratives and which they tried either to undermine by presenting the border as a space of possibilities or to uphold by gendering the two countries straddling the border. Johan Schimanski, whose essay is located in comparative literature, looks at texts from different European traditions, periods and contexts that deal with border crossings to 'show as wide a range of genderings as possible' in order to move towards a model of what he terms 'border poetics'. The chapters by Jane Aaron and Katie Gramich deal with the literature of the Welsh–English border. Like Yuval-Davis and Stoezler, Aaron suggests that women are more likely than men to 'tolerate the tensions of the border condition' and appreciate the fact that 'sanity resides in being of the border, rather than on either of its sides'. She examines four fictional texts written by women writers from either side of the Welsh–English border in the early twentieth century. In each of these texts, it is female rather than male characters who show the resilience to maintain border identities. Gramich examines representations of the Welsh borderlands in a wide range of twentieth-century fictional texts produced by men. She illustrates how cultural, linguistic, religious and temperamental differences between Wales and England are often inextricably linked to gender in these texts. She is concerned in particular with the question of the extent to which the texts feminize Wales as a place of quasi-colonial Otherness and whether this changes over time.

The third part sheds some light on the role that gender plays in constructing, sustaining and dismantling internal borders. Margaret Jacobs discusses a border that has received increasing attention in colonial history (see Stoler, 2006, for an introduction to colonial history), namely the 'intimate border', that is the border surrounding one's private self and body. She examines the efforts of white American women in the late nineteenth and early twentieth centuries to transform the homes of Native American women, and also their roles as surrogate mothers to Native American children in boarding schools and as employers of young Native American domestics. Her chapter illustrates that white women's crossing of Native American women's intimate borders involved social costs for Native American women. It also suggests that historians can learn more about the ways in which colonial relations were created and sustained if they shift their attention away from the public sphere of government to the private sphere of the home. As Jacobs illustrates, the homes of Native American women were not a private refuge or haven from larger colonial forces but another contested site of colonialism. The internal border explored by Siân Reynolds is that of the border between Scotland and England. She first explores the drawing of this border in the centuries leading up to the Act of the Union of 1707 and then examines the revival of Scottish national culture in the last thirty years, which has done much to rebuild the border between Scotland and England. Reynolds is concerned with the role that gender played in both processes. She clearly conveys that women were used as 'symbolic border guards' in the first and that the second was marked by a relative gender-blindness. Like Jacobs's essay, that of William Spurlin alerts scholars to the dangers of thinking in terms of dichotomies. He takes up the idea articulated by many postcolonial feminists that borderlands can be places from which to challenge hegemonic narratives. He focuses on the borderlands of culture and argues that if culture is seen as 'hybrid', it is not only possible to create more of 'a global/local tension rather than a privileging of one domain over the other' but also to disrupt and exceed the 'coherence of normative citizenship tied to the perpetuation of hetero-normativity'. He unravels his argument in a discussion of globalized representations of AIDS and HIV infection in Africa and localized queer and AIDS activism in post-apartheid South Africa. The last essay in this part, by Glenn Jordan and Chris Weedon, draws on the media and oral life histories to examine the construction of racialized borders in the multi-ethnic Tiger Bay area of Cardiff in the period immediately before and during the Second World War. It explores how individual perceptions of these borders were (and are) lived and negotiated in gendered ways in popular memory and argues that the thematic tropes and coping strategies that emerge from these life stories tell us as much about the present as the past.

Finally, in the last part of the book, Jocelyn Ahlers and Kimberley Knowles-Yánez set out some of the ways in which border studies programmes in universities can incorporate gender into the curriculum. Both authors teach on the border studies programme of the Liberal Studies department at California State University, San Marcos, which is located a forty-five-minute drive away from the US–Mexico border. After a brief summary of the history of the programme, they provide two case studies – language and land-use planning – to argue that gender in border studies programmes needs to refer to both the gendered experiences of living in a border region or crossing a territorial border and gender as a border-creating social construct.

The essays in this volume not only illustrate the wide variety of work undertaken on gender and borders but also suggest ways in which this work can be taken further. Like much of the existing scholarship, most of the papers presented here tend to equate gender with women. Future research should also explore, as Cohen has done, the lives of men who live in borderlands or have crossed territorial or metaphorical borders and the ways in which ideas about manhood influenced their lives, so that we can gain a fuller understanding of the ways in which gender acts as what Joan Wallach Scott has called a 'primary way of signifying relationships of power' (1988: 44). To do this effectively, it is also essential that scholars working on gender and borders examine gender in relation to other markers of difference, including religion, class, sexual orientation, race and ethnicity, because it is in the interplay with these other markers that gender helps constitute symbolic and cultural borders. Some of the essays in this volume have tried to do this. Jacobs, for example, examines gender's intersection with sexuality and race, and Jordan and Weedon are concerned with the intersection of race, gender and class. The essays in this volume shed more light not only on the workings of gender but also on the nature of borders, whether they be territorial, symbolic, cultural or conceptual. They convey most clearly that borders are not fixed and static but continuously contested, negotiated and reinterpreted, that they carry meaning and shape identities and that they are inherently contradictory, problematical and multifaceted. But, above all, the essays presented here illustrate that borders help to create and sustain asymmetrical and hierarchical relationships, suggesting that if we want to limit the oppressive effects of borders we need to have a fuller understanding of the interplay between gender and borders.

Bibliography

Abrams, Lynn and Karen Hunt (2000). 'Borders and frontiers in women's history', *Women's History Review*, 9, 2, 191–200.

Alexander, M. Jacqui and Chandra Talpade Mohanty (eds) (1997). *Feminist Genealogies, Colonial Legacies, Democratic Futures*, New York and London: Routledge.

Altink, Henrice and Sharif Gemie (eds) (2008). *At the Border: Margins and Peripheries in Modern France*, Cardiff: University of Wales Press.

Anzaldúa, Gloria (1987). *Borderlands: La Frontera. The New Mestiza*, San Francisco: Aunt Lute Books.

Beaumont, Caitriona (2000). 'Citizens not feminists: the boundary negotiated between citizenship and feminism in mainstream women's organisations in England, 1928–39', *Women's History Review*, 9, 2, 411–29.

Berriozabal, Maria Antonietta (2003). 'Una historia de una de muchas Marias', *Frontiers*, 24, 2–3, 155–67.

Bhabha, Homi K. (1994). *The Location of Culture*, London: Routledge.

Castillo, Debra A. and María-Socorro Tabuenca Córdoba (2002). *Border Women: Writing from La Frontera*, Minneapolis: University of Minnesota.

Constable, Nicole (ed.) (2005). *Cross-Border Marriages: Gender and Mobility in Transnational India*, Philadelphia: University of Philadelphia Press.

Curran, Sara R., Steven Shafter, Katherine M. Donato and Filiz Garip (2006). 'Mapping gender and migration in sociological scholarship: is it segregation or integration?', *International Migration Review*, 40, 1, 199–223.

George, Rosemary Marangoly (1996). *The Politics of Home: Post-colonial Relocations and Twentieth Century Fiction*, Cambridge: Cambridge University Press.

Humm, Maggie (1991). *Border Traffic: Strategies of Contemporary Women Writers*, Manchester: Manchester University Press.

Kirkpatrick, Kathryn (ed.) (2001). *Border Crossing: Irish Women Writers and National Identities*, Tuscaloosa: University of Alabahama Press.

Luibheid, Eithne (2002). *Entry Denied: Controlling Sexuality at the Border*, Minneapolis: University of Minnesota Press.

McManus, Sheila (2005). *The Lines which Separate: Race, Gender and the Making of the Alberta-Montana Borderlands*, Lincoln: University of Nebraska Press.

Masson, Ursula (2000). '"Political conditions in Wales are quite different" . . .: party politics and votes for women in Wales, 1912–15', *Women's History Review*, 9, 2, 369–88.

Mendez, Jennifer Bickham and Diane L. Wolf (2001). 'Where feminist theory meets feminist practice: border-crossing in a transnational academic feminist organization', *Organization*, 8, 4, 723–50.

Menon, Ritua (ed.) (2004). *No Woman's Land: Women from Pakistan, India and Bangladesh Write on the Partition of India*, New Delhi: Women Unlimited.

Mohanty, Chandra Talpade (2003). *Feminism Without Borders: Decolonizing Theory, Practicing Solidarity*, Durham and London: Duke University Press.

Morokvasic, Mirjana (2004). '"Settled in mobility": engendering post-wall migration in Europe', *Feminist Review*, 77, 7–25.

Morokvasic-Muller, Mirjana, Umut Erel and Kyoko Shinozaki (eds) (2003). *Crossing Borders and Shifting Boundaries*, vol. 2, Opladen: Leske and Budrick, 9–16.

Pearce, Lynne (ed.) (2000). *Devolving Identities: Feminist Readings in Home and Belonging*, Aldershot: Ashgate.

Piper, Nicola (2006). 'Gendering the politics of migration', *International Migration Review*, 40, 1, 133–64.

Ruiz, Vicki L. and Susan Tiano (eds) (1987). *Women on the US–Mexico Border: Responses to Change*, Boston: Allen and Unwin.

Rutherford, Jonathan (ed.) (1990). 'Interview with Homi Bhabha. The third space', in *Identity, Community, Culture Difference*, London: Lawrence and Wishart, 207–21.

Said, Edward (1978). *Orientalism*, London: Routledge and Kegan Paul.

Sánchez, Graciela (2003). 'La Cultura, la Communidad, la Familia', *Frontiers*, 24, 2–3, 75–86.

Schimanski, Johan and Stephen Wolfe (eds) (2007). *Border Poetics De-limited*, Hannover: Wehrhahn Verlag.

Scott, Joan Wallach (ed.) (1988). *Gender and the Politics of History*, New York: Columbia University Press.

Simelane, Hamilton Sipho (2004). 'The state, chiefs, and the control of female migration in colonial Swaziland, *c.*1930s and 1950s', *Journal of African History*, 45, 103–24.

Sinke, Suzanne M. (2006). 'Gender and migration: historical perspectives', *International Migration Review*, 40, 1, 82–103.

Stoler, Ann Laura (ed.) (2006). *Haunted by Empire: Geographies of Intimacy in North American History*, Durham and London: Duke University Press.

Tatsoglou, Evangelina and Alexandra Dobrowolsky (eds) (2006). *Women, Migration and Citizenship: Making Local, National and Transnational Connections*, Aldershot: Ashgate.

Vila, Pablo (2005). *Border Identifications: Narratives of Religion, Gender and Class on the U.S.–Mexico Border*, Austin: University of Texas Press.

Yuval-Davis, Nira and Marcel Stoetzler (2002). 'Imagined boundaries and borders: a gendered gaze', *The European Journal of Women's Studies*, 9, 3, 329–44.

I

MIGRATION AND GENDER

1

Outside the Border of the Modern: Mexican Migration and the Racialized and Gendered Dynamics of US National Belonging

DEBORAH COHEN

This chapter explores the impact of structuring unofficial membership in the US nation along a modern/non-modern divide and the ways in which one set of migrants to the US attempted to manoeuvre against this framing (also see Camacho, 2008, and Lim, 2006, on the modern as crucial to US national belonging). The migrants examined here are Mexican men who came during the Bracero Programme, a series of US–Mexico agreements under which Mexican men were sent to work in US agriculture, in particular in California. The programme, in effect between 1942 and 1964, brought nearly two million braceros, as participants were called, to the US to do stoop labour. More critical here, the Mexican state framed the men's journey (women were prohibited from the programme) as a modernizing one; it was to transform them into modern Mexican citizens who, upon return, would contribute to Mexico's modernization. When braceros arrived in the US, however, they lived and laboured in conditions that denied this framing. This denial, together with the definition of US membership and braceros' labour in terms of a modern/non-modern dichotomy, I suggest, situated these men as always already outside the US nation and the modern; they were positioned as outsiders/foreigners.[1] As various queer theorists and citizenship studies scholars have argued, the outsider-foreigner is not a neutral position but always gendered, raced and sexed, a national spectre against whom citizenship benefits are allocated along heteronormative lines (see, for example, Brandzel, 2005; Canaday, 2003a and 2003b; Duggan, 1994; and Summerville, 2005). Drawing on these scholars' insights, I argue in my reading of the braceros' place vis-à-vis the configuration of US belonging that the modern/non-modern configuration shaped the ways through which braceros fought for the benefits of migration.

In the first section, I discuss the programme and what the Mexican state anticipated that braceros would achieve. The second section turns to how braceros struggled for rewards of migration in a context of their exclusion and denial of these rewards. The last section analyses the implications of framing the braceros' journey as a modernizing one. Together, the sections show how braceros used the gendered strategies at their disposal to claim the benefits that the programme had offered and to which they saw themselves entitled.

The Bracero Programme

In 1942, not long after entering the Second World War, the US approached Mexico about establishing a formal programme to bring Mexicans to work in US agriculture, as growers were increasingly worried about projected shortages of cheap labour and lost harvests. Although Mexico was initially reluctant, it ultimately agreed. The agreement that emerged from these international negotiations reflected Mexico's (initial but short-lived) leverage. Very generally, it stipulated wage levels (initially higher than for US workers); provided migrants with transportation to and from the US and medical and workers' compensation insurance; and outlawed braceros' use as strike-breakers or to influence local salaries. Mexico furthermore demanded that part of the braceros' wages be withheld until they returned. Returning with capital and useful knowledge, the men were encouraged to purchase farm machinery and transform agriculture into a productive industry, a capitalization that would enable the country to meet its foodstuff needs. Mexico's insistence on these various conditions shows its goal for the programme: the transformation of peasants into yeoman farmers. This class transformation, it was assumed, would simultaneously bolster the patriarchal family as the unit of production, seen as necessary since many men sought to migrate precisely because they were unable to meet their patriarchal duties of supporting their wives and children. To accomplish this goal, the programme tried to prevent frivolous spending by withholding 10 per cent of braceros' wages. The goal was not achieved because during the early years of the programme some 70 per cent of braceros were aged under twenty-one and single (Dominguez, 1947).[2] That is, although migrants were assumed to be patriarchs too poor to fulfil that position, in reality most were proto-patriarchs being schooled for a future role. Nor did the expected class transformation occur. More than half of braceros had no prior agricultural experience and, of the few who did, only a handful returned fully to farming (Dominguez, 1948). Moreover, when the men returned, they could not access the capital that they accrued – it was lost in the process.[3] Without capital, returnees found it impossible to capitalize small farms.

In short, the programme was to be the quintessential modernizing transformation for men that the state regarded as unambiguously non-modern. That Mexico would see picking cotton and sugar beets as the road to capitalization and class transformation might strike one as disingenuous, even ludicrous, considering that braceros earned only $0.30 to $1.00 an hour. This aim makes sense only, however, if we understand that the Mexican state saw the migrants' labour as part of the nation's contribution to the Second World War, and that modernization, as encapsulated in modernization theory, was then the dominant worldview.[4]

As I suggested at the outset, the men charged with bringing the modern home through farm work came face to face with their inability to meet the conditions for being modern in the US. The braceros' position as Mexican, like that of all those of Mexican descent regardless of citizenship, racialized them as perennial foreigners and thereby made the modern off limits (Ngai, 2003: ch. 1). Moreover, at the time of the programme, US domestic farmhands were not covered by the National Labor Relations Act protections, part of Franklin D. Roosevelt's New Deal labour legislation. Growers, in arguments against covering agricultural labourers, had depicted them not as workers but as clients who were in a patron–client relationship with their employers. Clearly, then, all farmworkers at the time were seen as non-modern. Thus, braceros were sent to the US to be modernized by doing labour antithetical to modern work. Ironically, however, their non-modern labour made the modernization of US agriculture possible, as the low wages paid to braceros enabled growers to accrue the capital needed to invest in technology and thus modernize the sector. When the programme was terminated in 1964, over two-thirds of the crops were picked by machines, compared with 8 per cent in 1951 (Grove, 2000: 272, and 1996: 318).

Despite the two states' and growers' expectations for the programme, the men who came (or tried to come) did see something in it for themselves: the ability to maintain families and re-secure claims to manhood jeopardized by precarious economic conditions in Mexico. They would manoeuvre within circumstances that constrained their ability to advocate for themselves to get what they needed from the programme. The next section turns to these constrained circumstances: the world in which braceros lived and worked. As stated previously, Mexico sent braceros north expecting that this would modernize individual braceros and the Mexican nation as a whole. Yet, because of how the men lived and the work they did, their treatment as well as the history of racial exclusion in the US, they were denied the status of modern subject. Their exclusion from the modern was due to their racialized position as Mexican *and* to the homosocial arrangements under which they lived and worked that chipped away at the men's claim to upholding a masculine ideal. The next section, which looks at the spaces in which braceros worked, shows how these men, although cast as non-modern, struggled to be seen as modern and used a gendered language to do so.

The world of braceros[5]

The world of the braceros was largely a world of men. By day it comprised men working side by side engaged in back-breaking labour in the fields. By night, the braceros shared military-style barracks (often of several thousand men) or small shacks of five to seven men. In recalling their migrant surroundings, the men painted a benign picture of these same-sex environments. As one man put it, '[w]e worked together all day; we cooked together, we drank together . . . We spent all our time together.' 'I remember lying in bed at night', said Alvaro García, who lived in barracks. 'After we had . . . bought radios, you'd hear lots of music, all different kinds . . . some Mexican, some American . . . a circus of music.'

The differences between Mexico and the US that the braceros encountered included not just their sleeping arrangements but also the food eaten. Braceros, used to a diet of tortillas and beans, did not like the 'yellow cheese', their name for American cheese that accompanied the questionable meat and Wonder Bread. They longed for 'beans, chillies, and tortillas', because, as one man argued, 'it's who we are'. Not only what men ate but also who cooked marked their difference from Americans. Men who considered cooking the role of wives and mothers often found themselves preparing their own food. 'Where I went we had to cook our own meals', said Federico Garciniego, and 'shop, too'. Once

> it was my turn . . . I had only done it a couple of times before . . . [N]o one could speak English very well . . . no one could read . . . I saw these cans of what looked like meat . . . So [I] figured, 'buy them' . . . The meat wasn't great, but . . . on tortillas, with beans, it was okay.

Apparently, he had bought dog food.

The same-sex living arrangements contrasted sharply with Mexican domestic ones and affected the ability of the braceros to live up to their country's standards of masculinity. In Mexico, domestic arrangements were organized around natal and extended heterosexual family units from which all members derived their economic and social responsibilities and privileges. In return for family maintenance, a man exercised control over his wife's labour and sexuality and the children she bore. The inability to maintain a family, a fate shared by most poor and working-class Mexican men at the time of the programme, threatened their claim to their status as head of the family. Migration, with its prospect of greater economic security, opened up the potential, imagined and real, for recouping (or, among single men, looking forward to) this claim. Considering this particular masculine ideal, such mundane acts as eating *sans* chillies, beans or tortillas, and shopping and preparing food became significant. The braceros gradually began to recognize themselves as different from US nationals. This was reinforced by the fact that they lived in racially segregated farming communities. The individual and collective senses of self created north of the border contrasted markedly with the notion of being Mexican or American with which men left Mexico. These, instead, became representative of new gender subjectivities and set within an explicitly transnational context, even as they were threats to old ones.

How should we understand this process of subjectivity formation? At the time of the programme, the process of building a Mexican nation was underway yet incomplete. With the exception of those living in the capital and thus in close contact with the Mexican national state, most braceros did not always define themselves primarily in national terms but used more localized references. In this respect, for men who left the country as only tenuously Mexican, the programme functioned as a nation-building exercise, one tied to a specifically gendered transnational proletarian subjectivity.

Although most migrants had lived in Mexico under conditions organizationally, but not qualitatively, dissimilar from bracero quarters, their US living conditions were imbued with different meanings because their social organization undermined the hetero-normative logic from which their claims and rights as (proto)patriarchs were derived. Washing clothes and cooking subverted the men's claims as patriarchs and became points at which they would rally other reasons to their defence. Andrés Morales mentioned that 'local women would come and wash the men's clothes', but, because he wanted to save money, he initially washed his own. He soon, however, paid a woman to do his washing because 'after working all day, I didn't want to do it'. Andrés, then, tried to live up to the dominant masculine ideal. By not paying for laundry service, he had, as a proper patriarch, prioritized his family needs over his own, because the money he saved could be sent home to family. Yet employing someone to do his washing also did not undermine his attempt to be a patriarch, for proper patriarchs were supposed to have access to women's labour. It could be argued, then, that the ongoing struggle between spending money and making life easier or saving it and making life harder was implicitly one about rights to the title of proper patriarch. Moreover, it refashioned a gender subjectivity that was recognized as Mexican and was produced in a transnational, not a domestic, context.

The bar: space of seduction for cash

The same-sex working and living environment led the braceros, then, to question not merely their national but also their gendered identity. They employed a variety of means to recuperate patriarchal claims, in particular drinking with friends, socializing with women other than wives or girlfriends and distinguishing themselves from other Mexican migrants with regards to these two activities. Yet the line between properly gendered men and others was tenuous since the social privilege afforded to those who met gender expectations included the right to adventure, as well as practices like drinking, otherwise seen as deleterious to the family. Thus the men's descriptions of these practices suggest an inherent tension between a moral argument against drinking and socializing with women other than wives and their being seen as a reward for being a proper patriarch. Former migrants claimed that, although *they* 'didn't drink very much', 'almost *everyone* did'. Samuel Carrillo explained how 'every Saturday night . . . men went to the bar . . . I went sometimes . . . But I was never drunk.' Others, it seems, spent nearly all their leisure time 'with friends at the bar'. But, as another former bracero, Alejandro Medina, told me, since 'I had a family . . . I couldn't spend my week's wages in just one night'. 'I behaved myself.'

In the above quote, Alejandro hints at both the right to socialize with friends after a week of hard work and the limits of that right. As a husband and father, he had a family to support; however, he did not deny his right as proper patriarch to participate in these social rituals, only that it was limited. Men's testimonies then reveal their attempts to assuage the anxiety created by homosocial domestic arrangements they understood as threatening their heterosexual respectability.

More broadly, these testimonies suggest two ways of resolving the threats emanating from homosocial and thus disruptive domestic arrangements: either the men went to the bars and exercised their male privilege in an attempt to (re)secure their claim to manhood, or they refused to participate in these social rituals because of their need to send money home to families, asserting a moral argument to recoup their manhood. As many men asserted, they went to bars, they drank. But, if they did not have families or still sent money home, 'it was okay'. Thus, the critical caveat: as long as men fulfilled their responsibilities as men, they could justify their activities and still claim manhood and refuse the spectre of a destabilizing gender figure who resided in a sexually unregulated space: the drunk, carouser, womanizer and spendthrift.

Generating solidarity: the field, the barracks, the bar

The process through which the braceros reclaimed their manhood was generative of other identities, including those of nation, race and class, and drew upon a specifically Mexican version of citizenship. We can see this most clearly in the solidarity that developed amongst the migrants in the field, the barracks and the bar. Like the braceros' regimes of living and leisure, work, too, was a predominantly male world, one built on mentoring and friendships. Men 'helped *and* competed with each other'. One man recalled how he was part of a picking crew that was 'the fastest at filling those crates'. Another remembered himself 'as a champion. I beat out thirty people.' Long-time braceros brought new arrivals into this setting of competition and rivalry, orienting them to the structures of work. 'When I went the first time, I didn't know how to pick beets . . . [T]he first day . . . I took . . . my sack and started to pick . . . I watched the others and tried to imitate them. That helped, but not that much.' Finally, one man 'took me aside. "Like this," he said. "It's much easier." And it was . . . We got to be friends. And then later . . . I showed other men [the technique] . . . That's how it worked.'

The supportive and competitive relationships fostered in the fields were often anchored in particular identities: local, regional or national. 'We were Mexican,' Mauricio Herrera told me flatly, 'we learned from each other'. Men's subjectivities were under attack, even as they were being reformed vis-à-vis prior claims as patriarchs and local or regional (as opposed to national) identities. While often newcomers 'couldn't [read] the contract' and 'used to throw [it] away', long-time workers knew what it said. They 'talk[ed] about the clauses among ourselves in the camp', orienting recent arrivals to its provisions (Ignacio Ochoa Perdomo in *Seasonal Farm Laborers*, 2002, and Galarza, 1956: 66). Veteran migrants frequently had valuable knowledge and experiences, often organizing to demand better food or pressuring a grower to comply with the official pay scale. Ramón Avitia recounted a story of food complaints. 'One time', he said, 'a group of us, we didn't like the food . . . I had been going [to the US] for a while, so we, especially those with some experience, we threatened the boss', saying 'that we weren't going to work if the food didn't improve. It didn't, so we left, about ten of us . . . We found other jobs, without contracts, but the food was better. That's important.'

Male relationships flourished in this homosocial environment and long-time workers passed their knowledge on to newcomers. This transfer of information helped mediate the power of grower associations, which compiled and traded names of workers who 'caused trouble', a code word for attempting to improve working or living conditions or stop the rampant 'discounting' of wages. In sharing information, showing newcomers shortcuts and, in turn, helping them earn more money, returning migrants built a worker solidarity set against the particular practices of class, race and nationality in the US.

Migrants did not share only information about work; long-time migrants also taught newcomers about other aspects of bracero life, often about more 'recreational' activities. Alvaro García, for instance, recounted how, after receiving his first pay cheque, he and some friends met

> this man who had been [working] a while. He said he knew exactly what we needed. Now I figured . . . that he'd be taking us into town. We all needed clothes, you know, things . . . But do you know where he took us? Sure, he took us into town, but instead of taking us to buy clothes, we went to a bar . . . We went to this bar where everyone knew him. He had credit, he could drink as much as he wanted even if he didn't have the money . . . We all drank, we drank a lot. I spent almost my whole paycheck that night . . . It was fun, but I didn't do it too much, once in a while. He did it every weekend. After that, so did some others.

In analysing the migrants' living and working conditions, we begin to see how bracero experiences generated new subjectivities, ones in tension both with their positions as non-white agricultural migrants in the US and with the ways they had been led to think about themselves in Mexico. These migrants, who in the US were 'separated . . . from family and friends', 'isolated from American communities', 'confronted with new foods not to their taste' and with work under demanding bosses 'known to exploit them', were husbands, sons and brothers in Mexico. In Mexico they had lived in families – units of men, women, children and, often, older relatives. They had socialized with friends; had sex with their wives, and had courted girlfriends under the proprietary eyes of the community. In Mexico, they had derived their responsibilities and freedoms, which were very much age and gender compatible, as a part of the family unit and in relation to its other members and the community's customs. Thus they had tried to work outside the house and leave domestic chores to their womenfolk, a line they did not want to cross.

However, work in the US was all about crossing lines, both physical and imaginary. Here, migrants could not maintain even the appearance of this staunchly entrenched demarcation between 'women's' and 'men's' work, between 'men's' and 'women's' spaces. Forced to engage in what was seen as women's work, men had had strong feelings about these supposed gendered transgressions. 'We had to wash our clothes', they told me, 'we had to cook, we had to shop for our food, we even had to repair torn clothes. I didn't like it much; I didn't want to, but I had to do it. I wanted to eat.' Another man agreed. 'We arrived from a day's work', he said, only 'to work again . . . patting and flipping tortillas, preparing supper, preparing fried beans for the next day, cooking the meat – in a word, we did everything . . . we cooked, washed, ironed, and did all the housework' (Cockcroft, 1986: 22). Another commented how he 'didn't know how to cook' before he migrated, but how he learned to cook. 'Some of the other workers taught me . . . I still remember how so once in a while, I'll prepare something for my family.' One man eloquently summed up the experience:

> All day we worked in the fields; all day we picked. From lemons to tomatoes, we dragged our sacks and we picked. Then we went to our barracks and we cooked dinner; we washed our clothes, we cleaned, we went to bed . . . After doing men's work all day, every evening we did women's work . . . We did men's work, we did women's work, too.

These words bring into relief the previously unbridgeable divide between 'women's' and 'men's' work. Men's work, in their eyes, was physically taxing and demanded physical strength: men lugged around heavy sacks of fruits or vegetables; they got dirty, their bodies ached and they earned money. Men's work gave them men's worn and callused hands.

Yet herein lies the inherent tension: although these workers engaged in men's work not unlike that which they had done in Mexico, they had crossed an official border. It was not the *work* itself but the *space* in which it was done that demanded that these men also did the work of women. The words of the men bespeak both a pride and a sense of shame for having had to do tasks defined as women's work. 'It [women's work] isn't so hard', men repeatedly told me, especially when talking about cooking and washing clothes. Embedded in this phrase is the pride of self-sufficiency and of being able to do something not previously tackled. Still, the words contain another emotion: the shame of being forced to cross that previously uncrossed line, communicated as these same men discounted the difficulty of women's responsibilities, the same responsibilities that when done by them threatened their position as proper patriarchs.

The implications of braceros' predicament

Faced with the continual possibility of denial of their rights and privileges as proper patriarchs, braceros sought to overcome this threat by using what they had at their disposal; namely, their identity as workers. This identity was built on the homosocial space of the barracks, was transformed in the fields vis-à-vis their white and Mexican American bosses and foremen and their Mexican and American co-workers and was also shaped by their encounter with US and Mexican state officials. Accounts of clashes between the migrants and their foremen and bosses illustrate most clearly that braceros mobilized a worker identity to their own ends. For example, when thirty-five-year-old Francisco Hernández Cano was approached by a local newspaper reporter in 1956, he was on his way to Washington to 'get contract laborers fair pay and treatment' for himself and the Mexican 'nationals' with whom he worked in California's Imperial Valley. His co-workers, he told the reporter, 'had passed the hat to get [his] bus fare' and he was off to talk to the Mexican ambassador, whom he hoped would resolve 'complaints – of pay deductions for tools, blankets, and insurance, of bad food and housing, of days wasted waiting for work', which were all violations of the work contract. He mentioned that he could make 18 to 35 dollars a week under the contract but that most growers did not obey the contract. According to him, most growers paid only 5 or 10 dollars a week and there were some that even paid a few cents for a whole week's work.

According to the newspaper article, 'Hernández Cano – and the million other Mexicans . . . [who] came north to work [that year] – wanted their contracts enforced' because in Mexico, they 'had no land and no job'.[6] The paper, then, did not see the braceros as peasants because they lacked land. The braceros also did not see themselves as such but as wage workers who described their economic situation in terms of the amount of money that a man could make in a week. Like workers elsewhere, the men wanted their contracts enforced. While braceros were allowed to elect one man to represent them in disputes with their employers, this representative was not allowed to renegotiate any issue, such as salary, spelled out in the original contract. This, and the fact that the growers generally refused to meet with these worker representatives or negotiate with braceros more generally, meant that the workers had little choice but to engage in slow-downs, work stoppages and other forms of worker solidarity to increase their wages and improve their working conditions. This posed a dilemma, however, because their contract explicitly forbade them from striking or honouring strikes of other workers by refusing to cross their picket lines, the only resolution for which was the repatriation of workers, which they did not want. Many braceros tried to get around this dilemma by deserting and moving elsewhere. According to Immigration and Naturalization Service statistics, early in the programme nearly 15 per cent of braceros deserted (Ngai, 2003: 146). Hernández Cano and the other Imperial Valley braceros, on the other hand, refused to skip out on the contract and, instead, adopted a class-based strategy that transcended national ties: asserting their rights as workers.

Most workers, however, did not adopt this bracero-as-worker strategy. They did not do so not just because they did not know procedures for filing a complaint but also because this strategy seldom succeeded in improving their wages and working conditions. First, while some Mexican consular officials actively used the mechanisms that the contracts allowed to resolve disputes, many – especially in California and Texas, places with the longest history of abuse of Mexican and Mexican American workers – refused to do so because of potential personal gains from a good working relationship with the growers. These officials usually tried to discourage workers from filing a grievance. If unable to do so, they instead threatened braceros with removal and/or repatriation. Realizing that the men were heavily dependent on the wages earned, even though they were meagre, these officials anticipated that the threat would force the workers either to back down or to return home. Although men often responded as expected, in some instances, the official's threat did not work and he had no choice but to follow up on his threat to appease the growers. A second reason for the failure of the bracero-as-worker strategy was that the remedies at the disposal of those consular officials keen to help braceros in their disputes were limited to those outlined in the Bracero agreements.[7]

Thus, although the migrants could, to some extent, recoup their position as patriarchs and assert *that* particular aspect of modern agency, they were unable to claim the status of modern citizen because of their race. Like other poor and working-class people of Mexican descent, they were configured as forever foreign, which in turn meant that they were seen as racially outside the bounds of the US modernist project (see, amongst others, Ngai, 2003, and Foley, 1998). Their position as Mexican was never reconcilable with the US understanding of modernizing agent.[8] Recognizing this barrier, braceros asserted their worker identity. Many demanded that growers adhered to provisions of the contract and that the US state, as their official employer, honour its commitment to enforce the agreement; and they took the Mexican state to task. Yet, as we have seen, even as the state negotiated for stronger and more enforceable work agreements, local consulate officers often undercut the efforts. When officials refused to investigate claims against growers or made threats of deportation, angry mobilized braceros frequently called for other Mexican state officials to protect citizens-workers. As we saw, Hernández Cano was travelling to Washington on behalf of his co-workers to speak to the Mexican ambassador. If that failed, they left bracero positions and went in search of better jobs.

In sum, the foregoing analysis of the braceros' negotiation of their gender, class and national identity makes poignantly clear that the modern was not an 'empty discursive realm' but part of a larger framework with rewards and privileges; it tied together seemingly disparate categories of difference and ranked them hierarchically. According to Alicia Schmidt Camacho, for Mexican migrants '[t]o become *national* – and thus incorporated into the US nation-state – they had to become *modern*' (Camacho, 2000: 86). The Bracero Programme fostered an investment in the idea of the modern and its rewards, a world-view that *all* connected to the programme shared and *most* thought could be attained through this migration. By examining how braceros attempted to claim the position of ideal social actor in the modernist project, the foregoing has given us a window on to how the project itself was dependent not only on the visible labour of those supposedly ideal social actors, but, also, on that of those denied this status.

It can be argued, then, that the modern/non-modern dichotomy *was* the border that the braceros experienced, not only at the territorial line between Mexico and the US, but everywhere. This was the border for which they had to fight, the rewards that the programme promised, a struggle they waged in largely gendered terms. This border, I suggest, is still practised throughout the US today and serves to sustain the fiction of an absolute distance, crucial to the maintenance of the boundaries of US national belonging (Camacho, 2000: 210). Although this distance is fictive, the rewards for being categorized as modern *are* very real. Although braceros were always a temporary workforce and thus never meant to stay in the US, their portrayal as non-modern had implications not just for the financial rewards that they could reap but also how the US imagined itself as a nation.

Acknowledgements

I would like to thank Lessie Jo Frazier, Laura Westhoff, Rosario Montoya, Andrea Friedman, Jane Aaron, Suzana Maia and Henrice Altink for their assistance on this chapter. Financial support and writing time was provided by a University of Missouri Research Board Fellowship, the University of Missouri–St. Louis Research Award, the Center for International Studies at the University of Missouri–St. Louis, and Program of American Studies at Indiana University. This is taken from my unpublished manuscript, 'Bordering Modernities: Transnational Labor Migration and the Making of Mexico and the US'. In addition, some material, used here with permission from Cambridge University Press, was previously published in Cohen, 2006.

Notes

1 Being modern was, generally, cast as: industrialization (having an economy built around factory(-like) production), technology (having widespread access to and use of radios, phonographs and telephones), state-of-the-art infrastructure systems (having paved roads, running water, electricity and indoor plumbing), progress defined in terms of consumer goods within economic reach, rising wages and an increasing standard of living. Being modern was also thought to shape ways of knowing, thinking and feeling. It found visible manifestation in forms of taste, desire and value, and was set against what was deemed as backward or traditional. The modern countries, and people within them, were seen to meet (most, if not all, of) these benchmarks. My point is not whether Mexico or the US actually *was* modern, but that the ability to claim to be modern brought fundamental rewards.

2 By the late 1950s, dynamics maybe have changed (at least in California). Sampling 1,000 braceros there, Anderson (1964: 62) found that about two-thirds were married, over half having children. Almost 45 per cent were between twenty-one and thirty years old, over half with one year or less of schooling.

3 Often, returning braceros did not know that money had been withheld from their cheques. For those who did, they could not reliably access this

money because of the paperwork involved. Surviving braceros and their descendents have filed lawsuits in US courts, held protests outside the US embassy and invaded the hacienda of the mother of Mexican president Vicente Fox in an attempt to resolve the issue (Pitti, 2005).

4 Briefly, modernization theory was a by-product of the post-Second World War US rise as economic and military superpower; the challenge to its pre-eminent position by the communist Soviet Union and, later, China; and the connected processes of the disintegration of European colonial empires and anti-colonial independence movements in Africa and Asia. It posited a unidirectional process of social change that set stages common to all societies (evolution) and predicted homogenization (a trend toward convergence between societies). This process was seen as irreversible, transformative, progressive (suffering for a big pay-off), slow moving (explicitly not revolutionary) and based on the pattern followed by the US. While modernization theory was first and foremost an economic theory, the pay-off was much more than economic: it also was cultural and political. Economic modernity (advanced capitalist relations) was seen as part of an economic-political-cultural tripartite package, with democracy as its political component and particular (US and western European) values and relationships (mediated by and through consumption) as its cultural ones. It is, then, a theory about the production of modern subjectivities. These subjectivities deemed appropriate for citizens of modern capitalist democracies were framed as individualistic, not collectivist, and were seen to emerge from capitalist relations of production and consumption and were mapped on to relations vis-à-vis the state and other individuals and communities.

5 This section relies on newspapers, US government documents and the personal papers of farmworker advocates. All uncited quotes are taken from interviews with former braceros conducted between January 1995 and June 1996, in June 1999 and in July 2004 in Durango, Mexico. Most of the men interviewed went to California's Imperial Valley.

6 Ernesto Galarza papers; Box 18; folder 4: Braceros (conditions), health care and insurance, 1952–1956. Special Collections, Stanford University.

7 For example, the only option open to consular officials in resolving labour disputes was to remove braceros from the fields and return them to Mexico while the dispute was being resolved. Even supportive officials hesitated to use this remedy since they knew that workers did not want them to exercise this option.

8 Mexican Americans struggling for civil rights at this time recognized that benefits of US citizenship came through not actual citizenship, but claims to whiteness. They contended that the 1848 treaty, which ended the US–Mexico War and had enabled the official citizenship of former Mexican citizens before non-white people could be citizens, made them legally white and should thus guarantee those rights (Foley, 1998).

Bibliography

Anderson, Henry (1964). *A Harvest of Loneliness: An Inquiry into a Social Problem*, California: Citizens for Farm Labor.

Brandzel, Amy (2005). 'Queering citizenship, same-sex marriage and the state', *GLQ*, 11, 3, 171–204.

Camacho, Alicia Schmidt (2000). 'Migrant subjects: race, labor and insurgency in the Mexico–U.S. borderlands', Ph.D. thesis, Stanford University.

——(2008). *Migrant Imaginaries, Latino Cultural Politics in the US-Mexico Borderlands*, New York: New York University Press.

Canaday, Margot (2003a). 'Who is a homosexual?: the consolidation of sexual identities in mid-twentieth-century American immigration law', *Law and Social Inquiry*, 28, 2, 351–86.

——(2003b). 'Building a straight state: sexuality and social citizenship under the 1944 G.I. Bill', *Journal of American History*, 90, 3, 935–57.

Cockcroft, James (1986). *Outlaws in the Promised Land: Mexican Immigrant Workers and America's Future,* New York: Grove Press.

Cohen, Deborah (2006). 'From peasant to worker: migration, masculinity, and the making of Mexican workers in the US', *International Labor and Working-Class History*, 69, 1, 1–23.

Domínguez, Guillermo Martínez (1947). 'Los Braceros Mexicanos', *Revista de Economía*, 31 May, 69.

——(1948). 'Los braceros: experiencias que debe aprovecharse', *Revista Mexicana de Sociología*, 10, 177–95.

Duggan, Lisa (1994). 'Queering the state', *Social Text*, 39, 1–14.

Foley, Neil (1998). 'Becoming Hispanic: Mexican Americans and the Faustian pact with whiteness', in Neil Foley (ed.), *Reflexiones 1997: New Directions in Mexican American Studies*, Austin: University of Texas, pp. 53–70.

——(1999). *The White Scourge: Mexicans, Blacks, and Poor Whites in Texas Cotton Culture*, Berkeley and London: University of California Press.

Galarza, Ernesto (1956). *Strangers in our Fields: based on a report regarding compliance with the contractual, legal, and civil rights of Mexican agricultural contract labor in the United States, made possible through a grant-in-aid from the fund for the Republic.* Washington DC: n.p.

Grove, Wayne (1996). 'The Mexican farm labor program, 1942–1964: government-administered labor market insurance for farmers', *Agricultural History*, 70, 2, 302–20.

——(2000). 'Cotton on the federal road to economic development', *Agricultural History*, 74, 2, 272–92.

Lim, Shirley (2006). *A Feeling of Belonging: Asian American Women's Public Culture, 1930–1960*, New York: New York University Press.

Ngai, Mae M. (2003). *Impossible Subjects: Illegal Aliens and the Making of Modern America*, Princeton and London: Princeton University Press.

Pitti, Stephen (2005). 'Bracero justice: the legacies of Mexican contract labor', paper presented at the Repairing the Past: Confronting the Legacies of Slavery, Genocide, and Caste conference at Yale University.

Seasonal Farm Laborers Program: Sad Recollections (2002). Directed by Jorge Luis Vazquez; documentary, 26 minutes, with English subtitles.

Summerville, Siobhan (2005). 'Queering loving', *GLQ*, 11, 3, 335–70.

2

Accented Margins: Gendering the Borders of Diaspora

JANET BAUER

Lingering at the border: the illusions and realities of the borderlands

Early in my research with Iranian political asylum seekers, I met a young mother who described her arduous and difficult flight across the mountains between Iran and Turkey with a newborn. That border crossing, she declared, was 'the easy part'. For her, as for many on the other side of the border from home, living in exile and claiming a space for oneself was a never-ending process of what Lugo has called daily, racialized border inspections (Lugo, 2000).

As shifting markers arising out of dynamic interactions, borders are theoretically salient as catalysts of persistent tension, creativity and change. It was the borderlands research on the American southwest that established the border as a postmodern illusion – a porous, ambiguous space rather than an impermeable boundary with fixed parameters – something that invites transgression and resistance, albeit in the shadow of state and institutional power, and that can produce its own hybridities.[1] Hurtado suggests this when she writes: 'it is in *la frontera* that Chicanas situated their feminism as well as their claim to cultural citizenship to highlight a particular border culture and language that stood between the two nation-states . . . not fully belonging to either' (2005: 125). At this border, where Chicanas must confront the multiple boundaries of race, class and ethnicity and struggle to protect their core selves, Hurtado constructs her 'relational analysis of power', exposing the border as a potential site of oppression as well as expression.

The emerging interest in border theory coincided with cultural theory's enchantment with postmodern notions of culture as 'fragmented' and varying across situational contexts in contradistinction to notions of culture as shared and distinctly bordered (cf. Rosaldo, 1993). Though a more expansive notion of border possibilities arose out of dissatisfaction with a static notion of boundaries of place and an appreciation for the complexities of cultural 'mixing', the paradox or duality of borders – as both fixed and fluid, territorial and embodied – continues to be reinforced in literature and in personal life passages, as Iranian refugees move from life in Iran to resettlement in Turkey, Germany and Canada. Whether approached through the theoretical language of *ethnoscapes* (Appadurai, 1991) or *networks* (Bacon, 1996) on the one hand, or *hybridities* (Naficy, 2001) and *negotiations or third spaces* (Licona, 2005) on the other, there continues to be some tension between the essentialism and structure of boundaries and the social and political processes of bordering.[2]

Indeed, the paradox of reinforcing boundaries while crossing and dismantling borders has been noted in the lived experiences of the young elementary schoolboys who cross into the otherwise 'polluting' territory of the girls' play areas to taunt or tease them without getting 'cooties' in Thorne's study (1992) and of the Gur Hasidim of Israel, who depend upon the correct behaviour of their women to avoid the pollution of a consumerist, secular society, upon which they depend to support their distinctive lifestyle (El-Or, 1994). This perplexing quality of what Thorne calls 'borderwork' captures Iranian refugee women's experiences of recurring boundaries in the liminal spaces of exile.

Nevertheless, whenever I refer to 'borders' below, I understand them to retain a sense of promise, ambiguity, tension and innovation with the potency for destabilizing and transgressing rigid notions of difference, as I focus on the underlying politics of social relationships within and on the margins of the borderlands. Taking for granted that refugees are located in the interstices of the local and the global, I will focus on the daily interactions and negotiations *within and between* 'communities' of refugees as these eventually affect ongoing relationships with their reception societies. While attention is usually focused on the spaces of interaction between refugees and their host societies, the less-explored borders between refugees and those back home, other refugees in their communities and their own construction of self are also important places of tension, struggle and compromise.

Turning to these interior margins, I recognize that those 'phobias and panics' – the uncertainties of the liminal borderlands as described by Naficy (1996) – remain under-theorized for what Lugo described as the constant border inspections of race, sexuality and power in daily experiences (both in meetings with others and in interior self-inspections). As suggested in 'Dilemmas at the border', 'There is, as yet, a gap in the literature between the social theory of the "everyday" and the constitutive phenomenon of racism in the life world of the contemporary advanced industrial states' (Bauer and Prashad, 2000: 278). As Lugo suggests elsewhere, 'in order to understand its political and practical importance we must re-imagine border theory in the realm of the inescapable, mountainous terrains of power' (1997: 44). Otherwise, the possibility of stagnation without transformation or empowerment, particularly in the lives of individual Muslim, refugee women, persists. While policies and institutional structures provide the framework for the exertion of power over refugees, it is daily interactions through which borderlands are policed.

Below I will first explore the sexual and racial geographies of the border zones where Iranian exile communities, in which I have been conducting ethnographic research for the last twenty years, are engaged by their 'others' – before proceeding to examine the interior borderlands of refugee life.[3]

Moving targets: the sexual and racial geographies of the Iranian diasporic borderlands

Representing the shifting borders of communities of difference, Iranian (Muslim), refugee women are in many ways ideal subjects of border study[4] – something I observe whenever someone asks me what kind of research I do. Predictably, I am inundated with tales of their 'unexplainable' fears of Muslims and their heavily veiled women. It is here, then, on the bodies of Muslim women that the paradoxes of postmodern borders are inscribed. It is in them that the de-territorialization of a refugee or immigrant's status is contraposed with a woman's (especially a Muslim woman's) embodiment of specific, 'fixed' national and cultural boundaries, and where the spectre of the 'mixing' of cultures and diminishing borders is contraposed with a concern for preserving traditional culture. For Iranians themselves, the former condition is reflected in notions of *avareh* (a fear – perhaps panic – of homelessness and loss of one's culture) experienced at the border, and the latter is referenced in both historical texts and contemporary images of a nation's own women as 'points of access' (cf. Hatem, 1989; Stoler, 1989; Yeganeh, 1993).

The paradoxes of women's place-holding can be readily observed in the case of Iranian diaspora communities in North America and Europe. Detained at the margins of their respective reception societies, refugee and immigrant women are socially deployed as markers of the 'new' cultural and racial difference to which Stolcke (1995) alludes and that can be seen in recent hijab debates or skirmishes over 'Muslim' dress. From 'the other side', women may 'protect' the boundaries of 'traditional' culture for their own communities,[5] enduring those constant 'border inspections' of everyday life in the continuous surveillance of their clothing, mannerisms and demeanour. In other words, women play a key role in maintaining the illusions of boundaries for both home and host cultures.

Changes in immigrant women's dress or behaviour, especially that of Muslim women, have come to reflect the cultural and racial (non)integration of these communities. For those North American and European women who routinely express their fears to me in taxis and waiting rooms, the image of a shrouded and confined woman – and by extension, the 'Muslim' woman – causes an almost physical, visibly emotional reaction similar to that aroused in the hijab debates in France, as detailed by Joan Wallach Scott (2007). Scott's analysis of the French colonial and postcolonial positioning of north African Muslim women reflects a shifting, yet persistent and racialized, border (the civilized and the uncivilized) between the French and the 'other' embodied in Muslim women's dress and appearance. Iranian women are often at the centre of this essentializing and racializing of the 'other' perhaps because, as Scott points out in her introduction to *The Politics of the Veil*, the veil 'evoke[s] the specter of an Iranian style Islamic revolution' (2007: 23). Even other diasporic Muslim women, like those in Trinidad, have insisted to me that they are not oppressed or backward like they believe Iranian women to be.

Consequently, the trauma of the borderlands is acutely experienced by Iranian women (Muslim and non-Muslim) exiles, for whom the Iranian revolution and the Islamic Republic of Iran have prompted a turn towards a more secular Muslim identity – a possibility that is not often recognized by non-Iranian colleagues who privilege devoutness (as signified by hijab) as a marker of Muslim authenticity. While

Iranian refugee women in my ethnographic study represent a variety of educational, political, marital, class, educational and religious backgrounds and settle in different kinds of communities in Europe and North America, they experience similar essentialist (and often sexualized) images of the Middle Eastern or Islamic woman through the variety of relationships they form in their host societies. Such Western essentializing repositions Muslim immigrants along a border of religious difference that inhibits access to many opportunities they were expecting across the border. Thus, one of my subjects, Mina was not permitted to be herself and also speak about or represent Muslim women's perspective for her German colleagues.

These stereotypical misconceptions are constantly reproduced in interactions in which Iranians are confronted with visions of fanatical Islam in interactions with non-Iranians on the street, in print and visual media and in comments from co-workers. This experience was epitomized by reactions to them following the publication of *Not Without My Daughter* in the early 1990s, a book that portrayed, in quite racist language, the oppressive behaviours of one Iranian husband towards his American wife. The movie version of this book continues to appear on mainstream television channels and successive memoirs, like Azar Nafisi's *Reading Lolita in Tehran* (2003), continue to be criticized for contributing to the demonization of Iranian culture. As Mina said, these stereotypes and subsequent rejection or objectification are hurtful.

This new sense of a racial self is especially jarring for the political refugees who fought for egalitarian ideals and social justice. While Iranians were aware of race prejudice in the United States, they were not prepared to be 'black' in Europe (and to a lesser extent in Canada), to constantly feel, through the gazes of others, that they are intruders. Most have no contact with the mostly invisible communities of Afro-Iranians, a small minority of the Iranian population, and are unselfconscious about the Iranian *Siah Bazi* – a traditional theatre form in which an 'endearing' black-faced buffoon succeeds in ridiculing the elite.[6]

Worn on women's bodies, '"race" is essentially an essentialist narrative of sexualized difference' (Brah, 1996: 156). Iranians often refer to their 'black heads' (*kalle siah*) as the initial source of perceived public differentiation at the bakery or on the subway, but the effect, as Dyer suggests, is to 'reproduce racial power relations' existing between immigrants and their hosts (Dyer, 1997: 45). Muslim women in particular have been exoticized as different, something Iranian refugees have experienced and resisted in everything from daily encounters on the street and official or public discourse to the 'endearments' used by Western sexual partners in referring to them as their 'little dark girls'. The Muslim body as a racialized body is something with which the individual and community, devout or not, must engage (particularly since 9/11).

In the reality of daily life, however, women experience this racialization as the shifting borders of cultural and generational differences (as I will note later), hybridities, and slippages in refugee cultural identifications with home and host ('native' and 'immigrant') cultures, as well as in women's own desires and struggles for self-actualization among these various communities. Mina's feelings of acceptance on her trip to the US, for example, contrasted with her feelings of abuse and disrespect on the streets of Berlin. Women refugees not only embody the boundaries of these relationships, they are expected to provide the 'bridge' across the 'borders' of home community and reception societies through a variety of activities, including their labour and their interaction with state agencies and educational institutions, as well as participation in multicultural or pan-immigrant women's organizations (Bauer, 2000).

Unfortunately for Iranian women, there is a misleading but convenient convergence between cultural stereotypes about Iranian women's behaviours promoted by Iranians themselves (based on idealized religio-cultural notions of behaviour) and by outsiders (based on historical and contemporary media portrayals). The irony of the surface illusions of Muslim refugee women's difference (in both Western stereotypes and homeland cultural ideals) is their convergence toward exoticizing and racializing women in ways that impose restrictions on women's movement and choices. Consequently, women become the site for contesting cultural expectations and images, despite their own lives and experiences to the contrary.

While many individual women strive to assert their own perspectives (regarding their choice to balance family and studies or to testify in court against Iranians who have perpetrated domestic violence), they often find that the pull of the Iranian community to 'protect' its image or the rejection by the host community because they are identified as exotic others complicates attempts to define their own place of belonging. Even refusals through hybrid choices or rejection of hijab may only intensify not dislodge the impact of these negotiations of power in spite of all the hybridization and generational differences that reflect different kinds of engagement with the cultures of reference. Both refugees and immigrants develop, to a greater or lesser extent, hybrid or cosmopolitan lifestyles in which both cultures of reference – the native and the new – are changing and adapting in ways that make it difficult to maintain the boundaries distinguishing those cultures.[7]

The focus of attention in contemporary immigration studies remains on the borders between the host society and its immigrant minorities. With our intense focus on borderland interactions at the exteriors of refugee or immigrant and reception societies, the interior fringes remain under-explored areas of refugee life. Through the 'disciplining' and 'racing' of their new lives in the workplace and main streets,[8] some refugee and immigrant women have learned to submerge or transfer their search for subjectivity beyond the gaze of their reception societies within the boundaries of refugee communities. While often invisible to others and ever unstable, the dynamic exchanges beyond the central borders affect women's engagement as agents and subjects. I wish to draw attention to the shifting margins of immigrant communities themselves that give rise to gendered renegotiations in the borderlands – specifically, engagements in four sites – within refugee communities, with the homeland, with other immigrant groups and with interior notions of self. Indeed, the 'Iranian community' as an imagined affiliation reflects connectivities maintained through kinship, friendship and political association by virtue of technologies of travel and communication across different reception societies as well as back home. Of course, in the very hybridity of refugee adaptations across these communities (speaking, as they must, in the languages of different host cultures), refugee women challenge and destabilize gendered borders.

Re-gendering the borders: the arus posti *and Iranian refugee communities*

In the first decades following the 1979 revolution, debates over gender were central in renegotiating the boundaries of exile communities. In this process, women's behaviours and experiences and women themselves remained emblematic of meaningful cultural traditions and legacies, much as the discourse about the reputation of the country had historically rested on protecting the *namus* (modesty or honour) of its women (cf. Varzi, 2006). For example, within their own communities (as well as in their host societies), women asylum seekers who transgressed the trends toward re-traditionalization were accused by other Iranians of 'losing' their culture. The margins of dominant masculinity and femininity become muted or confused across cultural borders (cf. Brah, 1996), so that culturally acceptable affection among men or among women might be read as homosexuality by North Americans or Europeans – something many Iranian refugees became obsessed with avoiding. Moreover, despite the changing contours of marriage and divorce in Iran (cf. Mir Hosseini, 1996), refugee women who sought divorce and custody of their children abroad were publicly accused of destroying the Iranian family.

In the midst of these debates, the *arus posti* (or 'sent for brides') offer especially interesting insights on the re-gendering of the interior borders of Iranian exile communities in their relationships with *home*. The paradoxical role of Iranian women, in both representing an imagined past or national culture and challenging the boundaries of modernity, is epitomized by the *arus posti.* What happens to these brides may signify the perils, as well as possibilities, for those who linger at the border.

Brides were often 'posted' after an unmarried male asylum seeker or student, who had been abroad for some time, was pressured by his family or personal circumstances to reinforce ties to Iranian culture by arranging a marriage to someone back home. Perhaps this also reflects the men's degree of detachment from the reception society. Male asylum seekers who were prohibited from returning home could be married by proxy in Iran or travel to Turkey or Oman for the wedding, after which brides might return to Iran to await the arrival of their travel documents.[9] I do not mean to insinuate that all such arranged marriages are unhappy or inegalitarian, that they are completely devoid of free choice or that the bride is always the object of the search for a spouse, but only that the arrival of *arus posti* brides into the communities amplified or intensified the community debate over women's place and so-called traditional gender roles and family life in exile, especially for refugee women who were struggling to fashion a very different future for themselves. The presence of these brides challenged some of the central, yet contested, notions around which the community imagined itself as modern and forward-thinking.

Despite the transformation of social life and the rise of individuation in modern Iran (cf. Adelkhah, 2000), the exile community, and often the husband, expected to find a young, inexperienced and virginal 'traditional' Iranian girl. The brides themselves became emblematic of cultural ideals, especially traditions of domesticity in which wives are expected to reproduce the home culture. Much as Stoler (1989) positions the role of white women in colonial empires preserving home cultures abroad, sending for *arus posti* conveys an expectation that women (and heterosexual unions) should protect traditions, caring for the home, preparing Iranian cuisine, raising children who are conversant in the Persian language and who show ritualized deference (*ta'arof*) to their in-laws. This is a vision that challenges the more active and resourceful image being created by other refugee and immigrant women, who are quite critical of men's motivations in sending for or accepting these brides. Moreover, unlike a refugee husband or other refugee women, the bride will be an immigrant and will be able to move back and forth between Iran and her new place of residence, a constant reminder of the contrast between changing expectations in Iran and the exile condition.

The husbands of such brides were often quite a bit older than their sent-for brides and had often been in sexual liaisons, even long-term relationships with non-Iranian women, although they not infrequently expressed distrust of non-Iranian women's sexual faithfulness. Or, conversely, they expected Iranian women to be sexually faithful in a way that they could not expect from Western women. Consequently, refugee women felt some pressure to conform to idealized expectations within their communities (as well as in the host society). The brides, themselves, for the most part had imagined partaking in new opportunities and lifestyles abroad, including more egalitarian conjugal relationships and activities outside the home. Not only were expectations on both sides often disappointed but the parties themselves became the substance of object lessons and debates throughout their local diasporic communities and beyond. I will describe briefly two slightly different *arus posti* cases, which contributed to the central controversies arising over sex and marriage that are part of the dynamic of redefining Iranian diasporic communities.

In my study refugee women present themselves as more progressive and feminist and yet *arus posti* come with their own expectations for modern living, which question the positioning of both refugee women and the image of traditional women back home. Take the case of Ameh Sima, almost thirty, who had been married in Turkey although she insisted that her husband who could not return to Iran was only a student. When I met her she was finally expecting her first child, and at this point was no longer able to help her husband in a small tobacco stand business he had just started in a large German city. She had a set of Iranian women friends in similar circumstances but most of her husband's family were political refugees. Her sister-in-law, who constantly reminded me that she is not a *ta'rofi* (meaning culturally traditional) and had left such ritualized nonsense behind, was berating Sima in her own circles for not getting out of her bed with a very difficult pregnancy to come to pay respects in person after learning that her sister-in-law's father had died in Iran. This same feminist-leaning sister-in-law had forced Sima, under threat of an 'outing', finally to tell her husband that she had been married once before in Iran. Sima's own goals were to build a sound conjugal relationship and a family (children were essential) to make the best of living outside Iran. 'Somehow they have both made their peace with their situation', her sister-in-law told me. In other words Sima was able to get something out of the relationship. *Posti* brides, she told me, might not have everything as they wanted it, but they were clear about what they were after and ended up getting more of what they wanted than the men did.

Nahid, by contrast, set out on a different route to independence, divorcing her husband, engaging in a tentative relationship with a German that ended badly, and going out to clubs with other Iranian women friends. In our long discussions she emphasized that, although she wanted to know a certain kind of independence in her sexual explorations, she felt her own socialization made it difficult for her to act freely on this – especially after her German lover referred to her in racialized terms. Moving to a new home and distancing herself from the Iranian community did not help. On my last trip, Nahid asked me what I thought about an Iranian woman who might decide in middle age that she was a lesbian and explore that facet of her identity. This is the same Nahid whose German lover had endearingly called her his 'little black one' ten years earlier. Perhaps a bit of the *posti* resilience is having an effect on how refugee women are also examining the interiors of their own desires.

In another case, a very young Maryam agreed to marry her husband, fifteen years her senior, because, as a member of a religious minority in Iran, her educational and economic opportunities had been limited. In fact, her father had lost his job because of this. She had left Iran to get an education. Her one other requirement for the marriage was a lavish wedding in Oman, where her refugee husband could meet her and where they lived for five months awaiting her immigration documents. He was by popular accounts a 'loser', for after fifteen years in exile he was still a pizza delivery man. The first year was a struggle, although Maryam found a job, took her college entrance examinations and resisted her husband's pleas to get pregnant before he got too old to enjoy his children. He promised to help her take care of a child while she studied. However, at the same time, his forward-thinking male friends (and former political colleagues) were warning him that an educated wife would never remain satisfied in such a relationship. After giving birth to her first child, Maryam continued to run the household and take classes at a local college. Other women said that she was still young, energetic and optimistic but that she would tire. Maryam confided to me that she was troubled by thoughts of whether she should stay with her husband, whom she does not love, to have a second child before she was too old or whether she should leave after her studies were finished to find a partner of whom she was more enamoured. Kobra, Maryam's refugee friend, became irritated at 'the progress' she was making. Although unmarried, Kobra had been in a troublesome relationship with another Iranian refugee for about ten years, worked in several jobs and seemed to make little progress in her own studies, despite fewer pressures to have children and take care of the household.

While some brides may be considered more traditional, the individuality and independence of 'brides' like these mean that refugees were forced to rethink their position vis-à-vis women back home as well as their attempts to redefine idealized gender relations in exile. The *posti* brides did not see themselves as political activists – the self-image which defined post-revolutionary exiled womanhood. In contradicting community expectations, these women forced the diasporic community to rethink the way it defined itself. They not only maintained physical links back home (unlike many of the refugees who have been unable or unwilling to visit), but they were also constant reminders that life back home, against which the refugee community and refugee women understood themselves, is different than imagined, less political, less traditional, very much less Islamic, and that women are more open sexually (although the demand for hymen repair confirms the continued importance of maintaining the appearances of virginity).

More importantly, their presence challenged activist women's definition and positioning of themselves and threatened to be a source of misunderstanding vis-à-vis the host community if they were acknowledged as participants in 'arranged marriages'. Refugee and immigrant women had to rethink their relationships not only to their conceptions of the homeland and the women who were left behind but also to how they have tried to construct their own identities against stereotypes of perceived oppressions and limitations of women back home. *Posti* brides, then, were more likely to be positioned by other Iranians as comparable with those 'uncivilized' French hijab wearing girls to which French Iranians responded by giving 'sensationalist talks of women's lack of freedom in Muslim countries', according to Joan Scott (2007: 163). The tension between notions of home and reception culture created by the presence of *posti* brides in the community generates a re-examination of not only relationships to, but also the roles of women in both homeland and reception societies. Indeed, their integration into the community was occurring at a moment of expanding protest for reform in Iran and, of course, social oppression is a main reason why many women opted to become *arus posti*.

Thus the positioning of sent-for brides is central to attempts by women generally to rearrange understandings of gender roles, of the community's sense of itself and of relationships back home. To some extent *posti* brides reaffirm traditional family and gender roles, as well as connections back home to Iran, and it might be argued that these brides are a force for what Honig (1998) calls, in the American context, the revitalization of patriarchy or re-traditionalization of gender roles through marriage to foreign brides or brides from the homeland because these women are seen as less politically resistant to whatever we call traditional culture than the refugee women have been.[10]

Increased numbers of *posti* brides and stories about them have circulated throughout the communities, heightening tensions between *posti* brides, their husbands, who are suspected of wanting 'traditional' women, and others in the community. Through these discussions around *posti* brides, those idealized notions of submissiveness and domesticity remain alive in the communities. Falling back on idealized notions that sometimes contradict their own experiences before leaving Iran, men often anticipate Iranian brides who are modest, virginal and compliant. These brides, on the other hand, like refugee women, are themselves looking forward to enjoying new opportunities and companionate marriages with westernized spouses. In demonstrating some agency and transgressing the stereotypes of women back home, *arus posti* force the disaporic community to reconsider the way it has imagined itself, exposing the shifting boundaries of tradition. These brides become a shocking reminder that gender roles and relationships back home, against which refugee women have defined themselves as more active and resourceful, are changing.

The dilemmas of *arus posti* become occasions for destabilizing and readjusting those taken-for-granted notions about Iranian women in exile and back home. However, in contrast to the *arus posti*, who perhaps are not motivated to narrate their experiences because they are less anchored in the borderlands and more capable of remaining on the other side of the border, refugee women often turn to re-engage the interior margins of community and self before returning to exterior encounters with their hosts.

Out of the borderlands and back: shape-shifting narratives and feminist encounters

Hamid Naficy (1996) alludes to the importance of gender in the creative work of redefining the self within the liminal zones of diasporic, transnational space.[11] The advantage of conducting longitudinal observations lies in the opportunity to identify the shifting locus of gender negotiations in these border zones. Over the last twenty years, Iranian refugee women have at different times engaged in various discursive acts towards narrating the self between their sometimes colliding borders, often through participation in Iranian feminist dialogues like those at the annual international Iranian Women's Studies Foundation conferences or in memoir writing in two contexts: the seemingly borderless expanse of the virtual world and the traditional print media. Two things about these 'interior' worlds are noteworthy: their transnational dimensions, across national borders, and the deployment of debates on cultural relativism and multiculturalism for framing responses of non-Iranian activists who are accused of essentializing Iranian women. The transnational reach of virtual connections reflects the breadth of the more 'grounded' local communities in which refugees participate. On the whole, refugees have friends, colleagues and families dispersed throughout a number of countries as well as back home. These endeavours are important for women's rethinking and reshaping themselves as citizen subjects across territorial spaces of exile.

Iranian refugee women began early on in their exile to establish and participate in women's organizations, seminars and other activities, working to alter perceptions of Iranian women in both the Iranian and host communities, especially after the publication and showing of *Not Without My Daughter* (Mahmoody and Hoffer, 1991). They have also mounted campaigns in defence of women's rights in Iran. Women's associations have survived cycles of inactivity or dispersal and reformation, as they struggled to exit the borderlands, at times participating in cross-border collaborations with local non-Iranian women's organizations, before drawing back to focus on writing journal or Internet articles about their experiences as political activists and refugee women or to participate in Iranian social justice campaigns or meetings of the Iranian Women's Studies Foundation (IWSF). Their experiences of collaboration across the feminist boundaries (of East/West) have often been unsatisfying – particularly as the climate of racism has intensified in their reception societies.

Although Karpinski (1999) proposes the 'nomadic' spaces of diaspora as places for refashioning collaborative feminist subjectivities and challenging the 'dominant order', western feminists often redraw the borders around notions of Islamic authenticity so as to preclude the collaboration to which Karpinski alludes. Iranian feminists have responded to these transnational feminist borders (Islamic feminism versus secular feminism) with a energetic critique of the cultural relativism that marginalizes refugee 'authenticity' or makes it difficult to lay claim to hybrid identities, substantiating Beltran's claim that borderlands cannot erase boundaries of power (Beltran, 2004) and leaving only an illusion of transnational feminism, despite the hopefulness of Mohanty's *Feminism without Borders* (2004) or Eisenstein's 'poly/dimensional feminism' where 'liberal, Islamic and Africana womanists dialogue with each other while challenging the limits of each other's understandings and viewings' (2004: 21). Thus, Iranian women activists have often found cross-border feminist encounters unpleasant or unproductive, encountering what they perceive as the 'misrecognition' of Muslim women in the guise of feminist cultural relativism (Bauer, 2005).

However, the internationalization of Iranian women's networks has provided possibilities for expanding feminist activism within the trans-local Iranian community formed across state borders or boundaries of power. Websites like Irandokht (*http://www.irandokht.com*) and Internet chat rooms in Paltalk provide space for virtual, unbounded community dialogue.[12] Since 1989, the IWSF has hosted annual meetings, providing forums for debate and collaboration among Iranian women of different political affiliations, ethnic and religious backgrounds, generations and countries of residence – including those still living in Iran – all of which can become a source of tension and conflict. Still, participants attest to the importance of debating and contesting issues of democracy, cultural accommodation, intercommunal differences and disagreements with western feminists over cultural relativism as well as renewing ties within the community through these forums and creating a diasporic Iranian identity of sorts.

The yearly IWSF meetings constitute an opportunity to position and express oneself and learn the language of defining the self in the interior regions of the borderlands – in Persian. Here women from all backgrounds, like leftist activist Raziye Gholami-Schabani, share testimonial accounts of their lives of political struggle (cf. Bauer, 2007). The IWSF, like some of the virtual communities in which women participate, has become a place for women to 'narrate' themselves in a Persian-language venue for compatriots who can help negotiate their transitional experiences. The greatest challenges are those posed by attempts to incorporate second- and third-generation women whose identities and cultural competences are hybridized differently from their parents and grandparents, as will be seen in the intergenerational contestation of multiculturalism (below).

Narratives can be seen as organizing mechanisms for composing our lives, as well as a means of attempting border transgressions.[13] Kaplan (2002), in particular, explores the connection between testimonial memoirs, social activism and the integration of traumatized identities (like those of asylum seekers) in the diaspora. When telling their stories to non-Iranian activist colleagues became strenuous and repetitive, refugee women continued to record personal memoirs, share them in Internet chat rooms, or publish them on Internet sites and in Persian-language journals. Exploring these interior margins expands refugee women's opportunities for creating a self that traverses unbounded communities of cyberspace publics and often seeks to position women as citizens of particular reception societies. Jale Ahmadi's 1999 essay, for example, seeks to explain her own location in a de-territorialized space between 'fundamentalism' and 'racism' against a backdrop of global acts of patriarchal Islamic oppression.

Some of the first women's exile monographs to incorporate strands of memoir appeared (in German and English) in response to Mahmoody's publication of *Not Without My Daughter*, along with the publication of (largely Persian-language) refugee prison memoirs like those by Gholami-Schabani, who has also spoken at IWSF meetings to wildly appreciative audiences.[14] In these and the recent spate of memoirs published in host-country languages, women exiles have sought to make sense of their experiences. The latter memoirs, published in host-country languages by refugees, immigrants and 'bi-nationals' of different generations, like Bahrampour (1999), Moaveni (2005), Satrapi (2003), Hakakian (2004), Latifi (2004), Nafisi (2003), Rachlin (2006) and many others, can be seen as a means of exploring one's hybridized or translocal identities as well as an effort to reposition the borders of belonging by explaining the self to non-Iranian audiences (cf. Elahi, 2006; Malek, 2006).[15] Although Ahmadi suggested to me that she was much more capable of fully interrogating her own life than were the social scientists who solicited her participation in survey research about refugee adaptation, many recent Iranian memoirs have also been criticized for enhancing existing, unreflective western stereotypes of Iran and Iranian women (cf. Donadey and Ahmed-Ghosh, 2008).

Perhaps more importantly, they also bring immigrant women from interior sites of inspection back to the borderlands with their hosts in acts of individual performativity designed to locate and unify the fragments of self, which one second-generation woman wistfully described as 'neither here nor there'. In a context where location is embodied, the body (gendered or racialized, imagined or encountered), as May Joseph (1999) suggests, increasingly insinuates itself into everyday 'performances' in locating the self. Women's narrative self is taking form in both Persian publications and in those of host-country languages – bringing attention again back to those borders of immigrant and host society, where the battles around cultural relativism (in the hijab cases) abound.

These (discursive and non-discursive) efforts of narration to establish what Ritivoi (2002) calls 'the narrative self' work to reposition the borders of citizenship and belonging as reflected to some extent in Joan Wallach Scott's (2007) examination of hijab-wearing French school girls' attempts to assert their citizenship. However, in explaining how their performances of self were an incorporation of both the French and Muslim aspects of their identities, Scott draws on Mahmoud Darwish's notions of 'architecture of the self' to propose a different kind of Muslim relationship to the state (one mediated by borderless relations through God) in contrast to the 'unencumbered', autonomous self of the French non-Muslim girls. This notion of the self conveys less flexibility than the notions of the disaporic self proposed by Ritivoi's 'narrative self', Wekker's 'multiplicitous self' (2006), or Brah's 'diasporic subjectivities' (1996). These latter notions of self seem more capable of capturing the fluidity of de-territorialized experience, although Brah's conceptualization does not convince me of the agency of women because it fails to examine the interior contours of the self. Ritivoi's 'narrative self' seeks to create a sense of belonging and personal identity through transcending the borders, so to speak, by incorporating the shifting cultural and racial experiences of the immigrant. This self seeks to construct 'narrative unity' between an immutable personal identity and a self which is contingent upon shifting social, cultural and political contexts – in other words, a way to bridge the borders of one's identity.[16] Thus narrative (memoir) writing, blogging and film-making have become ways to 'explain the self' across borders – however much this is positioned within imperialist and unequal relations of power.

Do these efforts to identify the self (two acts in one – the interior and the exterior) reignite the notion of boundaries or provide a basis for transcending them? Women's new senses of self play off of a variety of relationships across the borders of home and host cultures, both of which are changing and adapting. The challenge for women is to transgress the boundaries of internal and external conceptions of themselves, balancing ties to their various communities.[17] As yet we have no efficacious models for detailing the processes for integrating different aspects of the changing self across cultural boundaries. The border sentinels – stereotyped images – may be deployed in ways reminiscent of Mary Douglas's notions of 'purity and danger' by which difference becomes a marker for exclusion and alarm.

In ordinary practice, encounters are not always raced or gendered in the same way and stereotype frames (or cultural or normative schemas) are not necessarily used consistently to interpret interactions in the borderlands. However, as Jale wondered, 'When will Muslim women become white?' Since the interplay of relationships can give rise to the persistence of boundaries with the illusions of borders of difference, maintaining some 'tension' in the borderlands may be an important part of the process of building a workable self within the structures of state and institutional power dominating them. To examine those possibilities, I turn to the experiences of the second generation along both the interior margins and outer borders.

There is no integration here: on the necessity of gendering border studies

Through regular exchanges and visits, the community of diasporic Iranians beyond localized boundaries is expanded and community debates assume a life without borders. However, new borders are constantly emerging and they are, to borrow Hamid Naficy's term, richly 'accented' to flavour the processes that give rise to and sustain difference. Immigrant lives are increasingly situated within disparate local host cultures, and within them – in various exile Iranian communities. Iranian refugees in different locations come to reflect the flavour of those places (the languages and lifestyles of their host communities – American, Canadian, German). The second generation, in particular, may claim only partial membership in their parents' communities as their language skills and connections to Iranian culture are more tenuous and their longing for connections to their host cultures more vibrant and meaningful. For them, debates over *arus posti* and of *ta'arof* are interpreted through a hybridized lens.

While the young Iranians (or hyphenated-Iranians) I interviewed in Canada and Germany appreciated the social support of Iranian community networks, they rejected the highly ritualized forms of politeness (*ta'arof*) around paying for restaurant bills, seeing them as anxieties over money rather than as the means of negotiating reciprocity and respect. Like teenagers everywhere, Sepideh's lip rings and punk looks are deprecated by some of her mother's Iranian friends. Yet she recognizes that her closest and best friends are Iranian or other 'foreign' teens in Berlin. Perhaps more immersed in the borderlands than their parents they sometimes become secular defendants of Islam vis-à-vis their host society, to the displeasure of their political refugee parents.

It is perhaps among these second- and third-generation young people that the possibilities of transcending or transforming borders will be realized, although Brown suggests that we do not choose to make changes so much as 'suffer' them in our lives (2003: 193). Already positioned differently at the borders, this generation enters debates about cultural relativism and relationships with Iran from a perhaps more 'uncluttered' perspective than their elders. There are notable examples of the ease with which they sometimes engage in activism across the borders with Iran. Nazanine Afshin-Jam (a Canadian-Iranian singer) organized an international human rights campaign to support another Nazanine in Iran who had been sentenced to death for killing a man who attempted to rape her. The second generation have in many ways led the charge with revealing personal essays on sites like *Iranian.com* and in confronting their 'elders' who continue to express and explore themselves in Persian-language accounts of prison torture, sexual experiences and ideas about gender roles. Youth activism and Internet writing recast and explore their hybrid identities with both Iranian and non-Iranian audiences.

Second-generation women's participation inside the Iranian Women's Studies Foundation, especially in recent debates around multiculturalism, brings the interior margins of the feminist self across generations and cultural contexts into sharper view and draws attention to their own projects to achieve a narrative unity across borders. Many first-generation activists have been particularly distressed by perceived cultural relativism and tolerance (even preference) for Islamic feminism among western feminists (Moghissi, 1999; Mojab and el-Kassem, n.d.). Following the 2005 IWSF conference in Vienna, some second-generation Iranian feminists launched an internet exchange to challenge the responses (of first-generation political exiles) to the speakers invited from Iranian universities who appeared in hijab. Despite being partially hindered by the boundaries of language (not being fluent in academic Persian or not being able to talk easily to one another across various host-country languages), they raised their voices to shift debate on multiculturalism towards their more hybrid positions regarding hijab-wearing as a matter of individual choice and showing tolerance towards Islamist feminists – positions identified by many first-generation participants as typical 'western', 'liberal' ones.

When Vijay Prashad and I were writing the introduction to a special border crossings issue of *Cultural Dynamics* (Bauer and Prashad, 2000), we asked ourselves, if 'borders' do constitute a metaphor for social theory and unending possibilities, encompassing everything with respect to social interaction, how could border theory be theoretically forceful? However, examining multiple borders (interior and exterior) draws our attention to important disjunctures of power and anxieties.

Contrasting the experiences of women (of different generations) seems central to understanding the processes (of racialization and sexualization) that give rise to the persistence of, and slippages in, unequal power relations in the borderlands (within/among immigrant communities or within oneself – topics less frequently addressed in gendering the borders, but important to explaining them). Refugee women have not only 'represented' their communities' experiences of navigating opportunities, institutions and resources 'along the border' but are also reclaiming the borders of immigration with their narrative forays. This seems important to theorizing diaspora and its borders as they are at the forefront of 'rewriting' and complicating borderlands history.

Despite the hybridizing of their experiences and prospects for multiple 'crossings' over, second-generation women ultimately find that, like their parents, they cannot escape embodied differences of *kalle siah* (or performing racialized and sexualized identities) in the borderlands. And their increasing acceptance of their borderland positions (like creating monthly Iranian youth events) signals a realization that integration, as they once understood it, is not a reality, nor perhaps even a desirable goal. It would seem that they are in a better position to address the issues that have plagued borderland relations by convincing their 'others' not only to hear them 'in their own terms' but to avoid the tendency to confuse their perspective as 'the others'' own (Wyatt, 2004). The salience of the boundaries confronting them remains or is reified and strengthened. Perhaps it is sufficient to capture and hold the tensions of these marginal spaces, destabilizing the production of difference. But it seems something is missing – beyond the narrative unity provided by the narrator for herself and her others, something not eliminated by references to a 'third space'.

The emergence of intergenerational and gender variations in engaging the borders of the narrative self points to the limits of 'subject formation' (and to the extent it is located within it, border theory) as a conceptual tool capturing the complexities of Muslim diasporic border identities. Subject formation, as conveyed by Brah (1996), suggests the need to transcend binary categories. However, current conceptualizations do not speak sufficiently to racialization and sexualization and the extent to which the body is integral to belonging. How can *subject formation* do justice to both the self-inscription of experience and the political economy of relations that fixes them? Or, as Brah suggests, the confluence of personal biography and social history is indeed complicated. The problem is to capture (or find the methods to capture) how structures of power, community and the state, infiltrate on-the-ground experiences of race and gender, producing the illusion of immutable differences. Those structures of power themselves are not illusions. Nahid, for example, was trained in a health profession before fleeing Iran. After a delay in the verification of her credentials, she received approval for employment in a lower-ranking, lower-paying health profession, which required 'dirtier' work and 'heavier' labour. Other women also complained about the obstacles they faced in gaining recognition for credentials or retraining themselves and having to settle for semi-professional work. The potency of the margins is that they are geographical guideposts to where those sources of power and its con-tradictions lie.

Muslim refugee women are still required to cross many incapacitating boundaries in the imagination of others in multiple sites. This is the danger of the liminal space of the borderlands, as structures of power located in the state and other special interest groups seek to maintain the salience of gendered differences – as in the headscarf debates. Iranians have found that other immigrants around them have responded by reconstituting yet other borders. Today in Germany (to a lesser extent in Canada which also dabbled with the idea of special *shari'a* (Islamic legal) courts), other (non-Iranian) immigrant communities have taken up these emblems of difference, for example, utilizing Islamic mores to patrol and protect the borders of their neighbourhoods against even non-religious dark-haired pedestrians who walk their way. Right now, as Nahid described, she has to confront not only herself and her community in the borderlands but also Muslim/ Turkish patients and co-workers pressing her to explain why she does not fast during Ramadan or dress 'properly'. 'I fled Iran,' she says, 'to escape from fanatics and now I'm back in the midst of them.' Indeed, refugees and their communities must develop multiple strategies for addressing the messiness of the borders.

Multiculturalism as the recognition of cultures offers no clear guidelines either to removing or to reinforcing borders of difference (cf. Phillips, 2007; Amir-Moazami, 2005). As young Sepideh said, she finds herself neither here nor there at a time when emblems of difference are becoming more politically salient in discussions of citizenship, multiculturalism and belonging in the New Europe, as well as in North America.

Notes

[1] Cf. Hurtado: 'The geographical area represented by *la frontera* has become the guiding metaphor for all border crossings Chicanas do on a daily basis' (2005: 125).

[2] This tension repeatedly emerges in works like Lamont and Molnar (2002), which reviews both the structures of boundaries and interactions that give rise to them or Martinez (2002), which illuminates Chicana writers' crossing the borders of expected sexual roles in the pursuit of self-realization and pleasure.

[3] Since 1988, I have been following and interviewing Iranian political asylum seekers, primarily in Germany and Canada, countries representing two very different 'reception' societies. Most but not all are Muslim-heritage refugees. Their 'communities' in exile, however, include Iranians who have other-than-refugee status but whose experiences of 'bordering', and racialization in particular, are similar to those of asylum seekers.

[4] James Clifford seems to concur when he writes, 'women's [diaspora] experiences are particularly revealing' (1994: 313).

[5] This echoes Mary Douglas's conceptualization of purity and danger – where difference becomes a marker for exclusion and ritual practices are created to protect the integrity of communities from the pollution of outsiders (2002).

[6] These feelings can be complicated for some by the acknowledgement of Iranian cultural racism toward others.

[7] Postmodern, theoretical discourses acknowledge (even celebrate) such complexities of culture and the processes of cultural hybridization as conducive to fostering multicultural environments (cf. Werbner and Modood, 1997). In my use of hybridization here I adopt an untheorized referent of 'the mixing' of cultural influences.

[8] See Lisa Lowe (1996), for example, on the impact of host-country institutions and policies in creating or socializing immigrant workers to their place.

[9] While some students and immigrants could return home to help conduct the search for an acceptable bride, refugee men, at least until recently, were unable to do so. Thus refugee men sometimes met their prospective brides and conducted courtships on trips to Turkey or Oman, as well as through video, cassette, letter and phone exchanges over a period of time, after their families had located and 'interviewed' likely candidates.

[10] See Schaeffer-Gabriel (2005) for a discussion of similar re-traditionalization of masculinities among American men choosing cyber-brides.

[11] 'The ideologies and practices of a "United Europe," "American firstism," Serbian "ethnic cleansing," Islamic Fundamentalism, . . . are all instances

of not only (re)creating actual, material borders but also of drawing new discursive boundaries between the self and its others' (Naficy, 1996: 138–9).

12 These expansive virtual communities encompass participants from Iran as well. See Nouraie-Simone (2005) on young Iranian women bloggers' participation in virtual worlds.

13 'Disaporic identities are at once local and global; they are networks of transnational identifications encompassing 'imagined' and 'encountered' communities' (Brah, 1996: 196).

14 Originally published in Persian as *The Story of One Tudeh Woman*, Gholami-Schabani's memoirs are forthcoming in English (Bauer and Bouseh, translators).

15 There are also recent filmic explorations of identity, like Sadegh-Vaziri's video *A Place Called Home* and Satrapi's recently released film version of *Persepolis*.

16 Likewise, Brah suggests, 'Identities are marked by the multiplicity of subject positions that constitute the subject' (1996: 123), although the 'multiplicity, contradiction and instability of subjectivity is signified as having coherence, continuity, stability, as having a core – a continually changing core but the sense of a core nonetheless – that at any given moment is enunciated as the "I"' (1996: 125).

17 The challenge to Iranian women may be complicated by traditions similar to what Suad Joaeph (1999) has called patriarchal connectivity in the creation of Arab women's relational selves through which family ties mediate women's subjectivities. However, following Patricia Hill-Collins, Zaytoun suggests that a woman's 'self' is not defined by escaping ties with others, reinforcing the notion of multiple and shifting identities (2006).

Bibliography

Adelkhah, Fariba (2000). *Being Modern in Iran*, New York: Columbia University Press.

Ahmadi, Jale (1999). 'Women between fundamentalism and racism', paper presented at Trinity College (translated from German by Johannes Evelein, with Janet Bauer and Jale Ahamdi).

Amir-Moazami, Schirin (2005). 'Buried alive: multiculturalism in Germany', *ISIMS Newsletter*, 16, 22–3.

Appadurai, Arjun (1991). 'Global ethnoscapes: notes and queries for a transnational anthropology', in Richard Fox (ed.), *Recapturing Anthropology*, Santa Fe: School of American Research Press, pp. 191–210.

Bacon, Jean (1996). *Life Lines: Community, Family, and Assimilation Among Asian Indian Immigrants*, New York: Oxford University Press.

Bahrampour, Tara (1999). *To See and See Again: A Life in Iran and America*, Berkeley: University of California Press.

Bauer, Janet (2000). 'Desiring place: Iranian "refugee" women and the cultural politics of self and community', *Comparative Studies of South Asia, Africa and the Middle East*, 20, 180–209.

——(2005). 'Accented feminisms: the *misrecognition* of Iranian gender and modernity in western (feminist) theory', in Golnaz Amin (ed.), *Gender Relations and Modernity in Iran*, Cambridge, MA: Iranian Women's Studies Foundation, pp. 67–99.

——(2007). 'The life story of an Iranian woman – an introduction to Raziye Gholami-Schabani, Raziyeh', in Golnaz Amin (ed.), *Secular Feminism*, Cambridge, MA: Iranian Women's Studies Foundation, pp. 132–40.

Bauer, Janet and Vijay Prashad (2000). 'Dilemmas at the border: an introduction', *Cultural Dynamics*, 12, 3, 175–81.

Beltran, Cristina (2004). 'Patrolling borders: hybrids, hierarchies and the challenge of Mestizaje', *Political Research Quarterly*, 57, 4, 595–607.

Brah, Avtar (1996). *Cartographies of Diaspora: Contesting Identities*, London and New York: Routledge.

Brown, Richard Harvey (2003). 'Narration and postmodern mediations of western selfhood', in Richard Harvey Brown (ed.), *The Politics of Selfhood: Bodies and Identities in Global Capitalism*, Minneapolis: University of Minnesota, pp. 189–226.

Clifford, James (1994). 'Diasporas', *Cultural Anthropology*, 9, 3, 322–38.

Donadey, Anne and Huma Ahmed-Ghosh (2008). 'Why Americans love Azar Nafisi's *Reading Lolita in Tehran*', *Signs*, 33, 1, 623–46.

Douglas, Mary (2002). *Purity and Danger: An Analysis of the Concepts of Pollution and Taboo*, London and New York: Routledge.

Dyer, Richard (1997). *White*, London and New York: Routledge.

Eisenstein, Zillah (2004). *Against Empire: Feminisims, Racism and 'the' West*, London: Zed Press.

Elahi, Babak (2006). 'Translating the self: language and identity in Iranian-American women's memoirs', *Iranian Studies*, 39, 4, 461–80.

El-Or, Tamar (1994). *Educated and Ignorant: Orthodox Jewish Women and Their World*, trans. Haim Watzman, Boulder, CO: Lynne Rienner.

Ewing, Katherine Pratt (1990). 'The illusion of wholeness: culture, self, and the experience of inconsistency', *Ethos*, 18, 3, 251–78.

Hakakian, Roya (2004). *Journey from the Land of No: A Girlhood Caught in Revolutionary Iran*, New York: Crown Publishers.

Hatem, Mervat (1989). 'Through each other's eyes: Egyptian, Levantine-Egyptian, and European women's images of themselves and of each other (1862–1920)', *Women's Studies International Forum*, 12, 2, 183–98.

Honig, Bonnie (1998). 'Immigrant America? How foreignness "solves" democracy's problems', *Social Text*, Fall, 1–27.

Hurtado, Aida (2005). 'Multiple subjectivities: Chicanas and cultural citizenship', in Marilyn Friedman (ed.), *Women and Citizenship*, Oxford: Oxford University Press, pp. 111–29.

Joseph, May (1999). *Nomadic Identities: The Performance of Citizenship*, Minneapolis: University of Minnesota Press.

Joseph, Suad (1999). 'Brother–sister relationships: connectivity, love, and power in the reproduction of patriarchy in Lebanon', in Suad Joseph (ed.), *Intimate Selving and Arab Families*, Syracuse: Syracuse University Press, pp. 113–40.

Kaplan, Temma (2002). 'Reversing the shame and gendering the memory', *Signs*, 28, 1, 179–99.

Karpinski, Eva (1999). 'Choosing feminism, choosing exile: towards the development of a transnational feminist consciousness', in Alena Heitlinger (ed.), *Émigré Feminism: Transnational Perspectives*, Toronto: University of Toronto Press, pp. 17–29.

Lamont, Michele and Virag Molnar (2002). 'The study of boundaries in the social sciences', *Annual Review of Sociology*, 28, 167–95.

Latifi, Afschineh (2004). *Even After All this Time: A Story of Love, Revolution and Leaving Iran*, New York: Harper Collins.

Licona, Adela (2005). '(B)orderlands' rhetorics and representations: the transformative potential of feminist third-space scholarship and zines', *NWSA Journal*, 17/2, 104.

Lowe, Lisa (1996). *Immigrant Acts: On Asian American Cultural Politics*, Durham, NC: Duke University Press.

Lugo, Alejandro (1997). 'Reflections on border theory, culture and the nation', in Scott Michaelson and David E. Johnson (eds), *Border Theory: The Limits of Cultural Politics*, Minneapolis: University of Minnesota Press, pp. 43–67.

——(2000). 'Theorizing border inspections', *Cultural Dynamics*, 12, 3, 353–73.

Mahmoody, Betty and William Hoffer (1991). *Not Without My Daughter*, New York: St Martin's Press.

Malek, Amy (2006). 'Memoir in Iranian exile cultural production: a case study of Marjane Satrapi's Persepollis series', *Iranian Studies*, 39, 3, 353–80.

Martinez, Elizabeth (2002). 'Crossing gender borders: sexual relations and Chicana artistic identity', *MELUS*, 27, 131.

Mir Hosseini, Ziba (1996). 'Women and politics in post-Khomeini Iran: divorce, veiling and emerging feminist voices', in Haleh Afshar (ed.), *Women and Politics in the Third World*, London and New York: Routledge, pp. 142–70.

Moaveni, Azadeh (2005). *Lipstick Jihad: A Memoir of Growing up Iranian in America and American in Iran*, New York: Public Affairs Press.

Moghissi, Haideh (1999). *Feminism and Islamic Fundamentalism: The Limits of Postmodern Analysis*, London: Zed Press.

Mohanty, Chandra Talpade (2004). *Feminism Without Borders: Decolonizing Theory, Practicing Solidarity*, Durham, NC: Duke University Press.

Mojab, Shahrzad and Nadeen el-Kassem (n.d.). 'Cultural relativism: theoretical, political and ideological debates', unpublished MS.

Naficy, Hamid (1996). 'Phobic spaces and liminal panics: independent transnational film genre', in Wimal Dissanayake (ed.), *Global/ Local*, Durham, NC: Duke University Press, pp. 119–44.

——(2001). *An Accented Cinema: Exilic and Diasporic Filmmaking*, Princeton, NJ: Princeton University Press.

Nafisi, Azar (2003). *Reading Lolita in Tehran: A Memoir in Books*, New York: Random House.

Nouraie-Simone, Fereshteh (2005). 'Wings of freedom: Iranian women, identity, and cyberspace', in Fereshteh Nouraie-Simone (ed.), *On Shifting Ground: Muslim Women in the Global Era*, New York: The Feminist Press, pp. 61–79.

Phillips, Anne (2007). *Multiculuralism without Culture*, Princeton, NJ: Princeton University Press, 2007.

Rachlin, Nahid (2006). *Persian Girls: A Memoir*, New York: Jeremy Tarcher/ Penguin Books.

Ritivoi, Andrea (2002). *Yesterday's Self: Nostalgia and the Immigrant Identity*, Oxford: Rowman and Littlefield.

Rosaldo, Renato (1993). *Culture and Truth: The Remaking of Social Analysis*, Boston: Beacon Press.

Satrapi, Marjane (2003). *Persepolis: The Story of a Childhood*, New York: Pantheon.

Schaeffer-Grabiel, Felicity (2005). 'Planet-love.com: cyberbrides in the Americas and the transnational routes of US masculinity', *Signs*, 31, 2, 331–56.

Scott, Joan Wallach (2007). *The Politics of the Veil*, Princeton, NJ: Princeton University Press.

Stolcke, Verena (1995). 'Talking culture, new boundaries: new rhetorics of exclusion in Europe', *Cultural Anthropology*, 36, 1, 1–24.

Stoler, Ann (1989). 'Making empire respectable: the politics of race and sexual morality in the twentieth-century colonial cultures', *American Ethnologist*, 16, 4, 634–60.

Thorne, Barrie (1992). 'Girls and boys together . . . but mostly apart: gender arrangements in elementary schools', in Juila Wrigley (ed.), *Education and Gender Equality*, London: Falmer Press, pp. 115–30.

Varzi, Roxanne (2006). *Warring Souls: Youth, Media, and Martyrdom in Post-Revolution Iran*, Durham, NC: Duke University Press.

Wekker, Gloria (2006). *The Politics of Passion: Women's Sexual Culture in the Afro-Surinamese Diaspora*, New York: Columbia University Press.

Werbner, Pnina and Tariq Modood (eds) (1997). *Debating Cultural Hybridity: Multi-Cultural Identities and the Politics of Anti-Racism*, London: Zed Books.

Wyatt, Jean (2004). 'Toward cross-race dialogue: identification, misrecognition, and difference in feminist multicultural community', *Signs*, 29, 3, 879–903.

Yeganeh, Nahid (1993). 'Women, Nationalism and Islam in contemporary political discourse in Iran', *Feminist Review*, 44, 3–18.

Zaytoun, Kellie (2006). 'Theorizing at the borders: considering social location in rethinking self and psychological development', *NWSA Journal*, 18, 2, 52–72.

3

Brazilian Women Crossing Borders

SUZANA MAIA

Introduction

As you drive by warehouses, sweatshops and the abandoned buildings of Queens Boulevard, or even the more lively commercial areas of Astoria, in the borough of Queens, New York, it is easy to overlook the discreet dark facades and neon lights announcing gentlemen's bars and clubs. Inside, the clientele varies from Hispanic and white working-class men to Greek construction subcontractors, Italians in the restaurant business, groups of black teenagers and a generation of Albanian immigrants, newly arrived in the city. Brazilian women are the majority of dancers, followed by women from Colombia. On a regular nightshift, from 7.30 p.m. to 4.00 a.m., ten to fifteen dancers work in a bar, and dancers take turns performing on stage. Each stage performance lasts for twenty minutes. In Queens bars semi-naked women, wearing G-string bikinis, at times topless, parade up and down a small platform located alongside the bar counter. Every now and then dancers stop to receive dollar bills from clients, which they put under the band of their bikinis. When not dancing, a woman is supposed to socialize with clients on the floor and encourage them to buy drinks, for which she receives a small percentage. Some bars also offer 'lap dances'. In this case a woman performs a one-to-one dance for a client, usually executed in a corner of the bar or in separate space. In Queens gentlemen's bars a dancer can make between $100 and $400 or more per night. Contrary to the belief that erotic dancing is a form of prostitution, there is no exchange of money for sex in gentlemen's clubs and, in fact, there are strict city and government laws defining the borders between prostitution and erotic dancing.

As I watch Brazilian women dancing semi-naked and receiving dollar bills, I wonder how many material and symbolic borders they must have crossed to be where they are, living a life that they most likely never thought of when growing up in Brazil. How did they come to inhabit that part of the city? How are their bodies re-inscribed with the transnational move as they take up work in specific labour markets and inhabit specific locations in New York City's racial, gender, class and sexuality hierarchies? To think about the contemporary global world is to think about material and symbolic borders and how they have been formed, reformed and continuously reconfigured. It is to think about the construction of nation-states and the ways in which people, objects, information and imaginaries move from one geographic area to another. For borders are not crossed at once. After crossing physical borders, there are others, more symbolic but no less real and effective, which must be crossed, transgressed, reinforced and reinvented in daily life.

In order to understand present-day border crossings, it is of central importance to look at borders as continuities of colonial relationships. This does not mean dwelling in the past but deciphering how the past leaves its traces in contemporary processes of subject formation. Nationalist ideologies that supported colonial projects were based on gendered assumptions that saw colonies as female, to be conquered and domesticated by the virile powers of European centres. However, in addition to gender, racial assumptions were also of course fundamental to the organization of colonial enterprises. Throughout history, Brazilian women have appeared in the global imaginaries that link race to sexuality/gender and nation. The stereotypical marking of Brazilian women has been created by historically rooted discourses about racial difference, in which the body of the mulatto woman becomes the symbol of an untamed land to be penetrated and civilized. In the colonization period, and later on, in the consolidation of colonized nation-states and their attempts at independence, the encounter between the white man and the dark woman became the foundational narrative of the nation (see Sommer, 1990; Parker, 1991; Schwarcz, 1999). In Brazil, skin colour, since colonial times, has defined one's location in the internal hierarchy of Brazilian society. The lighter the skin colour, the higher a person's position in the social scale, with people of African descent tending to occupy the lower social positions (see Twine, 1998; Burdick, 1998; Hanchard, 1999; Norvell, 2001; Sheriff, 2001).

Yet, despite racial hierarchy and racist ideologies, the romance between the white man and an idealized dark woman has been reinvented in the context of economic instability in which women in the Global South service European and North American men. In the past few years, Brazil has become one of the most important locations for sex tourism, after Thailand and followed by the Dominican Republic, Cuba and the Philippines (see Kempadoo, 1999). Concomitantly, Brazilian erotic dancers have become the majority of workers not just in New York City's outer boroughs but also in places such as Switzerland, and Brazilian dancers and prostitutes have changed the face of small towns in Portugal and Spain (CHAME, 2000). The extension of this phenomenon has only recently caught the attention of the news and media, and researchers have begun to look at how these processes happen 'on the ground'.

As recent studies of colonialism have argued, there is no simple duality between colonizers and subjugated (Stoler, 2006). Although such studies have emphasized differences among the various colonial powers,[1] less emphasis has been given to differences among the 'subjugated'. This becomes clear, for example, in the case of European and North American discourses of feminists, researchers, government and NGOs, when referring to immigrant sex workers. As suggested by Laura Augustin (2005), debates have been polarized between, on the one hand, those who see immigrants and particularly immigrant women in the sex industry as victims of a patriarchal regime represented both by abusive bosses and unscrupulous smugglers; and, on the other hand, those who argue that sex workers are free agents and that sex work is just another form of employment where workers make rational calculations in terms of costs and benefits.[2] Both these perspectives treat all sex workers as if they were part of a homogeneous group of people, tending to overlook the actual conditions and dilemmas faced by particular women.

My purpose in this chapter is to examine the differentiations and hierarchies among a specific group of 'sex workers' – Brazilian women who work as erotic dancers – and to probe the way in which characteristics acquired in the place of origin are reconfigured in the new setting. It is estimated that about one million Brazilians live in the US, most without proper papers.[3] This includes both people who overstay their tourist visas and those who cross the borders illegally. Unable to work legally and with limited language skills, Brazilians end up in the informal economy of US cities. Because dancers are considered independent contractors, and as such are not required to have work permits, dancing is one of the few jobs that 'undocumented' migrants can hold, alongside housekeeping and baby-sitting.[4] Erotic dancing becomes, then, a desirable job for women from different socio-economic and racial backgrounds, who at times work side by side. I begin by examining how Brazilian women from different socio-economic backgrounds are differently located according to the social segmentation and geographical distribution of gentlemen's bars throughout New York City.[5] I then look at the construction of social borders between women and men from different national, racial and class backgrounds within a particular bar in the borough of Queens. My data comes from fieldwork conducted between 2004 and 2006.

Hierarchies of bars and bodies

Brazilian women began to enter the gentlemen's bar scene as New York City was being transformed into the new world financial centre, a global city from which the global economy was managed and regulated (Sassen, 2001). This led to the gentrification of areas of New York City (Smith, 1996; Papayanis, 2000), a process articulated through the regulation of the city's sex industry, and involving a multitude of different and, at times, contradictory interests and agents. In 1995, the City Council and Planning Commission approved New York's new zoning code, which became a turning point in the way public sexuality was organized and managed.[6] Arguing that the concentration of sex-related business was the reason for the decline of strategic areas in Manhattan, such as Times Square, and certainly having in mind the renovation that was already in progress, New York City government opted for the dispersal of sex-related businesses. Thereafter, spaces for commercial and public sex came under the category of 'adult entertainment business'.[7] In accordance with the city's new zoning laws, sex-related businesses were barred from operating within 500 feet of each other, of residences, schools, houses of worship and hospitals. Businesses that did not comply with these restrictions were closed or removed to other areas. By 1998, most sex-related businesses in Manhattan had to relocate or change to non-sex use.[8] What used to be the heart of New York City's sex-related business, Times Square, had been highly gentrified, as small gentlemen's clubs, peep shows and stores for pornographic material closed down or moved to the outer boroughs outside Manhattan: Brooklyn, Queens and the Bronx. Not coincidently, those were areas that had received most immigrants in the past few decades.[9]

The gentlemen's bar scene of New York City thus became hierarchically differentiated according to race and class between the bars located mainly in Manhattan and the 'local' or 'neighbourhood' bars, which, in the process of gentrification of the city, were pushed to the outer boroughs. Due to the high costs for an establishment in Manhattan, most bars there can be classified as 'upmarket' gentlemen's bars. Located in privileged areas of the city, they cater to a 'whiter' clientele of businessmen, Wall Street brokers and investors, tourists and international politicians. These bars employ mostly white American women[10] as well as women from western Europe, such as Spain, Italy, England and Denmark. Some eastern European women are also employed, and a few women from a variety of Asian countries, such as Thailand and the Philippines. Women from Latin America are also common, but they must conform to the 'right' mixture of 'exoticism' for the target clientele.

A large number of dancers work in these clubs. At 8.00 p.m., when women from the afternoon shift meet women from the night shift, there can be sixty to seventy dancers in large midtown Manhattan gentlemen's bars. Upmarket gentlemen's bars constitute a space for conspicuous consumption and luxury, as well as the reinforcement of privileged upper-scale masculinity. The patrons sit at ease in lounge chairs while they closely inspect the bodies and performances of the dancers and choose from among the large number of women the ones most to their taste. After descending from the stage the women approach the clients and offer a dance, which can take place where the client is sitting (table dance), or in a reserved room or space, sometimes called the champagne room, where they perform lap dances. According to state laws, patrons cannot touch dancers, and dancers must touch patrons only on their shoulders and legs for the purpose of balance when dancing. However, while table dances are regulated by the gaze of the administration as well as other dancers and clients, lap dances are not.[11]

Although there are bars in Queens that can be considered more 'upmarket', like the ones located in Manhattan, most Queens bars would be better described as 'neighbourhood' bars. Queens bars are in general much smaller and the contacts between clients and dancers follow different conventions. In Queens the stage where the women dance, for example, is situated near the bar counter, in close proximity to bar patrons. In 'neighbourhood' bars there is less emphasis on the performance of the women as dancers and their main work consists in socializing and drinking with clients. Dancers make their tips mostly in the form of dollar bills when dancing on the stage, or when socializing with clients and encouraging them to buy drinks, for which dancers receive a small percentage.[12] During their shift the women dance for about twenty minutes. They then break for forty minutes during which time dancers sit and drink with clients. Most of the clientele are regulars or locals who come to the bar motivated by relations of friendship and familiarity with the dancers, as well as for the promise of love and attention. As in the case of the relationship between sex tourists and sex workers in different locations of the Global South (see Cabezas, 1999; Brennan, 2002), Brazilian women in Queens bars tend to develop relationships to bar patrons that go beyond the bar scene. Rather than just patrons, men who go to bars become their friends and potential husbands, partly because marriage is the only means that undocumented women have to legalize their status in the US. Because of the area of the city where they are located, bar patrons in Queens tend to be from very different social backgrounds from those of Manhattan, that is, from the working classes, either born in the US or migrants.

Owners of gentlemen's bars in Queens are often of Greek or Italian descent, whereas the managers are often Brazilian men or men from other Latin American countries. A number of clients are Greek and Italian men. As second- or third-generation immigrants from more established ethnic communities in the area, Greeks and Italians are usually the wealthiest of the clients. They are often owners of restaurants and other businesses, or construction subcontractors. Although their income level is high enough to propel them into the American middle class, they seem to be more comfortable among the working class or in the company of other immigrant groups (see Lewin, 2005). Dancers see the Greeks and Italians as the most generous clients. Recent immigrants, such as the Albanians, have an inferior status inside the bars vis-à-vis Greek and Italian clients. This echoes social relations in Greece where Albanian immigrants very often provide cheap labour. Corroborating dancers' perceptions, recent news has linked the Albanians with the new Mafia formations that are succeeding the traditional New York City's Italian Mafia. Despite their association with illegal immigration and illegal activities in the US, their European origins and the whiteness of their skin place the Albanians structurally above the 'Hispanics' in the hierarchy of Queens bars, though below the Greeks and Italians.[13]

The 'Hispanic' men, from a variety of countries of Central and South America, might well be from the middle classes back in their home countries but in New York they occupy the lowest income and status. They work in the lower levels of the restaurant business as bus boys or kitchen assistants, or in the construction sectors as temporary workers, day labourers, or gipsy cab drivers. 'White' Americans are subdivided into two groups: working-class third-generation Italian-Americans and Irish-Americans, who usually have unionized jobs and are likely to live in Long Island,[14] and the children of more middle-class Italian-American and Irish-American workers, who moved to the suburbs in the previous decades. Searching for better job opportunities and a more exciting lifestyle, some men have moved to Queens, where rents are lower, although they may work in Manhattan. They drop by the bars near their homes once in a while because it is considered an 'edgy' thing to do, according to new standards set by hip magazines such as *Time Out New York*. 'White' Americans and 'Hispanic' immigrants are in diametrically opposed positions both in terms of US class and racial stratification and in the dancers' perceptions.

It is with men from such different hierarchical strata that Brazilian dancers socialize on a daily basis. Encounters between men and women within the bars by no means only follow government rules that aim to control public sexuality and manage such a diverse population. Encounters, as they happen 'on the ground', also follow the workings of class and race, which allocate different social locations to different subjects as they cross borders of nation-states. For Brazilian women, relationships that may begin in the bar scene will have unambiguous consequences for who will or will not be incorporated as citizens and who will dwell on the marginal borders of the state. In the next section I provide two examples of women who, although working side by side in a gentlemen's bar in Queens, belong to distinct social locations and have undergone distinct trajectories in their moves between Brazil and the US.

Transnational encounters: divergent trajectories

Nana is a thirty-four-year-old woman from the north-east of Brazil who has a degree in sociology.[15] Although she had a relatively successful career while in Brazil, her salary was not enough to sustain the middle-class lifestyle to which she aspired. One of the immediate reasons that she gives for migrating was her desire to buy her own apartment. Nana migrated to New York using a network of women from her home location. This included a family of eighteen women from her home town who were already working in New York City as erotic dancers. When Nana arrived in New York, she already knew that she was going to work as a dancer and had a clear idea of what that job implied. She brought with her a suitcase containing various apparatus she could use as props in her new work, such as G-strings, sarongs, small shorts, high-heels and little bags, some of which had referential marks of place of origin, such as the colours of the Brazilian flag. Upon her arrival, she visited four gentlemen's bars where she could consider dancing, all located in the borough of Queens, where some of her friends worked as dancers.[16] They could introduce her to the managers and with their help Nana could communicate better with clients. After considering the advantages and disadvantages of different bars, Nana decided to start dancing in two bars located in different areas of Queens: Blue Diamond and La Casa.[17] The argument that she gave for preferring to work in these bars is that, following city regulations, no topless work or lap dancing is allowed in them. The women wear small tops and minuscule shorts or skirts and/or G-string bottoms and they make their money in tips when dancing on the stage. This, according to Nana, makes the atmosphere somewhat more 'familiar' and 'respectable'. Another important consideration is that the bars that she chose are either located near her home or with easy access to subway stations.

Blue Diamond, the bar where I chose to concentrate my fieldwork, is located in Astoria, a neighbourhood that occupies the first stripe of land across the Queens-Borough Bridge from Manhattan and is easily accessible by major subway lines. It was in Blue Diamond that Nana met Janice. Unlike Nana, Janice did not have the opportunity to go to college in Minas Gerais, the state where she was born in Brazil. Janice also used very different means and networks to get into the United States.[18] While Nana, being from the middle classes and able to prove that she had enough resources in Brazil, was able to get a tourist visa, Janice's venture to the US included a passage through Mexico City and a risky trip crossing the US–Mexico border with the help of a 'coyote'.[19] Janice told me she had been here for about two years and started dancing right after her arrival in New York. She said that in the beginning she worked from midday to 8.00 p.m. and then from 9.00 p.m. to 3.00 a.m. 'I could hardly walk', she said, 'I just worked and worked.' Her desperate financial need became clear to me when she told me she had a ten-year-old son and had recently paid for repairs to the house in which he lived with his father. 'His house', she said, 'would get all wet inside when it rained.'

Although an occasional visitor to Blue Diamond might miss the differences between the two women, a more careful observer would soon perceive how their different social locations were manifest in their behaviour and the relationships they established in the bar. In Queens bars, it is common for dancers to form cliques who socialize among themselves, while analysing the behaviour of other dancers. Gossiping as a form of social organizing, traditionally associated with women's forms of knowledge, is widely practised among dancers. While sitting around the counter or when counting money, redoing make-up, or resting in the dressing rooms, women comment on other women's behaviour, while asserting their own position of difference. For Nana, as for other dancers in my research, the speaking of English, an educational background and the perceived moral behaviour of dancers are common markers separating classes/races within the bars. This became clear to me on the night that I met Janice for the first time.

I had gone to the bar accompanied by Nana and we went directly to the dressing room, where dancers spend time getting ready for the performance. Janice had brought with her a bag full of go-go costumes that she distributed amongst other dancers. She said that some of them used to belong to her sister who had recently moved back to Brazil and some were her own, but she had gained weight and they no longer fitted her. Despite her generosity, the other dancers who belonged to Nana's clique still tended to ignore her. Nana, even after receiving a couple of G-string bikinis from Janice, still gossiped about her. Nana was the first to tell me that Janice had crossed the Mexico–US border, while expressing her horror about using a coyote and risking one's life to enter the country. She told me that Janice was once arrested on prostitution charges, and that she still goes out with clients. In addition to using a language of morality to separate herself from Janice, Nana also marked her distinction in terms of education and 'quality of life': 'Deus me livre (or God protect me)', she said,

> this is a miserable life, just working, killing herself to support her family in Brazil, she has no life of her own, she never went to school and never

> learned English. It is unbelievable these women here, they make so much money and they don't make anything of their lives.

Nana, at the time of this encounter, had been in the US for about four months and she was already enrolled in an English school that was part of the larger university system in New York. Not having to send money to her family in Brazil, unlike Janice and a number of other women in the bar, Nana had the time and financial means to invest in the education that she understood to be absolutely necessary for a successful incorporation into the US.

In addition to education, however, Nana, as well as Janice, knew that a successful incorporation would also involve acquiring the means to become legal in the US. Nana had come to the country with a tourist visa that was soon to expire, while Janice never had any kind of visa. For both, as for most of the other women working in the bars, one thing was clear: marriage to a man who had American legal residency or citizenship was the fastest and the safest means to secure their legal permanence in the country (see Brennan, 2002). Dancers' work schedules and their relative social marginality mean that the bars and the men they meet in them become their most likely source of incorporation into the US. The variety of backgrounds from which clients come entail diverse locations in US society and also different styles of masculinity that are differently valued by dancers.

When entering the bar scene, Brazilian women see clients as different possibilities of obtaining what they need in order to achieve a minimally comfortable stay in the country, or to become more permanently incorporated in it.[20] The Greek and Italian customers, for example, are usually already in their fifties and sixties and have stable disposable incomes. It is part of their performance of masculinity to help dancers out.[21] This 'help', described as 'sponsorship', becomes crucial in defining relationships both within and beyond the bar scene and can be a significant factor in dancers' economic survival. Some of these clients are married and even those who are not rarely express a desire to marry a dancer. Rather, they prefer to patronize their favourite dancers with generous tips and financial help that is not limited to the bar scene. The 'presents' that they give may vary from expensive dinners and clothing to financial help with paying rents or educational fees. Dancers may become their girlfriends or lovers, but these contacts are not to be confused with prostitution, which implies a direct exchange of money for sex. Many women, particularly at the beginning of their dancing career, become involved in this kind of relationship in order to gain help in settling into the city. Sooner or later, however, the limitations of sponsorship relations between dancers and clients become apparent when issues of legality and 'cultural citizenship' (Ong, 1996) start to matter more. Although both Nana and Janice had the chance to be involved in relationships with older Greek and Italian men, only Janice did so and for a short period only. Both knew that marrying was the only real chance they had of facilitating their incorporation in the US.

Nana and Janice also disregarded the possibility of relationships with Albanian clients, viewing them not only as lacking legal status in the US but also as engaging in illicit businesses, including drug dealing across borders. Albanians are classified by Brazilian dancers in the bar scene as 'the addicts', a categorization that marks the dancers' sense of their marginal position in the bar hierarchy. Two other kinds of clients seemed more capable of providing Nana and Janice with better means to reach the kind of legal incorporation that they needed: Hispanics who had achieved legal status and white Americans. Reproducing Brazilian racist ideologies, neither of the women, both of whom belonged to the whiter end of the spectrum of Brazilian racial hierarchy, considered having a relationship with African-American men.[22]

Janice's lack of English and her consequent limited interaction with clients definitely lowered her chances of integration into US society. In fact, women such as Janice end up socializing mainly with lower-status women and men in the bars, that is, with other Brazilian women from the working classes and Hispanic men and women. Janice did have the opportunity to engage in relationships with clients who could help her through their access to social mobility, but she did not quite succeed in her aims. Although she managed to marry a Puerto Rican who was a legal US resident, her husband was still in a somewhat marginalized position. Unable to gain the full incorporation she had expected, Janice divorced him after the two years required by law to gain legal status in the country. She then moved back to live with another dancer from her network in Queens, and socialized mainly with people from the bar scene, still living a somewhat marginalized life.

Nana, on the other hand, did not consider getting involved with anyone who she deemed to be of lower status than herself. From the beginning she distanced herself from working-class Brazilian women and associated only with women who were university graduates and from the Brazilian middle classes. Although, as required, she socialized with all types of clients in the bar, she kept this interaction separate from her personal life until she found what she considered to be the 'right' kind of man, that is, white American. She concentrated her efforts on learning English, even enrolling in a class that focused on learning the American accent, and was careful, with her bodily display and the way she dressed, not to look 'too Hispanic', as she put it to me. That meant that she did not use much make-up and kept her hair on her shoulders, arguing that the other women displayed an overtly sexualized behaviour, even beyond what was necessary for working in the bar. When Nana met a new client she made sure to say right up front that she held a university degree and that working in the bar was only circumstantial, something that she needed until she got something better. Only four months after her arrival in New York, Nana met Jimmy, a middle-class man of Italian and Irish descent. Having grown up in the American suburbs, Jimmy moved to New York looking for an exciting life, which included going once in while to a gentlemen's club located near his house. According to Nana, from the first time they met they both knew that they did not belong in the bar scene, and started meeting instead in cafes and other locations in the city. Before Nana's six-month visa had expired, Jimmy proposed marriage to her, in a ceremony that took place in the suburbs of Pennsylvania, initiating Nana's process of incorporation into the American nation.

Conclusion: beyond the bar scene

The geographical distribution and social composition of upmarket and neighbourhood bars in New York are very different and invite different sets of contacts between dancers and patrons. The ethnic composition of bars follows the demographics of the neighbourhood and the ethno-racial distribution of New York City's new population. In Queens, it is not only the dancers who are migrants, but also many of the men who frequent the clubs. The kinds of relationship that women establish with other dancers and with the different clients vary according to women and clients' social and ethno-racial background. The first large group to which a dancer belongs is nationality and, at the time of my research, in Queens neighbourhood bars, most of the dancers were either from Brazil or from Colombia. New Brazilian dancers immediately joined cliques of other Brazilian dancers. Besides this division, however, there are other differences among dancers likely to be less easily perceived by an outsider. These are differences of class and race as defined transnationally, with reference to the lives they had when still in their home country. Differences tend to be perceived and spoken about in terms of education, and they are seen as manifested in the relationships that dancers establish with clients in the bar scene.

While in Manhattan bars dancers' relationship with clients tend to be 'bounded' by the bar scene, in Queens bars are not just a workplace for Brazilian women. Rather, bars also constitute their main space of socialization. It is in gentlemen's bars that most dancers meet men who become their significant others, and who represent their linkage to society at large. The kinds of relationships that dancers have with clients are hierarchically organized within the structure of US society in terms of race and class, and represent different access to US legal and 'cultural' citizenship. Dancers' relationships to bar customers beyond the bar are a crucial arena through which the women become incorporated into US racial and class configuration. Marriage to an American citizen is for most dancers the only way they can achieve or maintain status in the US, for only if they are legal can they think of moving to other job markets, or, equally importantly, of moving freely between Brazil and the US. Depending on the conditions under which the different women entered the country and the bar scene, their chances of meeting people will be more or less restricted to gentlemen's bars and the people associated with them.

The trajectories of Nana and Janice illustrate how life conditions, as defined transnationally, affect individuals' mobility and their capacity to be incorporated in different national settings. In the contexts of such gentlemen's clubs, race and class constitute central means of access to citizenship, which allows both legal incorporation into the US and the ability to transit between nations. It is in this transit between borders that race and class are reconfigured, determining new and better opportunities for some, but, for others, marginality and instability. In micro-environments such as gentlemen's bars, distinctions of race and class, as based on a language of morality and education, for example, end up delineating privileges and opportunities for the different women. Racisms characteristic of Brazilian middle-class society are, in this way, reconfigured within a new and different context. From the perspective of most of these women, white US men are the most desirable. In the US and within a global hierarchy of race, class and cultural values 'whiteness' signifies social status and occupies a privileged position vis-à-vis other racial-ethnic and national variants. White American men present Brazilian women not only with access to legality, but also with access to membership of an imagined American middle class that they envisioned when still in Brazil.

With the intensification of migration, former colonizers and colonized now meet in the global centres. This is not to say that global inequalities between those nations located in the First World and those of the Global South have disappeared. Inequalities between nations persist, but the power relationships have become more complex with the intersection of people from different nation-states who occupy different social locations within their own borders. Gender continues to be central to defining the experiences of those who cross borders, but so are race, class and sexuality. In addition, processes of differentiation and subject formation are transnational and can be fully understood in transnational reference only by looking simultaneously at women's background and their social location both in the contexts from which they come and in those to which they migrate. It is also necessary to look at the differences among women from the same nation.

Feminist approaches to sex work have insistently called attention to the question of the agency of sex workers, particularly those who are migrants from countries located in the Global South. In gentlemen's bars, the agency of migrant women is defined by a series of interrelated variables and circumstances. Rather than being satisfied with abstract questions regarding all sex workers' conditions, research must look transnationally at women's social location regarding class and race in relation to both sending and receiving countries, in order to understand the differences between the subject formation of different individuals within given national groups. What matters is to explore the ways in which borders are formed and crossed while paying attention to the particular, finding points of convergence and divergence that allow for a fuller comprehension of what happens now and happened then, and what traces have persevered throughout history in different geographical locations.

Notes

[1] Whereas the English encouraged, or rather mandated, the separation between colonial men and native or African women, the Portuguese made the mixing of 'races' a cornerstone of its colonial rule. In both empires, race constituted a central category of differentiation (see Stolke, 2006).

[2] The first view is embraced, for example, by anti-pornography feminists who believe sex work is degrading to all women and harmful to society. Influential organizations such as NOW (National Organization for Women) and CATW (Coalition against the Trafficking in Women) emphasize the dangers and perils of sex work and associate women immigrants in the sex business with human trafficking and disease, particularly the spread of AIDS. The second perspective argues that sex work should be treated as a form of labour, sexual and emotional labour, and should be properly compensated and respected. A number of liberal organizations, such as COYOTE (Call off Your Tired Ethics) or Sex Workers Alliance, are examples of attempts to de-marginalize sex work.

[3] For an extensive bibliography of studies on Brazilian migration, see Margolis (2008).

[4] For the argument that, although there is a tendency in academic and activist literature to blur the experiences of domestic workers, brides and sex workers, it is also necessary to look at the differences among these categories of gendered migration, see Constable, 2003.

[5] For more in-depth conceptual discussions on how space and place are intersected and delineated by race, gender and sexuality, see Massey, 1994; Bell and Valentine, 1995.

[6] For an analysis of the workings of the state and the law in delineating how sexuality is regulated and managed, see Bernstein and Shaffner, 2005.

[7] See New York Planning Federation, 2008. In accord with *Zoning Amendment 12–10*, adult establishments are so classified when they 'regularly feature' or devote a 'substantial portion' of their business to displays that contain: 1. Live performances which are characterized by an emphasis on 'specific anatomical areas' or 'specified sexual activities'; or 2. employees who, as part of their employment, regularly expose to patrons 'specific anatomical areas'.

[8] With the new zoning restrictions the number of sex-related business in Times Square dropped from 120 to nineteen (*New York Post*, 25 February, 1998). A number of establishments converted a percentage (60 per cent in accordance to the zoning laws) of their areas or the material displayed to non-adult use. XX-rated movie rental places now have a portion of their material constituting of mainstream videos and tourist

paraphernalia (in the case of Times Square tourist areas); other video store facades contain a back portion of their space occupied by peep shows and all nude performances. Some gentlemen's bars have divided their area into spaces where the women cannot and another area where they can disrobe.

9 In 1990, Brooklyn and Queens accounted for 60 per cent of the total population of New York, and housed two-thirds of immigrants. According to the 2000 US census, Queens, where most of the women in my research live and work, had the largest absolute population increase of (277,781), a growth rate of 14.2 per cent. White non-Hispanics comprised 32 per cent of the borough's population, while Hispanics comprised 25 per cent, black non-Hispanics 19 per cent, and Asian non-Hispanics 17.5 per cent (New York City Census, 2000).

10 Although there are also upmarket bars that 'specialize' in black bodies, or that dedicate one night of the week to the offer of particular 'race' or 'national' bodies.

11 Each table dance costs about $20 dollars for a song or a few minutes, $15 paid to the dancer and $5 to the club. Usually a person or a group buys more than one dance. The champagne room costs $500 for an hour: the woman keeps $300 and the bar $200. Usually the men tip $100 more to the woman. In just an hour a dancer makes $400. Usually the customers stay for more than one song, and what in fact happens in the rooms depends on the agreements made between client/dancer. For further discussion of the meanings and regulations of 'lap dance', see Lewis, 2000.

12 Drinking with clients used to be optional. Recently it has become a requirement of the bars that a dancer must 'make' a minimum of five drinks a night. Every time a client buys a dancer a drink, the bartender gives the dancer a ticket that she can exchange with the management for cash at the end of the night.

13 Here I use the term 'Hispanic' rather than 'Latino/a' to be consistent with the usage of my subjects. See Beserra (2005) for an in-depth study of how, according to the class location they occupy, Brazilians tend to be perceived either as Latinos/Hispanics or Brazilians, when they reaffirm the particularity of Brazilian-ness.

14 In their studies of the construction of whiteness in the US, Brodkin Sacks (1994) and Frankenberg (1997) examine how Euro-Americans from the southern and eastern parts of Europe became incorporated into whiteness. Sacks argues that this shift in racial identity was parallel to the expansion of the American middle classes after the Second World War, and spurred by what she defines as 'affirmative action'. She points to the roles of the GI Bill, the Federal Housing Authority and the Veterans Administrations in promoting college education, home ownership and

suburban residence and lifestyle for Euro-Americans, to the detriment of African-American men.

15 In order to protect the identity of my subjects, both the names of the women and of the bars where they work are fictional.

16 In order to start dancing, it is necessary to book an audition beforehand, which a dancer friend could easily do just by asking the manager of the bar. Although there are agencies that mediate between dancer and bar, most women have a friend who makes the arrangement for them. The managers are often willing to employ new dancers as clients are allured by a constant variety of bodies and faces.

17 Since the bars must offer a variety of dancers each night, dancers usually rotate among a number of bars (two or three) through the week.

18 But she too knew what to expect: while Nana had the help of a network of women from her home city, Janice had a sister who had worked as a dancer and married a Colombian with American citizenship.

19 According to Rohter in the *New York Times* in June 2005, more Brazilians than any other nationality after Mexicans were crossing the Mexican–US border illegally: in two days alone the border patrol agents in Texas detained 232 Brazilian men and women. One city in Brazil issued 140 passports in one day to Brazilians who wanted to leave the country.

20 But, as Constable (2003) notes in the case of Chinese and Philippino women who engage in mail-order marriages with American men, the fact that these relationships are so embedded in political economic factors does not mean that they are devoid of emotions and affection.

21 For an analysis of sex tourists in Third World locations and their use of the language of 'help' in their 'performance of masculinity' and relationships to both sex workers and girlfriends, see Cabezas (1999).

22 The only form in which Brazilian women were involved with men of African descent was through engaging in paid marriages which cost about $10,000 in New York, at the time of my research.

Bibliography

Augustin, Laura (2005). 'Migrants in the mistress' house: other voices in the trafficking debate', *Social Politics: International Studies in Gender, State and Society*, 12, 1, 96–117.

Bell, David and Gill Valentine (1995). *Mapping Desire: Geographies of Sexualities*, London and New York: Routledge.

Bernstein, Elizabeth and Laurie Shaffner (eds) (2005). *Regulating Sex: The Politics of Intimacy and Identity*, London and New York: Routledge.

Beserra, Bernadete (2005). 'From Brazilians to Latinos? Racialization and Latinidad in the marketing of Brazilian carnival in Los Angeles', *Latino Studies*, 3, 1, 53–75.

Brennan, Denise (2002). 'Selling sex for visas: sex tourism as a stepping-stone to international migration', in Barbara Ehrenreich and Arlie R. Hochschild (eds), *Global Woman: Nannies, Maids, and Sex Workers in the New Economy*, New York: Owl Book, pp. 154–68.

Brodkin Sacks, Karen (1994). 'How did Jews become white folks?', in Steven Gregory and Roger Sanjek (eds), *Race*, New Brunswick: Rutgers University Press, pp. 78–102.

Burdick, John (1998). *Blessed Anastácia: Women, Race, and Popular Christianity in Brazil*, London: Routledge.

Cabezas, Amalia L. (1999). 'Women's work is never done: sex tourism in Sosua, Dominican Republic', in Kamala Kempadoo (ed.), *Sun, Sex, and Gold: Tourism and Sex Work in the Caribbean*, New York and Oxford: Rowan and Littlefield Publishers, pp. 93–123.

'Census 2000 data for the State of New York', *http://www.census.gov/census2000/states/ny.html.*

CHAME (Centro Humánitario de Apoio a Mulher) (2000). *Migração Feminina Internacional: Causas e Conseqüências*, Salvador, Brazil e Zurich.

Constable, Nicole (2003). *Romance on a Global Stage: Pen Pals, Virtual Ethnography and 'Mail Order' Marriages*, Berkeley: University of California Press.

Frankenberg, Ruth (1997). 'Local whiteness, localizing whiteness', in Ruth Frankenberg (ed.), *Displacing Whiteness*, Durham, NC: Duke University Press, pp. 1–33.

Hanchard, Michael G. (ed.) (1999). *Racial Politics in Contemporary Brazil*, Durham, NC: Duke University Press.

Kempadoo, Kamala (1999). 'Continuities and change: five centuries of prostitution in the Caribbean', in Kamala Kempadoo (ed.), *Sun, Sex, and Gold: Tourism and Sex Work in the Caribbean*, New York and Oxford: Rowan and Littlefield Publishers, pp. 3–35.

Lewin, Tamar (2005). 'Up from the holler: living in two worlds, at home in neither', in *Class Matters*, by correspondents of the *New York Times*, New York: Times Books.

Lewis, Jacqueline (2000). 'Controlling lap dance: law, morality, and sex work', in Ronald Weitzer (ed.), *Sex for Sale: Prostitution, Pornography, and the Sex Industry*, New York: Routledge.

Margolis, Maxine (2008). *http://sitemason.vanderbilt.edu/files/iSwFIQ/Margolis%Bibliography._Bib.doc.*

Massey, Doreen (1994). *Space, Place, and Gender*, Minneapolis: University of Minnesota Press.

New York Planning Federation (2008). 'Everything you ever wanted to know about adult entertainment regulations', *http://www.nypf.org/adult_ entertainement.htm.*

Norvell, John Michael (2001). 'Race mixture and the meaning of Brazil: race, class, and nation in the Zona Sul of Rio de Janeiro', Ph.D. thesis, Cornell University.

Ong, Aihwa (1996). 'Cultural citizenship as subject-making: immigrants negotiate racial and cultural boundaries in the United States', *Current Anthropology*, 37, 5, 737–62.

Papayanis, Marilyn Adler (2000). 'Sex and the Revanchist City: zoning out pornography in New York', *Environment and Planning D: Society and Space*, 18, 3, 341–54.

Parker, Richard (1991). *Bodies, Pleasures and Passions: Sexual Culture in Contemporary Brazil*, Boston: Beacon Press.

Piscitelli, Adriana (2004). 'Entre a Praia de Iracema e a União Européia: Turismo Sexual Internacional e Migração Feminina', in A. Piscitelli, Maria F. Gregory, and Sergio Carrara (eds), *Sexualidades e Saberes: Convenções e Fronteiras*, Rio de Janeiro: Garamond, pp. 283–318.

Rohter, Larry (2005). 'Brazilians streaming into US through Mexican border', *New York Times*, 30 June.

Sassen, Saskia (2001). *Global Cities: New York, London and Tokyo*, Princeton, NJ: Princeton University Press.

Schwarcz, Lilia Moritz (1999). *The Spectacle of Races: Scientists, Institutions, and the Race Question in Brazil, 1870–1930*, New York: Hill and Wang.

Sheriff, Robin E. (2001). *Dreaming Equality: Color, Race, and Racism in Urban Brazil*, New Brunswick: Rutgers University Press.

Smith, Neil (1996). *The New Urban Frontier: Gentrification and the Revanchist City*, London and New York: Routledge.

Sommer, Doris (1990). 'Irresistible romance: the foundational fictions of Latin America', in Homi Bhabha (ed.), *Nation and Narration*, New York: Routledge, pp. 71–98.

Stoler, Ann Laura (ed.) (2006). *Haunted by Empire: Geographies of Intimacy in North American History*, Durham, NC: Duke University Press.

Stolke, Verena (2006). 'O Enigma das Intersecções: classe, "raça", sexo, sexualidade. A formação dos impérios transatlânticos do século XVI ao XIX', *Estudos Feministas*, 14, 1, 15–42.

Twine, Frances Winddance (1998). *Racism in a Racial Democracy: The Maintenance of White Supremacy in Brazil,* New Brunswick: Rutgers University Press.

4

Teacher Supply and the Wales–England Border, 1922–1950: a Gendered Perspective

SIAN RHIANNON WILLIAMS

Introduction

In 1944, the McNair Committee reflected on what it considered to be the 'high regard' with which teachers historically were held in Wales, and concluded: 'Consequently, Wales has always been able to recruit for its own needs and also for service in England' (McNair Report, 1944: 124). Indeed, for much of the twentieth century, teachers were referred to jokingly as one of Wales's three chief exports; the others were, famously, coal and water. Welsh-born teachers, many of them Welsh speaking, became a significant presence in the schools of the London area, the Midlands, north-west England and elsewhere. Many 'came home' to Wales in due course while many others remained in England, either by choice or circumstance, and were joined by the next generation of migrant newly qualified teachers (NQTs). It is estimated that around 70 per cent of London's teachers were of Welsh origin in 1957 (Beddoe, 2000: 142), a reminder of the scale and intensity of the out-migration.

This chapter will examine aspects of cross-border movement of teachers from the perspective of gender. A discussion of gender is relevant in this context, not merely because of the gendered training and occupational structure of the teaching profession in a period when issues of supply and demand were closely related to debates around gender issues, but also because migration itself often involves a renegotiation (or consolidation) of gender roles and affects men and women differently (see Willis and Yeoh, 2000: xi–xxii). Migration is also bound up with issues of cultural and national identity which, in turn, have a gendered dimension.

Method

The study is based largely upon the material gleaned from the personal testimony of twenty-four former elementary teachers – eighteen women and six men (the imbalance is representative of the dominance of women in teaching) – who entered training between 1924 and 1947. Most were interviewed as part of a larger oral history project also involving secondary teachers, and the interviews were recorded and transcribed in 2001–2. A questionnaire was sent to eight who could not be interviewed, several of whom were in England. The focus of the project was on the teachers' professional histories, and not on migration as such, but the interviews revealed that almost all those who had trained as elementary teachers had spent some time in England, either for training or employment, usually to obtain their first post. A shorter questionnaire, focusing more specifically on migration, was later sent to a further six retired Welsh-born teachers living in England who had trained before 1950 (five were women), and their responses have also informed some of the questions raised by the original material.

Greater use has been made of interviewing as a research method in migration studies in recent years, while oral history has always been a core methodology in women's, gender and labour history, including the history of women teachers (see, for example, Willis and Yeoh, 2000; Weiler and Middleton, 1999). Reviewing the tradition of oral history, Bornat and Diamond mention the 'enormous role' it has to play in the growing field of migration studies. They quote Thompson and Bauer, two pioneers of the method, who claim: 'It is only though life story evidence that we can unearth the process of migration . . . the help from kin and friends in getting work and lodging on arrival, the long term outcome . . .' (Bornat and Diamond, 2007: 31). Certainly, these interviews have been extremely valuable in providing qualitative personal detail and a rich sense of atmosphere, although their limitations as historical evidence are constantly kept in mind. Documentary and archival sources have also been utilized to provide a complementary context to the life histories.

The focus here is on certificated, college-trained teachers, that group of NQTs who, on completion of training, found that they had little choice but to move out of Wales to find employment. The main emphasis is on south Wales where the interviews were conducted, but the documentary material reflects a wider geographical picture. The period between 1922 and 1950 has been chosen to incorporate the respondents' training years, and also because cross-border movement of teachers occurred on a larger scale during this time than ever before.

Several of the informants were interviewed in Welsh. In Welsh, the significance of crossing the border when travelling to England is emphasized by common use of the phrases '*dros y ffin*' (over the border) or '*dros Glawdd Offa*' (across or over Offa's Dyke). Some informants reflected this awareness through their use of these terms, while those using English referred to 'crossing the border' or 'going away' to England.

Reasons for moving

A large-scale study of internal migration in Britain has demonstrated that there was little difference in the frequency of migration between men and women after the mid-nineteenth century, although women became increasingly likely to migrate as time progressed. Overall, they were more likely to move for family reasons than for employment (Pooley and Turnbull, 1998: 72–7). However, migration patterns vary according to circumstances of time and place. In the case of teachers, women comprised the majority of migrants and were, like the men, moving to obtain employment. This is not to deny the importance of personal, cultural and social factors, such as family expectations or the presence or absence of friends or lovers in the decision taken by these young people to move. The comparatively greater social freedom allowed to some women by the 1930s and the assistance given by relatives and friends in the reception area are two such influences which increased the likelihood of migration. Reasons for return are also studied here. In this sample (which has a strong local bias) twenty-one of the twenty-four interviewees returned to their home area, mostly within five years, although six women subsequently returned to England, five to join husbands or fiancés, while one made a second return home. The respondents were all in their late teens or early twenties at the time of their first move, and although anecdotal evidence points to instances of teachers moving or returning to England in mid-life to improve their career prospects, this was predominantly a migration of young, single people.

Migration for training

Despite the increase in provision for teacher training in Wales in the two decades preceding the First World War, the continued growth in the numbers of potential teachers and a greater emphasis on the importance of training meant that provision was still inadequate. The tradition of training in England, a feature of the mid-nineteenth century, therefore continued, even when local provision was available. The element of individual choice and motivation was stronger when a decision to move to England was made prior to training rather than afterwards, although the degree of independent decision making was limited, especially for girls. It was less common for female students to move out of Wales for training in the early 1920s than later in the period, partly because of protective attitudes towards women at that time, but also because relatively more training places were then available locally. Later, the over-supply of teachers in Wales led to a reduction in training college places at a time when competition, especially for women's colleges, was greater, thus necessitating moves to England. However, the evidence suggests that most applicants, both men and women, preferred to train locally. Aspiring elementary teachers of working- and lower-middle-class backgrounds would usually make a local training institution their first choice, mainly for financial reasons, but increasingly, training places were limited (see Williams, 2005).

The main reason for attending a local college was a wish to be close to home and family. The evidence suggests that this was a more significant reason for girls if either of their parents, but particularly their mothers, was in poor health. It was girls also who faced most family pressure to train locally due to parental anxiety regarding their safety and well-being. Fears of the unknown and of moral corruption of daughters were primary concerns of parents, although not always explicitly articulated. Even for local colleges, there were worries. As MB (female, Swansea Training College (TC), 1940–2) exclaimed, 'you'd think we were going to America, not just to Swansea or Barry!' Yet, knowledge of a local institution and, in particular, of a principal whose reputation was for close supervision of girls, made these colleges a more reassuring choice for parents, whose views, as several interviewees emphasized, were not ordinarily opposed. The question of allowing their daughters to venture further afield, particularly to an English city where greater dangers might be lurking, was a source of much heartfelt worry. Once war broke out there was the additional risk of bombing. HW, who had made Goldsmith's College in London her first choice, attended an interview there in 1940, chaperoned by her chapel minister. She later declined her offer of a place because her mother wanted her closer to home. She obtained a place at Swansea Training College (where her uncle knew the principal), through clearing, and, ironically, witnessed there some of the worst bombing in Britain.

The availability of training for particular subjects or sectors was another key determinant of the need or wish to migrate for training; again, this was gender specific. Wales was comparatively well endowed with general training institutions but with the exception of 'the Domestic Arts' and agriculture, training for teaching technical and specialist subjects was lacking. Men wishing to obtain specialized training in craft subjects, and all students wishing to attend a designated physical education institution, would need to cross the border, for example, to Bedford (women) or Loughborough (men). EP (Shoreditch TC, 1948–50) mentioned that there was also a 'lack of sympathy' with his subject (handiwork) in Wales. In the early years of the century, nursery and kindergarten training courses (awarding National Froebel Union certificates) were available at Bangor and Cardiff, but these were later discontinued, forcing young women wishing to teach very young children to train outside Wales (PRO ED/86/94).

Religious background was also a factor. Most potential teachers from Wales were Nonconformists and attended a non-denominational institution. For those students who were Church of England adherents there were more openings in England than in Wales. The Anglican colleges would refer applicants to related institutions. One informant who had made St Mary's Training College, Cheltenham, her first choice was directed to St Mary's, Bangor, while another, who had chosen Bangor, went to Lincoln. There were sixty places a year for men at Trinity College, Carmarthen, but a rejection meant crossing the border. The training college clearing house system also facilitated moves. Those not accepted in Wales usually attended a college in England.

Recruitment methods employed by English training colleges, advice given by secondary school teachers or a local tradition of former pupils having attended particular colleges were also influential in deciding cross-border moves of school leavers. The principal of Portsmouth Training College (for women) actively recruited in Wales by holding interviews in Cardiff and Newport for which 'there were always plenty of applicants', and made it known that the institution welcomed Welsh students (DEB, letter to the author, 2001). DEB, who left Penygraig, Rhondda, for Portsmouth in 1936, estimated that around 25 per cent of students were from Wales during her time there. Three informants from Maesteg, Glamorgan, testified to a tradition among local girls to apply to Dudley College in Warwickshire. DR remembered seven Maesteg students, as well as several others from elsewhere in the south Wales valleys there in 1940–2. The Maesteg group were, in her words, '*fel y* Mafia *'na, wrth gwrs*' ('like the *Mafia* there, of course'), a reference to their familial closeness and otherness vis-à-vis the English institution.

To leave Wales at eighteen, particularly for young people such as these who had been brought up in a close-knit environment, was a life-changing event and required determination. MD's recounting of her (independent) decision to leave Llanelli, Carmarthenshire, to train at Avery Hill in London in 1938 conveyed a sense of rebellion. She described the move as an opportunity to escape patriarchal authority and restrictive social norms linked to chapel-going. As a Welsh speaker, she was under some pressure from the Welsh lecturer at Swansea Training College to stay in Wales (see below), but resisted. Awareness of her mother's worries did not dissuade her either. Avery Hill was evacuated to Huddersfield soon after her arrival there, so the increased distance from home and the war situation meant that, for several years, she saw her parents only rarely. In contrast to the Maesteg girls' experience in Dudley, MD had little or no contact with other students from Wales since they were located in various parts of the college. Reflecting upon it, she wondered whether separation may have been a deliberate policy.

The fact that MD had an aunt in London went some way towards helping her mother come to terms with her daughter's departure, and it is clear that networks of family and friends were of great importance in facilitating and encouraging cross-border moves for training. This is also evident in the history of those who moved to find employment.

Migration for jobs

The main reason for the outpouring of young certificated teachers in this period was the lack of employment opportunities in Wales. As potential state employees, NQTs were at the mercy of the vicissitudes of government and local education authority (LEA) policy, which in turn, was determined by the ups and downs of the economy. It is not possible to give a detailed account of the changes in supply and demand and the effects on different parts of Wales within such a short chapter, but it is clear that the over-supply which affected both England and Wales after 1922 was especially marked in Wales (see Burnham Report, 1925: 46; Partington, 1976: 26). The measures taken by LEAs in an attempt to reduce the effect of drastic cuts in finance on NQTs all had repercussions for gender issues in teaching. These included restrictions on the intake to training colleges, the introduction of marriage bars, the employment of a greater proportion of uncertificated and supplementary teachers (mainly women, who were cheaper to employ), combining infant and junior departments and placing head teachers in charge of classes in smaller schools.

Despite these efforts and the introduction of a quota system by the government, unemployment among NQTs in Wales continued to grow. The deep industrial depression intensified and prolonged the situation in the south Wales valleys in particular. Notwithstanding the coming of war, which caused a shortage of men teachers, the over-supply of NQTs continued into the 1940s. By this time, the vast majority of students in Welsh training colleges did not expect to be employed in Wales on completion of their course. Tellingly, all respondents from south Wales who had trained in the 1930s and 1940s stressed emphatically the near impossibility of securing a job in the area: it was a similar situation in north Wales.

The scale and timing of the exodus is reflected in 'first destination' figures of individual training institutions. In Bangor Normal Training College in north Wales (for men and women), the percentage of students obtaining employment in Wales decreased sharply in 1925, as shown below (Welsh Language Report, 1927: 119–20):

1923	50.0% (69/126)
1924	55.0% (76/138)
1925	18.8% (23/122)

The vast majority of these were Welsh-domiciled students. According to the principal of the college, 78 women who qualified in 1924 had found employment but only as uncertificated teachers (see Partington, 1976: 26). In 1925, the percentage of men students leaving Trinity College, Carmarthen, who obtained a post in Wales was 18.6 per cent (11/59), a similar proportion to Bangor (Welsh Language Report, 1927: 119). By the 1930s the situation had worsened and migration intensified. Table 1 below shows the effect on the women leaving Glamorgan Training College, Barry, all of whom were from the industrial valleys of Glamorgan and Monmouthshire. The male students at Caerleon Training College, Monmouthshire, were experiencing similar problems obtaining work. In 1936, 12 NQTs from the 1934 cohort of 65 (18.5 per cent) and 15 (36.5 per cent) of the 1935 cohort (of 41) were still unemployed, but unwilling to move. Caerleon's inspectors commented: 'It is possible that these figures look worse than they really are, owing to the reluctance of some students to apply for, or take up, posts away from home, preferring to await the chance of a local appointment' (Caerleon Report, 1937: 13). Interestingly then, these men were, it seems, no less eager than women to remain close to home. It is reasonable to suggest that the cost of accommodation (for lodgings were relatively expensive), young men's wish to continue to have their domestic needs serviced by their mothers, as well as an attachment to home or to Wales might provide an explanation of their motives. Two of the respondents were trained at Caerleon in the 1940s. One, GM (1942–4), moved to Birmingham: 'There were no jobs in south Wales, and I applied . . . I didn't have an interview or anything.' The other, DW (1941–3) who did not want to go far because of his father's illness, had no choice except to take a job (again, there was no interview) in a small school in Herefordshire, where scales of pay were lower than at home.

TABLE 1:
Employment destinations, Glamorgan Training College, Barry 1932–6

	1932	1933	1934	1935	1936	
					May	July
Employed	82	72/77	62/73	50/62	27/62	50/62
Employed in Wales*	29 (35.4)	20 (27.5)	8 (13.0)	8 (16.0)	5 (18.5)	No information
Employed in England*	53 (64.6)	52 (72.5)	54 (87.0)	42 (84.0)	22 (81.5)	No information
Unemployed	0	5	11	12	35	12

Source: Barry Report (1937: 3).
* Percentages in brackets.

TABLE 2:
First destinations of students leaving Bangor Normal Training College in July 1934 and obtaining employment by September 1935

	Men	Women	Total
Number in cohort obtaining employment	39/42	78/90	117/132
Employed in Wales*	24 (61.5)	24 (30.7)	48 (41.0)
Employed in England*	15 (38.5)	54 (69.3)	69 (59.0)
Unemployed*	3 (7.1)	12 (13.3)	15 (11.3)

Source: Bangor Report (1936: 12).
* Percentages in brackets.

Figures taken from the inspection report on Bangor Normal Training College in 1936 enable a direct comparison of male and female employment destinations to be made (see Table 2). Nineteen women and 4 men at Bangor Normal were originally from the north of England. All of these found jobs, and may well have been returning home. In commenting on the employment situation in relation to the students' origin, the report stated:

> Despite the general tendency of the students to seek employment so far as possible in the region of origin . . . the number . . . securing employment in Wales is less than half of the number recruited from Wales . . . England takes about three times the number which it sends to the college. (Bangor Report, 1936: 13)

A larger proportion of women moved to England; those who were employed locally took longer than the men to find posts (8 women did not obtain employment until September–December 1935). A point of note is that the male students at Bangor undertook one teaching practice placement in Liverpool, thus crossing the border during the course of training.

Unemployment affected the male college-leavers from Caerleon (south Wales) more intensely than the men students from Bangor (north Wales) in 1934. Similar numbers of female students from Glamorgan Training College, Barry and Bangor Normal moved to England in 1934 (54 from each). In Barry this constituted a higher proportion (74 per cent), thus reflecting even fewer local employment opportunities in the south.

The precise destinations of NQTs from south and west Wales are given in a record of the 75 women students who left Swansea Training College in the summer of 1943, of whom 54 (72 per cent) were employed in England. Of these, 17 (22.6 per cent of the cohort) went to Essex, 12 to Warwickshire (mainly Birmingham) and 11 to Middlesex. Only 3 were employed in the border counties of Hereford, Gloucester and Shropshire. Of particular interest is the clustering in certain towns and schools. Although this level of detail is incomplete in the document, Barking, Romford, Ilford, Hornchurch and Upminster in Essex were evidently the most popular destinations. Some schools in Hornchurch and Romford employed two or more students each (PRO ED78/171). Testimony of former Swansea and Barry students who qualified in the 1930s and 1940s confirmed clustering of Welsh NQTs in certain parts of Essex and the Midlands. GMD (GTC, Barry 1939–41) remembered LEA representatives from various districts interviewing at the college: 'Wednesbury came first so we all applied, so thirteen of us were chosen to go to Wednesbury, then, later on, Walsall came, you know, which isn't far away, . . . then Wolverhampton.'

Not all Barry's former students headed for the Midlands or London. Even in 1929 it was reported that the Barry 'old girls' were 'scattered all over England, as far north as Yorkshire and as far south as Folkestone; in the west Midlands and east London' (*Tan y Ddraig Goch*, 1929: 43). By the 1930s, branches of the college's 'old students' society had been set up in London, Bristol, Romford, the Midlands and Yorkshire. As one correspondent commented, 'It seems that Education Committees are eager to admit young ladies trained in *Coleg y Barri*' (*Tan y Ddraig Goch*, 1929: 43; 1930–9).

Migration was encouraged by English LEAs' practice of recruiting directly from colleges in Wales. In 1927, the departmental committee report on *Welsh in Education and Life* described how 'London, Liverpool, Sheffield, Hull and other great municipalities send representatives who are experts in the art of selection to various colleges . . . and naturally choose the best' (Welsh Language Report, 1927: 120). Interviews took place in May, and had the effect of 'creaming off' the most able students before the Welsh authorities advertised their vacancies or reserve lists (Bangor Report, 1936: 13). Although controversial, this recruitment method encouraged friends to apply together and, presumably, helped make the process of application and the prospect of moving out of Wales less intimidating.

For most students who were not appointed early, finding a post entailed applying for as many jobs as possible, wherever they appeared. Some college friends were determined to stay together. BD (female,

Swansea TC, 1939–41) and her friend answered an advertisement in *Teacher's World* for two jobs in Reading, were interviewed together and appointed to the posts. MM (female, GTC, Barry, 1937–9) described how groups of friends would scrutinize a shared issue of *The Schoolmaster* and send for multiple copies of application forms in order to save on postage. She found herself at a girls' school in Newcastle-under-Lyme, a place of which she had not previously heard. Despite feeling completely isolated on arrival, she soon discovered that an NQT from Cardiff had arrived at the corresponding boys' school that same day. They were soon brought together by their respective head teachers, and later married.

Moving

As noted above, there was some reluctance on the part of both male and female NQTs to leave Wales, even though it was evident that very few jobs were available locally. In the case of the women, the delay before applying in England was due partly to the protective attitude of their families, as in the case of training. It was not unusual for girls to return to the parental home and help keep house while searching for a job locally, which might take up to a year or more. MJ, who left Glamorgan Training College, Barry, in 1926 and who was unemployed for eight months, said that hers was the first cohort to face unemployment on a large scale, and that for a girl to move away to work would have been unthinkable in her family at that time. It was only later, when the problem became intractable, that families such as hers began to accept that women as well as men would have to migrate.

Even in the 1930s, when it was more common for young female teachers to move in search of work, 'girls did not go away initially, because their mothers wished them to – [stay], because they would be, well, endangered in different ways' (DB interview, 2001). In the 1940s parents still wished to keep the girls locally. MB was kept at home in Dowlais by her parents in September 1942 for five weeks after term had started because they were 'desperate' for her to stay to see if a job would turn up. The fact that it was wartime added to their anxiety. Eventually, she took a job in Barking. EH (GTC, Barry, 1940–2) from nearby Rhymney, was also waiting throughout that month. She felt that she had been extremely fortunate when a girl who had originally been appointed to a post in her village school decided to move to Birmingham, and she replaced her.

Yet, many young women, like men, did venture to move, even without the promise and assurance of a permanent post. GE (female, GTC Barry, 1932–4), after filling in 'thousands' of forms unsuccessfully, travelled to March in Cambridgeshire where she knew no one, to seek work as a supply teacher. This was common when permanent employment was difficult to find, and many of my respondents started their careers in this way. The story of GE's first night's stay at a temperance hotel full of teachers from Wales and Scotland, and of finding lodgings at an isolated farmhouse, was recounted as a classic tale. She felt that it was the fact that her brother and his friends were already teaching in England (though not in Cambridgeshire) which made her move more acceptable to the family, though they would have preferred her to have stayed locally.

Both men and women used same-sex networks to help find a job. Some had friends in high places: AH (female, Swansea TC, 1934–6) referred to a friend who, unlike herself, had 'no problem' since her uncle was director of education in Enfield. MJ (female, Swansea TC, 1936–8) followed a friend who 'knew someone' in Essex and who urged her to 'Come up! If you come up you are bound to have a job because if you go to the office on a Monday morning there'll be somebody absent somewhere.' Her mother was unwilling, but she went nevertheless. For most it was more difficult; but still, networks were important. DB (male, Bangor Normal TC, 1933–5) lodged with relatives who kept a shop in London for a week while he visited the offices of Middlesex, London, Surrey and Essex education authorities. There were no vacancies so he returned to Wales, leaving his relatives' telephone number with clerks in each office. His uncle was instructed to give 'the stock answer' if contacted: DB was out looking for work but would be in school by half past ten the following morning, if required. This is how he got his first day's teaching in Surrey. The other 'wheeze' he used with the LEA personnel was to mention that he had a friend teaching in a school in each authority.

The vividness with which the informants recounted their migration stories and the detail in which they remembered their arrival underlines the importance of the move in their lives. Several women admitted to feeling isolated and homesick away from home, but this did not feature as strongly in the men's accounts. MB, whose new landlady had left her alone in the house, recalled her arrival in Barking:

> Oh, dreadful, dreadful. Dreadful! It made you grow up. And the first Sunday I was in my digs . . . In this house that was all eerie and sort of – I felt awful and I didn't know a soul. And there was no phone. I was crying, I had *hiraeth* [a yearning for home], I couldn't contact my parents, there were no phones . . . And that was my first night. And that, I can honestly say, although I have had terrific sadnesses and upsets since then, but I think that's one of the worst horrors. And I went to school on the Monday.

Conversely, DB's move held no such horrors. For him, being in London 'wasn't odd since we'd had family up there'. He stayed with relatives before moving into his 'digs' with other teachers from Wales. The 'trauma' of crossing the border was cushioned by the presence of other young Welsh teachers in a similar situation. Men and women teachers organized their own networks based on existing family, college or school contacts to find a job and lodgings and get established. DB described how the Welsh people 'ganged up, in the better sense of the word, to go into "digs" with people' (known as 'digging'). Co-inhabitants of the 'digs' were often from the same college or region of Wales. Although his future wife (who had trained in Glamorgan Training College, Barry) shared digs with three women and a man, teachers usually lodged with same-sex colleagues.

Socially, too, much of their contact would be with professional colleagues of their own sex, especially if teaching in single-sex schools. Leisure activities included, for women, meeting friends (mainly other Welsh teachers) in the nearest town for shopping and the cinema, while men would meet through rugby or cricket. For women (former Barry students in particular), the local branch of the old students' society of the college was an important point of contact, but college societies were not mentioned by male teachers in this study. Sport, and rugby in particular, dominated the discussion of the experience in the case of the men. Rugby was particularly important socially for male teachers from Wales. Furthermore, rugby, and the masculine culture and qualities which accompanied it, also defined their professional credentials. As DB put it,

> I can say this truthfully. If you had the qualification of coming from Wales, and that you had a big interest in rugby and that you were also a good disciplinarian, and that was really the criterion by which I had my job and probably the one by which my friend got his.

Many English cities, such as London, Liverpool and Birmingham, already had well-established Welsh communities based around sports clubs, cultural societies and chapels, and these reinforced professional networks. MB, on her arrival in Barking, followed her parents' advice and went in search of a Welsh chapel, though she failed to locate one on her first Sunday there. The chapels provided a safe haven in parents' minds, but it was largely through the chapel activity that the two sexes mixed. Several interviewees described how, in London, they would go to cafes in Oxford Street after chapel on Sunday evenings and thence to Hyde Park for communal hymn singing. Gangs of boys would get 'hooked up', as DB described it, to gangs of girls. Two interviewees met their future spouses in this way. Others met their partners through attending Welsh social activities in Birmingham, Romford and elsewhere. The comparative freedom of living beyond the border after a sheltered home and two years in a restrictive training college environment would have allowed for a degree of sexual experimentation and consolidation of sexual identity, despite close monitoring of behaviour by landladies.

For those moving to rural England, however, there were no large Welsh networks and social life was more limited. In those cases, the character of the 'lodgings' was all important. DW lodged with three different landladies during his short stay in Herefordshire. Two of the 'lodgings' exacerbated his sense of isolation while the final one 'was home from home'. Despite this he 'was not particularly happy' and applied for a post 'back home' across the border in his native Monmouthshire as soon as the war ended.

AH was one teacher who travelled from Surrey to central London on Sundays to attend chapel and the singing in Hyde Park to 'get a bit of home'. Yet her experiences in the London area also brought her into contact with a different way of life, and one which signified more freedom for women. After working as a supply teacher around Croydon for a while, she got a job at Hackbridge and lodged with a family, originally from the east end of London, who took her with them to the local pub:

> It was the first time for me to see a woman sitting down enjoying a drink . . . I'd never seen a woman in a pub. 'Twas terrible down here [south Wales] for women to go drinking . . . and they'd have a knees-up . . . I thought it was great. It was the first time I'd seen anything like that, coming from the valleys – chapel morning, afternoon and night, no enjoyment in life. I don't know how the women here put up with it.

Whether or not the teachers met with different attitudes towards gender roles and accepted new cultural norms depended to an extent on the families with whom they lodged and the friends they made. By socializing mainly with co-migrants, the gender norms of home may well have been reinforced, despite the upheaval of migration. However, women teachers were, to some extent, challenging gender norms by the very act of moving away in search of work, although it should be remembered that other groups of unmarried female workers (domestic servants in particular) were also crossing into England and had done so for many years previously (though not without much social angst in Wales concerning the effect on their morals). As independent earners, both men and women teachers sent money home to help supplement family income if they could afford it, though not all could. Several female respondents supported widowed mothers or siblings from a distance for a substantial period before eventually moving home. In returning to Wales, often to care for and support ailing parents, women teachers were also conforming to traditional expectations of dutiful daughters.

Returning

As noted at the outset, the interviews were conducted with migrants who eventually returned to Wales, while the questionnaires were completed mainly by those who had remained in England. Despite the imbalance in favour of the returners, both sources contribute towards our understanding of the decision-making process and the circumstances which facilitated or militated against return. Many of the respondents' families wanted their daughters, in particular, to return home, and a large number did so, either completely voluntarily or partly so, in response to parental pressure or a sense of duty. In England, 'Welsh girls' gained a reputation for returning home at the first opportunity. MM's first headmistress in Newcastle-under-Lyme welcomed her with the words: 'I told them I didn't want anybody from south Wales. I'll be using all my energy showing you how to teach, then you'll be leaving me.' In recounting the story, MM added, '*A 'na beth netho'i wrth gwrs*' (And that's what I did, of course). GD (female, Swansea TC, 1943–5) stayed at her first school, a girls' school in Oldbury, Worcestershire, for eighteen months, six months longer than the headmistress had predicted:

> She was a very strict head and not very kindly disposed to Welsh people because, of course, they were always coming, but the first opportunity they had they were back home again, you see, and I think that quite rightly, they trained these girls you see, and just when they were getting a bit useful, off they went, back home again . . .

Not everyone returned home; some moved to the London area for higher pay, or to be with friends. GMD moved on from Wednesbury: 'We didn't stay that long, we headed for the big city then. We went to the London area.' This was for both economic and professional reasons; 'Barking was an autonomous authority, a very good authority – Scale 4 with a London weighting.' She also had a married sister in London, which was an additional attraction. But it was the pull of home which was most clearly articulated by both those who returned and those who stayed.

Of those who returned, many (both men and women) did so at the first opportunity. Often, this was several years later. The Board of Education report for 1947 noted that 'Many authorities have for years had waiting lists of teachers wishing to be considered for vacancies in their old home areas' (Board of Education Report, 1947: 77). MD from Llanelli had her name on Carmarthenshire's waiting list for six years before a vacancy arose. To return was to sacrifice one's promotion prospects, at least initially. Almost all returners to south Wales came back to supply teaching or temporary positions, and many did not secure a permanent post for several years. Most of my informants were eventually promoted, but were not returning to promotion.

Families at home monitored the job situation. Fathers in particular were on the lookout for vacancies for their daughters. BD returned to Abercynon after three years in Reading after her father had sent her an advertisement from the local paper. The sense of responsibility was pressing, though nothing was said: 'I don't know what he felt, but reading between the lines, I felt, they are getting on, they'd like me to come home.' As it transpired, BD did not remain at home for long and left her parents to return to teach in England, this time in Milston in the west Midlands, near her new husband's school. He had not been appointed at the local south Wales secondary school (located in a Labour-controlled district) allegedly 'because he came from a Liberal family', but got a job easily in Darleston. Her parents understood that she 'had to follow' her husband, despite their sadness at losing her once again. Some young teachers, like VM (female, Swansea TC,

1937–9), whose school in Gravesend had been evacuated first to East Anglia and then to Kent, did not settle and were 'anxious to go home to live'. In her case, a vacancy arose in her home village because a male teacher had joined the army in 1941.

Not all those who wished to return were able to do so. DEB 'wanted to teach in Wales' because she thought she 'owed it' to her parents. However, she asserted that 'it was impossible to obtain a teaching post if you had trained outside Wales'. On the other hand, some of those who did return would have preferred to have stayed in England. Several single women informants returned home to care for elderly parents, to provide companionship for widowed mothers or to support younger siblings. The interviews illustrate a strong sense of duty, but also the tensions experienced. Some of the married men teachers who returned also did so at times of family crisis, either in their own or their wives' families, and came back so that their wives could take up a caring role. Several of the women teachers who had married during or soon after the war returned to Wales to live with their parents while their husbands were abroad or, post-1946, in emergency training colleges. The war also brought some back to work temporarily. MD's school in Kensington was evacuated to Aberystwyth in west Wales, where she taught her class from England to sing in Welsh.

The evidence collected strongly suggests that those who were able to speak and teach in Welsh were advantaged in the scramble for jobs back in Wales, at least in Glamorgan. The employment of bilingual teachers is related to the policy of the Welsh Department of the Board of Education to extend and improve the teaching of Welsh in schools. Historically, women in particular, as mothers and teachers, were expected to remain faithful to the Welsh language and to transfer it to the next generation. With the decline in the use of Welsh at home, schools came to be seen as the main agents of language maintenance. The loss to Wales caused by the exodus of Welsh-speaking teachers, including women who had been specially trained, and, in the case of Barry students, nurtured and strongly encouraged to feel that they had a mission in this respect, was felt acutely by those who campaigned for Welsh in the school curriculum. Yet, even though they greatly regretted the loss of teachers who were particularly qualified to meet the needs of Wales, they admitted that those returning were 'presumably better teachers as a result of their experience in the wider sphere' (Welsh Language Report, 1927: 119; see also Williams, 2006).

If crossing the border to teach in England had been a professional 'culture shock', then returning home also took some adjusting to. Some of the interviewees who had taught in London and elsewhere in this period had been employed by forward-looking authorities, worked in new buildings, or observed innovative teaching methods and, consequently, found it difficult to return to old-fashioned, poorly equipped schools in the south Wales valleys or rural Wales. Several single women returners said that they missed friends and colleagues in England and one (GMD) felt that she had left the prospect of marriage behind her when she returned home to live with her elderly mother. For women like this, the financial independence that teaching offered allowed them, after the war, to spend holidays in England to continue friendships with former colleagues there.

Conclusion

For many young men and women teachers from Wales, crossing the border to England was a liberating experience. They welcomed the escape from parental authority and cultural norms felt to be restrictive and limiting. Women, in particular, were allowed more freedom and independence than they might have had in Wales. Migrants' journeys across the border were often ones of anticipation and excitement and most teachers were not disappointed by their new life and its possibilities. While many felt the change acutely and suffered trauma and *hiraeth* (at least initially), the move was less difficult for those who had relations or close friends in well-established Welsh 'expat' communities. Moving together and lodging with colleagues from Wales considerably eased the transition.

However, most of these young professionals did not cross the border by choice. On the contrary, they were forced to do so as a result of the economic and political circumstances of their time. A sense of rejection, of exile or of being uprooted is evident in many accounts, even in the responses of those migrants who had settled comfortably in England and had felt welcome among the English there. Some accepted stoically the fact that their service and skills were not required in Wales. They hardened themselves to the reality that they would never return home: 'I had no illusions about being able to work in Wales, so was not affected (by moving away)', said DEB. Others found this truth harder to accept, and seem to have comforted themselves by socializing almost exclusively with fellow migrants from Wales. Those who worked or worshipped together often intermarried and, as couples, continued to keep in close contact with home. Several respondents testified to feeling their sense of 'Welshness' more intensely when in England. 'Homesickness – *hiraeth*' and 'the clan thing' were among the explanations given for this. In HW's case, the experience of mixing with so many other young Welsh speakers in London changed her attitude towards the Welsh language and inspired her to work enthusiastically for Welsh-medium education on her return to south Wales.

The question of the impact that teachers from Wales made as a professional group and perceptions of them on the other side of the border is only briefly touched upon in the evidence amassed to date, and awaits further research. Such a substantial migration over a considerable period of time created distinct professional communities in certain areas of England, which were also able to integrate with host communities. The migrants' experiences recounted here suggest that Welsh teachers' professional identity was defined not merely by their national and regional identities, but by their gender identities too. To some extent at least, gender norms in Wales continued to influence their attitudes and behaviour in their new surroundings. Gender was also a determining factor in the decision (or pressure) to return home to teach despite the economic disadvantage which that move often entailed.

Bibliography

REPORTS AND PAPERS:

(1925). Board of Education. *Report of the Departmental Committee on the Training of Teachers for Public Elementary Schools*, London: HMSO.

(1927). *Welsh in Education and Life: Report of the Departmental Committee appointed by the Board of Education to Inquire into the Position of the Welsh Language . . . in the Educational System of Wales*, London: HMSO.

(1944). Board of Education. *Teachers and Youth Leaders: Report of the Committee appointed . . . to consider the Supply, Recruitment and Training of Teachers and Youth Leaders*, London: HMSO (McNair Report).

(1947). *Board of Education Annual Report*, London: HMSO.

Bangor (1936). Board of Education (Welsh Department). *Report of Inspection of Bangor Normal Training College held in the session 1935–6.*

Barry (1937). Board of Education (Welsh Department). *Report of Inspection of Glamorgan Training College, Barry by His Majesty's Inspectors, 1936–7.*

Caerleon (1937). Board of Education (Welsh Department). *Report of Inspection of Caerleon Training College, by His Majesty's Inspectors, 1936–7.*

PRO ED/78/171 (1943). Report by Principal of Swansea Training College, 23 December.

PRO ED/86/94. Memorandum by Professor Olive Wheeler, MacNair Committee Papers, Paper 91.

OTHER WORKS:

Beddoe, Deirdre (2000). *Out of the Shadows: A History of Women in Twentieth Century Wales*, Cardiff: University of Wales Press.

Bornat, J. and H. Diamond (2007). 'Women's history and oral history: developments and debates', *Women's History Review*, 16/1.

Partington, G. (1976). *Women Teachers in the Twentieth Century in England and Wales*, Reading: National Federation for Educational Research.

Pooley, C. and J. Turnbull (1998). *Migration and Mobility in Britain since the Eighteenth Century*, London: UCL Press.

Tan y Ddraig Goch/Under the Red Dragon (1929, 1930–9), 14–24.

Weiler, K. and S. Middleton (1999). *Telling Women's Lives: Narrative Inquiries in the History of Women's Education*, Oxford: Oxford University Press.

Williams, S. R. (2005). '"The only profession that was around": opting for teaching in the south Wales valleys in the inter-war years', *Llafur: Journal of the Welsh People's History Society*, 9, 2, 45–58.

——(2006). 'Welsh for all: experiments in bilingual teaching in the inter-war years', in C. Redknap, W. G. Lewis, S. R. Williams and J. Laugharne (eds), *Welsh-Medium and Bilingual Education*, Bangor Educational Transactions, Bangor: School of Education, pp. 37–59.

Willis, K. and B. Yeoh (eds) (2000). *Gender and Migration*, Cheltenham: Edward Elgar.

II

GENDERING NARRATIVES OF BORDER CROSSING

5

Reading Gender in Border-crossing Narratives

JOHAN SCHIMANSKI

Ironic masculinities

What would a masculine narrative of border crossing be like? In 1890, the Norwegian author Knut Hamsun published what was to become a classic text of male modernism, *Sult* (*Hunger*, 1996). Readings of this text have often concentrated on its existentialist themes and modernist narrative strategies but, as globalization and cultural identity have become more important in literary and cultural studies, it has also become easier to recognize the restless sense of mobility and border crossing in such texts, written as they were within a nineteenth-century form of globalization, against a background of social change, colonization and migration. Postcolonial theorist Homi K. Bhabha talks of 'the melancholic homelessness of the modern novelist' in approaching similarly positioned texts such as Joseph Conrad's *Heart of Darkness* (Bhabha, 1994: 123). This homelessness had clearly marked the life of the young Hamsun, who already had an attempt at emigration to the United States behind him, and who wrote *Sult* while living as a cosmopolitan in Copenhagen. The book, with its tale of a male protagonist attempting to survive economically, artistically and psychically in the urban environment of Kristiania (today's Oslo), addresses themes of estrangement and literary creation. However, it is also suffused with a sense of Kristiania as a cultural interstice, a place in between the Norwegian nation and its outside. Mark Sandberg has argued that Hamsun describes Kristiania as if it were a much larger city, making it a dislocated version of Hamsun's experiences in Chicago (Sandberg, 1999). The author-protagonist must escape from this space, and he does so physically in a border-crossing scene at the end of the book: wandering down to the docks, he leaves Kristiania, and Norway, by sea.

Borders are explicitly mentioned in Hamsun's novel only once, in a scene towards the end of the book which prepares some of the symbolic ground for the protagonist's final border crossing, and which also suggests that the act of border crossing is a gendered one. The protagonist confronts the cake woman he has met near the beginning of the book, trying to explain why he should be allowed to take some cakes from her in 'return' for a gift of money he has made her earlier:

> I tried another tack, spoke sharply and refused to listen to any nonsense. Hadn't it ever happened to her to be paid in advance in the same way? I asked. Of course, I meant by people who were well off, some of the consuls, for example? Never? Well, it wasn't fair that I should suffer because she was unfamiliar with this social custom. It was accepted practice in foreign countries. But maybe she had never been abroad? [*udenfor Landets Grændser?*, outside the country's borders?] Ah, there you are! Then she didn't have a word to say in this matter . . . And I made a grab for several cakes on the table. (pp. 179–80)[1]

The male protagonist pretends to superior knowledge of foreign parts, on a par with that of the various consuls, representatives of foreign nations (the title *Konsul*, in a country with almost no aristocracy, was a marker of social status). His attitudes and actions are invasive: grabbing the cakes, he symbolically crosses the border into the cake woman's intimate sphere. At the same time, the superiority he claims is undercut by the pervasive irony of the novel, his version of foreign custom clearly being a fiction, and his own status being that of a penniless outsider.

That the protagonist's encounter with the cake woman is in fact gendered (and that the hierarchies he constructs are not just based on class) is confirmed by symbolic connections made with other motifs in the novel. The lack of cosmopolitan competence or provinciality of the people around the protagonist is a recurrent theme, with the cosmopolitan being explicitly connected to the erotic: 'These easily satisfied, candy-chewing students who thought they were cutting loose in Continental [*europæisk*, European] style if they could feel a seamstress's bosom!' (p. 96) A sense of the foreign as feminine and erotic – and of the feminine as foreign – is also a major element in the book's sub-narrative about the protagonist's relationship to the woman Ylajali. Sitting on a bench on the Railway Quay (the site of the border crossing at the end of the book), he drifts into a daydream:

> The dark monsters out there would suck me up when night came on, and they would carry me far across the sea and through strange lands where no humans lived. They would bring me to Princess Ylajali's castle, where an undreamed-of splendour awaited me, exceeding that of all others. And she herself will be sitting in a sparkling hall where all is of amethyst, on a throne of yellow roses, and she will hold out her hand to me when I enter, greet me and bid me welcome as I approach and kneel down: Welcome, my knight, to me and my land! (pp. 53–4)

'Ylajali' is the orientalizing name he has given to a woman seen on the street who becomes his object of desire. In this description, which continues with a focus on the erotic, her imagined role as a princess is also one of a border guard, welcoming him to a foreign land. The borders of land and body are made to overlap.

Many of the protagonist's movements and daydreams while in Kristiania are clearly preparatory versions of his final border crossing at the end of the novel. Here gender ambivalence becomes gender polarity: The erotic femininity of the foreign is denied, as the protagonist gets down to the hard work of the sailor in a wholly male sphere. The reality of the ship disavows the daydreams of oriental princesses. Ylajali is definitively left behind in the book's final sentence: 'Once out in the fjord I straightened up, wet with fever and fatigue, looked in toward the shore [*Land*] and said goodbye for now to the city, to Kristiania, where the windows shone so brightly in every home' (p. 182). The mention of windows – a typical border figure – refers back to a key scene from the protagonist's unsuccessful affair with Ylajali, in which he follows her to her home, and sees her opening the window in her flat and looking down at him (p. 13). Also, in this last sentence, the subtle, parodic reference to the coasts and the *Hjem* ('homes') of Norway's national anthem, makes Ylajali the representative of a rejected national class. Thus positioned she reminds us of the role traditionally played by women in national discourse, as symbolic 'border guards', nurturers of language, culture and new generations (Yuval-Davis, 1997: 28–31). This is the world the protagonist rejects, identifying the feminine now with a national homeliness to which he has no access. Whether this denial is successful is not clear; once the protagonist is on the ship the word *Arbejde* ('work') is repeated almost manically, suggesting an uncomfortable form of social integration (p. 182). Before presenting himself as a potential sailor, he removes his glasses in order to fit into the world of the ship, pointing to an insecurity about his own masculine virility in line with the general irony of the novel (pp. 181–2).

The erotic plot is present in many of Hamsun's later texts, often with male protagonists who are positioned as social outsiders, and also as foreigners. A border experience on the part of the protagonist brings about a switching of his image of a woman from a foreign to a denied domestic other. The underlying narrative is similar to that of national romance as described by Doris Sommer (1990) in the nineteenth-century Latin-American context, in which the nation is formed through a union across an allegorically gendered internal difference. In this standard narrative, an exoticized, active female Other plays a key role in the creation of the nation, only to be relegated to a passive, nurturing role once the job is done. Only Hamsun constantly avoids, in a typically modernist move, actual union and thus also the allegorical creation of nation.[2]

Critical masculinities

The woman-as-foreign and the spatialization of the symbolic difference between women and men as a national border, with all their potential ambivalences and complexities, are tropes often activated in male narratives of border crossings. In 1953, Islwyn Ffowc Elis published what became one of the most popular novels written in Welsh in the twentieth century, the late realist political family romance *Cysgod y Cryman* (*Shadow of the Sickle*, 1998). Elis grew up in a Welsh-speaking community atypically near to the Welsh–English border and stated that the presence of the border had a guiding influence on his writing. In his novel, an Englishman, Paul Rushmere, engaged to marry a Welsh woman, Greta Vaughan, is first seen driving over the border in his car. As the border sign flashes by, Rushmere becomes embroiled in reflections on the sign, on the border, on Wales and on the woman he is to marry. These reflections are uneasy: the cryptic and uncanny otherness of Wales, as he sees it, disturbs him, though he is attracted to Greta Vaughan's otherness. There is 'some Celtic magic around her' – creating a border intimately connected with her body (Elis, 1998: 34). Like Hamsun's protagonists, he is attracted by the foreign, but he does not share their restlessness. His discomfort seems to lie in a wish that the borders of nation, of culture, of language and of Greta Vaughan's body should overlap more closely, so that he can retain control of the situation. The speed of his car seems to compensate for the deterritorialized spaces with which he finds himself confronted.

While *Cysgod y Cryman* and its sequel, *Yn Ôl i Leifior* (1956; *Return to Lleifior*, 1999) allow for differing interpretations, it is possible to follow an underlying nationalist ideology in the diptych, in contrast to the texts by Hamsun presented above. Rushmere, unlike Hamsun's protagonists, is hardly an object of identification for the author, the narrator or the reader; he is an enemy figure, threatening Greta in her role as a 'border guard' of Welsh national identity. The scene with the car puncturing the Welsh border is certainly invasive, even phallic; and in the sequel the national allegory connects back to this image when Rushmere is killed in a car accident while driving again from England to Wales. But the national allegory also implicitly critiques Rushmere's masculine narrative, though not from a specifically feminist viewpoint.[3]

The critique of the masculine border-crossing narrative is clear in *My Son's Story*, published by the South African author Nadine Gordimer in 1990, the year negotiations leading to the dissolving of apartheid began. The novel's late realist mode is suited to the problems of representing an apartheid state criss-crossed by internal boundaries, including the geographical boundaries of townships and Bantustans (cf. Engle, 1989: 115; Jacobs, 1990; and Pechey, 1998). The problematic protagonist and narrator, Will, documents a personal crisis following a love affair that his politically active father, Sonny, has with a white human rights monitor, Hannah Plowman, a crisis exasperated when his sister Baby and his Mother Aila join the resistance against apartheid. As the family makes a politically inspired move across the border into a white area, Will experiences his household and family becoming increasingly divided as its outer boundaries collapse. The political borders of apartheid invade his space, which he had thought was held together by his mother.[4]

Growing up, Will has experienced white areas as both forbidding and attractive magical territories, to be visited only on Saturdays. He likens their borders to the walls of Kafka's castle or his gates of the law (p. 17), but these borders are transformed by his father into 'a charmed circle' around their own life (p. 20). The comics Sonny brings to Will and Baby from the white town are full of heroic tales and 'romantic fables' (p. 20). As he gets older, whiteness and the blondness he later associates with Hannah become the stuff of another kind of fantasy (p. 14). Will's asocial attitudes make it often difficult to sympathize with him and, while Gordimer's critique is systematic and not individual, the book both connects Will's narratives of border crossing to a strong desire for fixity and ascribes them to the masculine.[5]

These masculine narratives of border crossing are fed rhetorically by metaphors of gender polarity based around heterosexual desire and, while they are often spatialized on a national scale, they are also figured to a large extent as a potentially invasive and violent meeting on the micro-scale of individual bodies. Symbolic differences and especially polarities of this kind are particularly easy to spatialize and to figure as territories. However, following Deleuze and Guattari, any such territorialization must be susceptible to deterritorialization, a destabilization of any fixity in term of space or also of meaning (1986). Discrepancies between different overlapping border planes, such as those between territorial, cultural, linguistic and bodily planes which cause Rushmere discomfort in *Cysgod y Cryman*, can threaten the standard masculine narrative by disseminating the border, thus transforming it from a line into a wider zone. Any kind of refiguring of the border (say as a seam rather than a wall) or of gender (say as Derridaean *différance* rather than as a binary) will also be potentially destabilizing.

Inverted masculinities

In the French author Jean Genet's writings one would expect a certain queering of gender and, as a consequence, a deterritorialization of masculine border-crossing narratives of the type described above. Hélène Cixous allowed Genet into the canon of *écriture féminine* in her essay 'Le Rire de la Méduse', 1975 (translated into English as 'The Laugh of the Medusa', 1976) and devoted portions of her book *Three Steps on the Ladder of Writing* to readings of the crossings of national and stylistic borders in Genet (Cixous, 1993). It is clear, however, that Genet continually plays with the standard masculine narrative, citing it from a distance. In his autobiographical fiction *Journal du voleur* (1949; *The Thief's Journal*, 1967), the masculine narrative is especially connected to its strand of thriller or adventure fiction, but is always ready to be transformed and inverted in the lyrical terms of a revived French classicism. Cixous's avowed ideal is one of fluidity in the border crossing, but she accepts that Genet's texts exhibit a doubleness: 'Cuts keep interfering in Genet's texts. Inside the pieces there is no cut since he has a double economy: while the text is clear-cut, inside there is a circuit of the order of "feminine" continuity' (Cixous, 1993: 133).

Working within his dominant motif registers of crime and homosexuality, Jean is always approaching a border, poised to transgress, only to pull back at the last moment, submerged in a shame which in turn supplies him with his greatest epiphanies. Cixous writes: 'In Genet's scene of passing the border there is always an ambivalence, do we pass or don't we?' (1993: 122). When Jean and his lover Michaelis attempt to return to Czechoslovakia from Katowice in Poland, for example, the plan is to threaten the hired driver if he refuses to cross the border illegally:

> Sitting in the rear, with one hand on my weapon and the other in the hand of Michaelis, who was stronger than I though just as young, I would gladly have fired into the driver's back. The car was going slowly uphill. Michaelis was supposed to leap to the steering-wheel, but just then the chauffeur stopped right in front of a border post that we had not seen. This crime was denied me. Escorted by two policemen, we returned to Katowice. (Genet, 1967: 89)

The car, the revolver, the potential violence – together with closeness to his partner – trace the outlines of a masculine narrative of border crossing. Jean almost reaches the limit constituted by the capital crime of murder, which he dreams of yet does not commit. But it is after the border crossing is frustrated, in the office of the chief of police in Katowice, that he experiences 'the anxious joy, fragile as the pollen on hazel blossoms, the golden morning joy of the murderer who escapes. Though I had not managed to commit the crime, I had at least been gently bathed in the fringe of its dawning' (p. 89). The classicist imagery which here suffuses the text suggests another, precisely more fragile and receptive eroticism and the more deterritorialized, disseminated border figure of the fringe (in plural in the original) or of the dawn. Jean has successfully positioned himself in the flickering half-light of the border, as a border subject. To use the border terminology of Jacques Derrida, he participates without belonging, reaching insight in the 'blinking of an eye' (Derrida, 1992: 227 and 231).[6]

The border crossing in Genet's 'journal' which has received the most critical attention is a crossing from Czechoslovakia into Poland, which Jean associates with the image of the Lady with the Unicorn, of the famous medieval tapestry in Musée de Cluny in Paris (see Caron, 2001: 90–2; Cixous, 1993: 136–45; Héron, 2003: 120–2 and 141–2). In this crossing he focuses on, among other things, erotic and heraldic images of Poland: the blondes of Poland, the heraldic eagle of Poland and the birches on the other side of the border. Genet then states that he would become part of the image rather than of the actual country on the other side of the border: 'The crossing of borders and the excitement it arouses in me were to enable me to apprehend directly the essence of the nation I was entering. I would penetrate less into a country than to the interior of an image' (1967: 39). Note the sexual sense activated by 'penetrate' but also an inversion of inner and outer, since Genet wishes to enter an image which is inside himself – a form of infolding of the border. This kind of inversion of inside and outside, according to another reader of Jean's border crossings, David Caron, is central to Genet's subversive practice:

> While Genet's famous motto, 'J'encule le monde,' ['I bugger the world'] implies that he is *in* the world (coming in, as it were, through the back door), his desire to be fucked (that is, the fact that he embraces his identification as a 'passive' homosexual) also implies that the world is in him as well. Of course, this is logically impossible – which is why the 'central' theme in *Journal du voleur* is the border. That, in a sense, is Genet's poetic challenge: to take us to the impossible moment when there is no inside/ outside, and therefore no system. (Caron, 2001: 64)[7]

Genet's insertion of himself into a border position later resurfaces in other splittings and doublings of agency and passivity. Jean's flight from another country, Belgium, and another lover, Armand, the last border crossing of the book in chronological terms, takes place on a train which, on crossing the border, enters a forest:

> In the Maubeuge forests, I realized that the country which was so hard for me to leave, the enveloping region for which I felt a sudden nostalgia as I crossed the last frontier, was Armand's radiant kindness, and that it was made up of all the elements, seen inside out, which composed his cruelty. (1967: 170)

The scene centres on a juxtaposition of a division between lovers and a division between countries, allowing nations and characters to enter into figural relations with each other. Thus Belgium becomes the enveloping region of Armand's radiant kindness (again, rays of light are evoked, as in the fringes and dawn above). The border becomes a place of inversion (*à l'envers*[8] – 'inside out'), and simultaneously a part of nature and a nostalgia for kindness, though crucially a kindness capable of doubling into cruelty. The theme is reaffirmed in an adjacent footnote:

> But what will prevent my destruction? Speaking of catastrophe, I cannot help recalling a dream: a locomotive was pursuing me. I was running along the tracks. I heard the machine puffing at my heels. I left the rails and ran into the countryside. The locomotive cruelly pursued me, but gently and politely it stopped in front of a small and fragile wooden fence which I recognized as one of the fences which closed off a meadow belonging to my foster-parents and where, as a child, I used to lead the cows to pasture. In telling a friend about this dream, I said, '. . . the train stopped at the fence of my childhood . . .'. (Genet, 1967: 171)

Here gentleness and cruelty are paired, on an idealized rural border: the small and fragile wooden fence surrounding his childhood. This spells out clearly the strong link between the rural and childhood in *Journal du voleur*, but at the same time we find repeated another variant of a drama taking place between kindness and cruelty. To use as figures terms taken from psychoanalyst Melanie Klein, already applied in a biographical-genetical fashion to other scenes in *Journal du voleur* by Gisèle Child-Olmsted (1997), we are here presented with a good and a bad mother – the good mother who is one with the child in an enveloping security, and the bad mother who (from the child's perspective) withholds that security, paradoxically allowing the child to enter into selfhood as a separate being.[9] Besides reconfirming the sense of the border being a primordial or primal scene – an originary liminality – these descriptions of danger and security, risk and plenitude, also allow Genet to present 'good' and 'bad' borders, suggesting that besides the catastrophic border of cut-off stories of love and penetration, which are variants of the cut which removes the child from the mother, there exists also a primordial, fragile border: the border as a join to the mother.

To follow the theories of another practitioner of psychoanalysis, Bracha Lichtenberg-Ettinger, the border as a join would be the matrixial borderspace, which she describes as an ideal form of the border, taken as a place of communication symbolized by the join between the child and the mother within the womb – an internal outside. This is the true beginning of the child's identity, before the violence of the Lacanian cut between the child and the mother, which we may mistakenly believe to be the basis of our status as fully developed selves (Lichtenberg-Ettinger, 1994). This is the fragile fence of childhood, and, with reference to the frustrated border crossing with Michaelis, the fragile fringes of pollen and dawning light.

Gendering border crossing

Again we must ask: what would a masculine narrative of border crossing be like? The question makes it instantly clear that gender is not just a matter of the feminine, which would be simply to reproduce a common hierarchical binary of universal versus female. In answering it, one risks, however, searching for some essence of the masculine against which to correlate various descriptions of border crossing. Any reading of gender must treat the category as contingent on cultural and historical contexts, contexts that furthermore must contain within them the reader in a transhistorical hermeneutics. Masculinity and femininity must be read as ascriptions and teased out in careful interpretation, if we are to avoid turning the descriptive into the normative. Some contexts carry with them highly naturalized conceptions of gender as a hierarchical polarity, easily territorialized and bordered; others may suggest alternative models of gender. Cixous's and Lichtenberg-Ettinger's ascriptions are also contingent on the figuration of the feminine or matrixial border as a fluid space or a join. Their practical advantage is that such a conception of the border is in itself a reminder not to essentialize, and that it is not necessary to read biological differences in, say, Lichtenberg-Ettinger's version of psychoanalysis literally.

While accepting their contingency, it likewise makes sense to take seriously – within the contemporary historical context of global migration and minority discourse – suggestions that women often deal better with post-border trauma, or that women are less likely to figure borders as places of melancholy and conflict (cf. Castillo, 2007: 116, and Aaron, 2007: 211). Both suggestions tend to support the case for feminist nomadism (as suggested by Braidotti, 1994), a concept which has come under some criticism as being possible only for a privileged global elite. Feminine narratives of captivity and victimization can, however, easily be read as parts of a mirroring, working in tandem with masculine narratives of fixity and invasion. Reinhold Görling's work with borders in Turkish-German cinema suggests that the films he studies portray masculine insecurities about gender in male immigrants, on their confrontation with an Other which allows female mobility, that can lead to forceful denials of female subjectivity and a forcing of women into captivity. Women, on the other hand, 'living in-between an Islamic and a liberal secular culture seem to create new subjectivities more easily than men – when they get enough space and freedom to do so' (Görling, 2007: 154).

Deterritorializing femininities

Female captivity or victimization is a strong theme in some border-crossing narratives. Norwegian author Dag Skogheim's novel *Sulis* (1980), the first volume of the meta-historical Sulis-Valby Quartet (1998a and 1998b), ends by describing the flight of the Norwegian woman Janny Olsen from war-torn Finland in 1918. Janny, who grew up in the north Norwegian mining community of Sulitjelma (the 'Sulis' of the title), flees the industrial town of Tammerfors/Tampere in Finland, where the white forces have overcome the reds in the decisive battle of the Finnish civil war. She takes with her the baby of a friend, forces her way on to a Swedish hospital train carrying the wounded, crosses the border into Sweden at Torneå/Tornio, survives a night of horror in Swedish town of Boden, takes the train to Narvik in Norway and then the boat onwards to Bodø and home to Sulitjelma.

The topographical border that Janny has to cross is disseminated across a wide border zone, beginning with the meeting with the guards around the Swedish hospital in Tammerfors, including the crossing of the Torne River on the actual Finnish–Swedish border and ending with the meeting with soldiers outside the mining community of Sulitjelma, who prevent her from actually reaching her destination. Along the way, the border is personified as a 'border guard' functioning as her opponent, usually male, against whom she pits herself in the role of a woman accompanied by a baby. Her status as a carer and the presence of the child function as supplementary passports, something made clear at the final, though in this case unsuccessful, border crossing by the state cordon outside Sulitjelma: 'A letter of passage? – She had nothing of that nonsense, but she did have a sick newly born baby, if they would like to see what he looked like?' (Skogheim, 1998a: 314, my translation).

Two passages are particularly critical, the first being the actual border on the ice-covered river, where Janny, as luck would have it, is hidden from the border guards by a sudden squall of drifting snow (p. 287). The second is the night in a hotel in Boden, where Janny and the child must take refuge to escape the cold (pp. 288–95). It is here that the hotel receptionist claims payment in the form of sexual 'services'. In transgressing ethical borders, the receptionist installs his own personal 'state of exception', on the basis of her identity as a refugee and a member of a potentially revolutionary proletariat, reducing her to 'bare life' in political theorist Giorgio Agamben's terms (Agamben, 1998 and 2005). The metaphorical and narrative connections to the national border make this scene of bodily border crossing readable as an allegory of state sovereignty, according to Agamben intimately connected with the right to install a 'state of exception'.[10] Following Rüdiger Görner's related suggestion of connecting body and territory through the legal concept of habeas corpus, the right to one's own body is put out of play on the national border (Görner, 2007: 62–3). It is at such borders that we allow the state to demand of us our identities and to carry out body searches. To refer to an example discussed by Agamben, the 'state of exception' installed by the US government at Guantanomo Bay is precisely in a border enclave on the island of Cuba (Agamben, 2005: 4).

While Agamben does not address the status of women directly in *Homo sacer* and its sequel *Stato di eccezione* (*State of Exception*), his theories do have applicability to gendered social relations in many different societies. Janny does not succumb wholly to the violence of the receptionist, however; the guile which has helped her on other occasions allows her a position of resistance. That she has the presence of mind to steal the receptionist's money and to use hotel furniture instead of the firewood he denies her, thus saving herself and the child and providing her passage on the train onwards to Norway, is due to the general adaptability and mobility learned during her upbringing in Sulitjelma (known as 'Lapland's Hell').

What Janny faces is a general spatialization of class borders into national and other territorial borders. She is, as a working-class woman, doubly marginalized; as the narrator claims on introducing her, 'She was to stand outermost on the wings of the proletariat for all her days, marked and scarred after bloody, life-and-death clashes in the hidden history of the North' (Skogheim, 1998a: 42). After her flight from Finland she is marginalized a third time, moving to the outer edges of northern Scandinavia, to the fictional coastal town of Valby, and starting a new life running a cafe. Valby is the main setting of the last three books of the quartet, and Janny's move sets a hidden trail of memories in motion, the uncovering of which is the theme of the last book, *Sølvhalsbandet* (1986, The Silver Necklace; Skogheim, 1998b). All through the quartet, Skogheim is careful to emphasize a female strand to the cosmopolitan proletarian history he uncovers, centred on the silver necklace – in Debra Castillo's terms, an 'umbilical object' connecting the exiled present across the border to a distant past (Castillo, 2007).

While Janny's story of border crossing starts out as a feminine narrative of successive momentary captivities and victimizations, it does deterritorialize gender through its element of guile and fiction. The exchange of sex for a roof over the head, though claiming to be 'in natura' (Skogheim, 1998a: 291), was never a real exchange, and the motherly connection between Janny and her dead friend's child is a subversion of naturalized relations. The crossing of the Torne River is in itself an act of smuggling. So, even though this female narrative of border crossing starts off as a dialectic response to the kind of masculine narrative I have been discussing above, it ends up deterritorializing gender just as much as it deterritorializes the bordered geography of the Scandinavian north.[11]

Although the Viennese, Sephardic-Jewish author Veza Canetti (born Venetiana Taubner-Calderon) wrote half a century or more before Skogheim, her writings exhibit some of the same concern for working-class narratives, supplemented by a grotesque irony corresponding to the fabulist, meta-historical elements in Skogheim. Her story 'Geduld bringt Rosen' ('Patience Brings Roses', Canetti, 2006),[12] first published as a serial in the Vienna *Arbeiter-Zeitung* in 1932 under the pseudonym Veza Magd, is, like Janny's narrative in *Sulis*, a tale of smuggling. The smugglers here are not the oppressed proletariat but, rather, their rich oppressors, personified by the Prokop family, émigrés from Russia, who through their miserly lack of concern bring about the tragic downfall of a gullibly servile family of the underclass, the Mäusles. The contact between the two families, brought about by their living in the same extended block of flats (a typically Viennese arrangement of locating both rich and poor in the same building), consists of various symbolic border crossings. At the beginning of the story, the Prokops have had their factories in Russia confiscated and are placed in a risky zone of dislocation; the tragedy of the Mäusles is brought about by a combination of the irresponsibility of the Prokops's profligate son Bobby and the false consciousness (to use a convenient Marxist term) of Herr Mäusle. In the final symbolic scene, as the Prokops return to the house after their daughter Tamara's marriage and the Mäusles leave it to bury their daughter Steffi, Tamara asks to have her flowers placed on Steffi's coffin. The person she asks to do this is Ljubka, a poor orphaned niece of the Prokops whom they have brought with them from Russia, and who acts as a go-between between the families and displays a correspondingly hybrid identity.

However, the story begins with a border crossing, with the Prokops and Ljubka crossing the border of Russia on the way to Vienna. The scene establishes the character of the Prokops as smugglers of character, respectable on the outside, but grotesquely unethical on the inside; this characteristic is established through an act of actual smuggling, as Frau Prokop (Herr Prokop is dead, as a result of losing his factories) has distributed the family jewels around the persons of the family. Ljubka does not know that they are smuggling; more seriously, she is ignorant of the fact that some of the smuggled goods are planted on her own person, baked into the bread that she is carrying. On discovering this afterwards, when the family is safely across the border, she realizes that they set her life in danger out of sheer greed.

There is a strong element of bodily border crossing, of invasion, in Frau Prokop's actions, though in this case, as opposed to my earlier examples, the invader is a woman (albeit, crucially, upper class):

> In what would have been less than an hour's walk from the Russian border, Mrs Prokop took the bag containing the rolls from her niece. She hurriedly broke one open and, her nostrils quivering with greed, plucked a ring from its inside, a ring with diamonds the size of hazelnuts. Everyone looked in amazement at the ring. Ljubka blanched. 'But auntie, they can execute you for that!'
>
> 'God looks after the innocent,' Mrs Prokop said, pointed towards God, who was apparently enthroned on the luggage rack, and, broke off a piece of the roll, which she passed to Ljubka. Then she opened up each roll after the other and filled her pockets with jewels. (Canetti, 2006: 23)

The religious subtext, which includes a parody of the Christian communion, strengthens the threatening identification between Ljubka's body and the rolls of bread. The implication of this identification is an image of her body being pierced or torn by the knowledge of Frau Prokop's treachery and the acknowledgement that Ljubka might have become the victim of capital punishment.

The motif of piercing bodily borders is thus given an epistemological dimension, which is now turned back against the Prokops, revealed as grotesque inside. As her mother hands over one of the smuggled pieces of jewellery to her, Tamara laughs and this laughter becomes a grimace, revealing a disturbingly doglike face behind her delicate features:

> How that fine face was now contorted! Rough lines, bare gums, wrinkles which reached as far as her temples, and then her ears – it was her ears which drew one's attention more than anything else. They were like a dog's when you pull his flaps, twisted, brown sockets, and her whole laugh betrayed no sign of joy, but just a meanness which could not be hidden. (p. 24)

The reader is reminded of this image in a later description of the disabled Steffi Mäusle (p. 28). Where Tamara is respectable on the outside and grotesque on the inside, Steffi is grotesque on the outside and respectable on the inside. As Alexandra Strohmaier points out in an article on Canetti's grotesque physiognomies, there is in 'Geduld bringt Rosen' an irony in its use of physiognomic conceptions of character popular in the interwar period (Strohmaier, 2005: 126). In the description of Tamara, the interpretative crossing between appearance and psyche is played out as a penetration and subversion of the outer surface of the body. The onlookers, presumably including Ljubka, penetrate her mask, cross the borders of her body and discover her smuggled identity.

Canetti's dominant focus in this story is class relations; the ascription of gender in this reading of territorial, bodily and epistemological border crossings in 'Geduld bringt Rosen' is dependent on a contextual interpretation involving, first, the historical role of female servants in Viennese society; secondly, the prominence of such figures in Canetti's stories; and, thirdly, Canetti's self-performance by signing this story 'Veza Magd' – *Magd* is the German word for 'maid'.[13] This interpretation is further strengthened by the association with the crippled Steffi, disability also being a common motif in Canetti's stories (and Canetti had only one arm); one can argue that this and the instability of Jewish identity that Lisa Silverman finds in Canetti's stories – which she connects to the permeability of urban boundaries in Canetti's Vienna – are part of a circulation of symbolic borders through the intersections of class, gender, (dis)ability and ethnicity (Silverman, 2006) .

The maid in the figure of Ljubka is, as Willi Huntemann points out, the only figure in this story who is not physically or ethically grotesque (Huntemann, 2000: 192). She has access to two worlds: she provides a third space of witness to the class conflict central to the story. To use Derrida's phrase again, she 'participates without belonging' (Derrida, 1992: 227). She is a border subject, negotiating inversions of inside and outside in a way similar to Jean in Genet's *Journal du voleur*. I would claim that this position is based partly on her feminine gendering, and again exemplifies a negation of the mirrorings of fixity/ captivity, invasion/ victimization.[14]

Gendering the border concept

I have here presented readings which apply the strategies of border poetics (cf. Schimanski, 2006a; Schimanski and Wolfe, 2007b), posing each a question which I have been asking myself for some time, that of the role of gender in border crossings. I have concentrated on a variety of fictional or heavily fictionalized narratives from different historical and social contexts in order to show as wide a range of genderings as possible and to provide for potential aesthetic distancing and critical estrangement of naturalized categories. I believe the question posed to be necessary not only in literary, cultural or social approaches to borders, but also because it raises important theoretical issues concerning the functioning of border poetics. The question may thus be posed more radically: is gender an integral part of the border concept and all reconceptualizations of the border? Gender, conceived not only purely as a binarity, but as part of embodiment and of subject formation, also becomes part of the formation of our concept of borders.

Recurrent in these readings is a gendering of the opposition between home and the unhomely, the border between the private and the public. While a certain kind of masculine border crossing is concerned with fixing the other, borders cannot in response be erased by, for example, an ideal, homeless nomadism. Lichtenberg-Ettinger's psychoanalytical theory asks us, rather, to be open to new conceptions of the border as a join and a space, in her terms a matrixial borderspace, in which inside and outside are confused (Lichtenberg-Ettinger, 1994). In Jacques Derrida's partly gendered terms, placing ourselves within the 'double invagination' of the border opens us to moments of insight (Derrida, 1992). A parallel reconceptualization and refiguring of the border into an in-between space of negotiation is central to Inge E. Boer's feminist and Bhabha-inspired border readings, and to her critique of Braidotti's nomadism.[15] Negotiation signifies for Boer a willingness not to take the border as a given, absolute line (Boer, 2006: 18, 193), but to adopt a flexible approach to the border, to let the border function as a place of 'contention and contestation' (pp. 33–4). As her readings of Algerian-French writer Nina Bouraoui make clear, together with some of the readings above, borders are places of inversion (p. 38). In their book of readings of women's writing from the Mexican–US borderlands, Debra A. Castillo and María-Socorro Tabuenca Córdoba conclude that women are both asked and ask themselves to inhabit an 'almost impossible borderbeing'; they ask themselves to do so 'as a way of rearticulating alternative forms of be-ing outside dominant culture's ideological imperatives' (Castillo and Socorro, 2002: 228). Ultimately, the crossing of the border and the meeting with the border reflect upon the subject, making the subject a contested, in-between, inverted space as well. Without border crossings we would not be able to discover the Other in ourselves.[14]

Acknowledgements

Many thanks to Ulrike Spring for her readings and support in preparing this text, and to the many discussants and readers who have heard or read earlier versions of the individual analyses.

Notes

1 References to the original wording are to the first edition, Hamsun, 1890.
2 See Schimanski, 2006b and 2001a, for further readings of *Sult* and the related text, 'Dronningen af Saba', Hamsun, 1892.
3 For a detailed reading of this scene, see Schimanski, 1996: 2–19.
4 See Bhabha, 1992: 13–15, and, for a feminist application of Bhabha's reading, see Boer, 2006: 50–51.
5 See Schimanski, 2003, for more detailed readings.

6 For a more detailed reading of this passage in Norwegian, see Schimanski, 2001b.

7 Caron does not use the word 'inversion' here, though the term fits his discussion well, since it has been used as a technical term for buggery and for homosexuality.

8 Héron points to the pun with the place-name Anvers (Antwerp), the scene of Jean's relationship to Armand (2003: 71).

9 Gisèle Child-Olmsted connects the good and the bad mother to Genet's biographical foster-mother and biological mother (1997).

10 Agamben cites Carl Schmitt and Walter Benjamin (Agamben, 1998: 64).

11 For a more detailed reading in Norwegian of border crossings in the Sulis-Valby Quartet, see Schimanski, 2008.

12 At the time, Canetti still bore her maiden name. I use the name attached to the current publications of her texts.

13 Canetti's bourgeois background and the Jewishness of her name may have forced her to adopt pseudonyms when writing for the social-democratic press – she herself cites Jewishness as the reason in correspondence (Canetti, 1990: 182–3) – and the choice of *Magd* may imply that by doing so she is acting as the maidservant of the working class. However, there is also a potential identification with the oppressed in the choice. Dagmar C. G. Lorenz writes concerning the gendered focus of this and other stories: 'Here, as in her later works, Taubner-Calderon uses women characters to express her main concerns' (Lorenz, 1995: 277). Julian Preece implies a subtext criticizing her socialist editors, who subordinated the role of women in their class struggle (Preece, 2007, 63; see also pp. 85–99 for a discussion of the figure of the maid in Canetti's writing). For a discussion of Canetti's identifications through the name *Magd* and her other pseudonym 'Veronika Knecht' (*Knecht*, serf), see Banasch, 2002: 31–2.

14 Where Canetti's perceived oppressor–victim dialectic is concerned, I follow Spreitzer, 2005: 11, who sees this overcome by her use of the grotesque, and Iversen, 1996, who points to her irony.

15 Boer, 2006, is primarily critical of nomadism as a critical concept because it reproduces orientalist attitudes. Sadly only her texts can now take part in this discussion.

Bibliography

Aaron, Jane (2007). 'Border blues: representing the Welsh border in twentieth-century Anglophone literature', in Johan Schimanski and Stephen Wolfe (eds), *Border Poetics De-limited*, Hannover: Wehrhahn, pp. 199–216.

Agamben, Giorgio (1998). *Homo Sacer: Sovereign Power and Bare Life*, trans. David Heller-Roazen, Stanford, CA: Stanford University Press.

——(2005). *State of Exception*, trans. Kevin Attell, Chicago: University of Chicago Press.

Banasch, Bettina (2002). 'Zittern als eine Bewegung des Widerstands: Veza Canettis frühe erzählungen "Geduld bringt Rosen" und der Roman *Die Gelbe Straße*', *Text+Kritik*, 156, 30–47.

Bhabha, Homi K. (1992). 'The world and the home', *Social Text*, 31/32, 141–53.

——(1994). *The Location of Culture*, London: Routledge.

Boer, Inge E. (2006). *Uncertain Territories: Boundaries in Cultural Analysis*, Amsterdam: Rodopi.

Braidotti, Rosi (1994). *Nomadic Subjects: Embodiment and Sexual Difference in Contemporary Feminist Theory*, New York: Columbia University Press.

Canetti, Veza (1990). *Die gelbe Strasse: Roman*, München: Hanser, 1990.

——(2006). 'Patience brings roses', in *Viennese Short Stories*, trans. Julian Preece, Riverside, CA: Ariadne, pp. 23–50.

Caron, David (2001). *AIDS in French Culture: Social Ills, Literary Cures*, Madison: University of Wisconsin Press.

Castillo, Debra A. (2007). 'Borders, identities, objects', in Johan Schimanski and Stephen Wolfe (eds), *Border Poetics De-limited*, Hannover: Wehrhahn, pp. 115–48.

——and María-Socorro Tabuenca Córdoba (2002). *Border Women: Writing from La Frontera*, Minneapolis: University of Minnesota Press.

Child-Olmsted, Gisèle (1997). 'Transfigurations of the mother in Genet's *Journal du voleur* and *Un Captif amoureux*', *French Review: Journal of the American Association of Teachers of French*, 71, 1, 44–54.

Cixous, Hélène (1976). 'The laugh of the Medusa', *Signs*, 1, 4, 875–93.

——(1993). *Three Steps on the Ladder of Writing*, trans. Sarah Cornell and Susan Sellers, New York: Columbia University Press.

Deleuze, Gilles and Félix Guattari (1986). *Kafka: Toward a Minor Literature*, trans. Dana Polan, Minneapolis: University of Minnesota Press.

Derrida, Jacques (1992). 'The law of genre', trans. Avital Ronell, in *Acts of Literature*, New York: Routledge, pp. 221–52.

Elis, Islwyn Ffowc (1998). *Shadow of the Sickle*, trans. Meic Stephens, Llandysul: Gomer.

——(1999). *Return to Lleifior*, trans. Meic Stephens, Llandysul: Gomer.

Engle, Lars (1989). 'The political uncanny: the novels of Nadine Gordimer', *Yale Journal of Criticism*, 2, 2, 101–27.

Genet, Jean (1967). *The Thief's Journal*, trans. Anthony Blond, Harmondsworth: Penguin.

——(1995 [1949]). *Journal du voleur*, Paris: Gallimard.

Gordimer, Nadine (1990). *My Son's Story*, London: Bloomsbury.

Görling, Reinhold (2007). 'Topology of borders in Turkish–German cinema', in Johan Schimanski and Stephen Wolfe (eds), *Border Poetics De-limited*, pp. 149–62.

Görner, Rüdiger (2007). 'Notes on the culture of borders', in Johan Schimanski and Stephen Wolfe (eds), *Border Poetics De-limited*, pp. 59–74.

Hamsun, Knut (1890). *Sult,* København: P. G. Philipsens Forlag.

——(1892). 'Dronningen af Saba', *Samtiden*, 3, 361–79.

——(1996). *Hunger*, trans. Sverre Lyngstad, Edinburgh: Canongate.

Héron, Pierre-Marie (2003). *Journal du voleur de Jean Genet*, Paris: Gallimard.

Huntemann, Willi (2000). 'Nicht verzöhnt: Veza Canettis Erzählung "Geduld bringt Rosen" als antihumanistische Groteske', *Convivium*, 8, 179–203.

Iversen, Karsten Sand (1996). 'Veza Canetti (1897–1963)', *Standart*, 10, 4, 8.

Jacobs, Johan U. (1990). 'Narration in No-Man's Land: the imagined outland in two contemporary South African novels', in Roger Bauer, Douwe W. Fokkema and Michael de Graat (eds), *Proceedings of the XIIth Congress of the International Comparative Literature Association / Actes du XIIe congrès de l'Association Internationale de Littérature Comparée*, München: Iudicium, vol. 2, pp. 124–9.

Lichtenberg-Ettinger, Bracha (1994). 'The becoming threshold of matrixial borderlines', in George Robertson (ed.), *Travellers' Tales: Narratives of Home and Displacement*, London: Routledge, pp. 38–62.

Lorenz, Dagmar C. G. (1995). 'Social criticism in Veza Taubner-Calderon's novel *Die gelbe Straße*', in Donald G. Daviau (ed.), *Jura Soyfer and His Time*, Riverside, CA: Ariadne, pp. 275–86.

Pechey, Graham (1998). 'The post-apartheid sublime: rediscovering the ordinary', in Derek Attridge and Rosemary Jolly (eds), *Writing South Africa: Literature, Apartheid, and Democracy 1970–1995*, Cambridge: Cambridge University Press, pp. 57–74.

Preece, Julian (2007). *The Rediscovered Writings of Veza Canetti: Out of the Shadows of a Husband*, Rochester, New York: Camden House.

Sandberg, Mark B. (1999). 'Writing on the wall: the language of advertising in Knut Hamsun's *Sult*', *Scandinavian Studies*, 71, 3, 265–96.

Schimanski, Johan (1996). 'A Poetics of the border: nation and genre in *Wythnos yng Nghymru Fydd* and other texts by Islwyn Ffowc Elis', unpublished Dr. art. thesis, Oslo.

——(2001a). 'Den litterære grensen: Knut Hamsuns "Dronningen af Saba"', in José L. Ramírez (ed.), *Att forska om gränser*, Stockholm: Nordregio, pp. 141–70.

——(2001b). 'Jean Genet og den europeiske grensen', in Ragnhild E. Reinton and Irene Iversen (eds), *Litteratur og erfaring*, Oslo: Spartacus, pp. 149–66.

——(2003). 'Genre borders in a border novel: Nadine Gordimer's *My Son's Story*', in Beata Agrell and Ingela Nilsson (eds), *Genrer och genreproblem: Teoretiska och historiska perspektiv / Genres and Their Problems: Theoretical and Historical Perspectives*, Göteborg: Daidalos, pp. 505–13.

——(2006a). 'Crossing and reading: notes towards a theory and a method', *Nordlit*, 19, 41–63.

——(2006b). 'Hamsuns koloniale nonsens', in Even Arntzen and Henning H. Wærp (eds), *Tid og rom i Hamsuns prosa (II)*, Hamarøy: Hamsun-Selskapet, pp. 81–116.

——(2008). 'Grensen – litterært faktum med romlig form', in Clas Zilliacus, Heidi Grönstad and Ulrika Gustafsson (eds), *Gränser i nordisk litteratur/ Borders in Nordic Literature*, Åbo: Åbo Akademis förlag, pp. 19–37.

Schimanski, Johan and Stephen Wolfe (eds) (2007a). *Border Poetics De-limited*, Hannover: Wehrhahn.

——(2007b). 'Imperial tides: a border poetic reading of *Heart of Darkness*', in Johan Schimanski and Stephen Wolfe (eds), *Border Poetics De-limited*, pp. 217–34.

Silverman, Lisa (2006). 'Zwischenzeit and Zwischenort: Veza Canetti, Else Feldmann, and Jewish writing in interwar Vienna', *Prooftexts: A Journal of Jewish Literary History*, 26, 1–2, 29–52.

Skogheim, Dag (1998a). *Sulis / Café Iris*, Oslo: Tiden.

——(1998b). *November -44 / Sølvhalsbåndet: Merkedager*, Oslo: Tiden.

Sommer, Doris (1990). 'Irresistible romance: the foundational fictions of Latin America', in Bhabha (ed.), *Nation and Narration*, London: Routledge, pp. 71–98.

Spreitzer, Brigitte (2005). 'Veza Canettis Roman *Die Gelbe Strasse* im Kontext der literarischen Moderne', in Ingrid Spörk and Alexandra Strohmaier (eds), *Veza Canetti*, Graz: Droschl, pp. 11–31.

Strohmaier, Alexandra (2005). 'Groteske Physiognomien: Zum semiotischen Konzept des Körpers in den Texten Veza Canettis', in Ingrid Spörk and Alexandra Strohmaier (eds), *Veza Canetti*, Graz: Droschl, pp. 121–47.

Yuval-Davis, Nira (1997). 'Gender and nation', in Rick Wilford and Robert L. Miller (eds), *Women, Ethnicity and Nationalism: The Politics of Transition*, London: Routledge, pp. 23–35.

6

Taking Sides: Power-play on the Welsh Border in Early Twentieth-century Women's Writing

JANE AARON

Introduction

In 1933 Sigmund Freud announced that he had 'discovered' in the female psyche a lower stratum below the oedipal. 'A woman's identification with her mother allows us to distinguish two strata', he suggests: 'the pre-Oedipus one which rests on her affectionate attachment to her mother and takes her as a model, and the later one from the Oedipus complex which seeks to get rid of her mother and take her place with her father'. Though these attachments date from earliest infancy, they retain their grip into adulthood, for 'neither of them is adequately surmounted in the course of development' (Freud, 1973 [1933]: 168). The terms with which Freud describes the consequences arising from this stratification of the female psyche by now seem very dated. Divided by their loyalties to opposing female and male models, throughout their lives women are at a serious disadvantage, he argues, for under such fragmented conditions, 'the formation of the super-ego must suffer; it cannot attain the strength and independence which give it its cultural significance' (p. 163). Faced with the opposites father/mother the female does not take sides in the way that the male infant does, and according to Freud that weakens her. Women, he argues, have historically failed to contribute as richly as men to world cultures not because they have been economically and educationally disadvantaged in comparison with men, but because their split psyches have distracted them from single-minded goals and bifurcated the driving force which should have been spurring them on to creative achievement.

It does not seem to occur to Freud that strong and independent superegos, capable of operating single-mindedly without diverging from their goals to consider more than one side of a question, may not necessarily constitute the highest cultural ideal. But, since the 1970s, with the shift in values that marked the second wave of the women's movement, feminist revisionists have queried Freud's assumptions in a manner which, I want to suggest in this chapter, throws interesting light on the literary representation of gender difference in border subjects, that is, the inhabitants of border locations.

In her highly influential study *The Reproduction of Mothering: Psychoanalysis and the Sociology of Genre* (1978) Nancy Chodorow agrees with Freud that, for a girl, 'turning to her father does not substitute for her attachment to her mother. Instead a girl retains her preoedipal tie to her mother . . . and builds oedipal attachments to both her mother and her father upon it.' But she attributes this stratification not to any essentialist aspect of biological femininity but solely to the fact that it is still primarily women who rear babies and young children. The female infant identifies with her female carer in a way that the male does not, but would do were both sexes cared for equally by males as well as females. For Chodorow, however, the consequence of multiple identifications for the female subject is not so much a weaker superego as a greater capacity for empathy with others. 'From the retention of preoedipal attachments to their mother, growing girls come to define and experience themselves as continuous with others', she says; 'their experience of self contains more flexible or permeable ego boundaries' (p. 129). This empathic experience later enables them to suspend their own ego needs in order to mother the next generation. But, when this pattern of gendered behaviour continues into a new era in which equality between the sexes is seen as desirable, the situation it gives rise to, in which only one sex is conditioned to develop the necessary flexibility to put others' needs first, obviously becomes fraught with tensions. This is not to say, with Freud, that the capacity for multiple identifications of necessity weakens the ego, but to recognize that, unless they are deliberately revolutionized, gendered patterns of child-rearing will perpetuate themselves in a manner which limits the potential of both sexes: of men for nurturing and for empathy with others, and of women for all achievements which require single-minded, goal-driven preoccupation.

Post-Chodorow, subsequent feminist analysis, in a more complete reversal of Freud's value-structures, saw the greater flexibility of the female ego as of worth in itself, quite apart from its usefulness in child-rearing. In a seminal essay, the poet and critic Rachel Blau DuPlessis, for example, posited the greater capacity of women to see both sides of a question as a hitherto undervalued but in humanitarian terms much needed 'female aesthetic'. 'Not positing oneself as the only, sol(e) authority', the female, unlike the male, for DuPlessis has 'both/and vision . . . the end of the either/or, dichotomized universe' (1986 [1979]: 275–6). From her point of view, to acquire 'more flexible or permeable ego boundaries' is all to the good, for the happiness of the individual and of the species. To be capable of diverse identifications and have a 'both/and' mindset which does not feel obliged to 'take sides' is seen as to the subject's advantage, and that of society generally. Entitled 'For the Etruscans', DuPlessis's text looks back to earlier, pre-patriarchal cultures, now lost in history, but possibly similarly enlightened. Relics left by earlier cultures do indeed testify to the fact that an undivided identity and a single-minded consciousness have not always been thought of as unquestionably admirable and a necessity for cultural achievement. Popular images of the deities in early Celtic cultures, for example, include double- and triple-faced gods and goddesses (see Ross, 1967: 73–81), tricephaloi and janiform figures who would clearly experience some difficulty in whole-heartedly, or at any rate whole-headedly, operating single-mindedly and identifying with one side only in any debate. The male, along with the female, has not always been imaged as ideally unified into one seamless whole; the capacity to look in more than one direction has been depicted as an attribute of the gods, to be aspired to and emulated by both genders. From this historical and, indeed, pre-historical perspective, the late nineteenth-century bourgeois culture in which Freud was reared, which would have imbued him with the conviction that single-mindedness was essentially masculine and necessary for cultural achievement, seems obviously dated, its militarism redolent of an imperialistic patriarchy in which conquest rather than the appreciation of another's point of view was the goal.

That patriarchal culture has, of course, since been eroded by successive waves of anti-imperial and feminist movements, though its bulwarks cannot yet be said to have been entirely overcome. In her essay, DuPlessis draws support for her ideas from the work of an array of early modernist women writers, in particular Virginia Woolf and Dorothy Richardson. She quotes, for example, Richardson's 1929 description of 'the unique gift of the feminine psyche . . . to do what the shapely mentalities of men appear incapable of doing for themselves, to act as a focus for divergent points of view' (Richardson, 1929: 347). This characteristic 'of being in all camps at once' is seen by Richardson as very much a positive attribute, potentially healing of those divisions which had but lately brought the world to catastrophe during the First World War. I was reminded of these feminist works from the 1970s, along with Freud's account of the female's pre-oedipal stratifications, on re-reading another interwar text, located on the Wales–England border and centrally concerned with divided identities, that is, Margiad Evans's 1932 novel *Country Dance*. Hilda Vaughan and Dorothy Edwards, two further Welsh writers of the interwar period, also published texts set in the Welsh border country to which issues of identity were central, while another earlier novel of the border, Violet Jacob's *The Sheep-Stealers* (1902), similarly features a protagonist fractured by internal conflicting identities. In the next three sections of this chapter I would like to explore these fictions in the light of these psychoanalytic theories of the female subject to see what they can contribute to the current understanding of gender relations in border locations.

Divided loyalties in Violet Jacob's The Sheep-Stealers

At first glance it would appear that *The Sheep-Stealers*, written in the first years of the twentieth century when Freud was initially developing his theories of the unconscious, is virtually a fictionalization of his ideas. It reads like a warning lesson on how not to mother – or to father, for that matter – and the parental dysfunction is much exacerbated by the fact that the family inhabits a border zone. Violet Jacob, the novel's author, was herself no stranger to the experience of divided loyalties: born in Scotland to a Welsh mother and a Scottish father, she was living in India as the wife of an Irish major in the British army when she wrote *The Sheep-Stealers*, her first novel. Later, after she and her husband had returned to Britain, they settled for a while on the Welsh border, near Hay-on-Wye, but Jacob must have known the area well before she went to India, for her descriptions of it in her novel are specific and convincing. The text's opening pages dwell in some detail on the character of both the landscape and the communities of the border:

> Soon after leaving Hereford, the outline of the mountain might be seen raising itself . . . over green hedges and rich meadow-land from the midst of verdure and civilization . . . The 'hill-people', as the slower-witted dwellers in the valley called them . . . were neither entirely mountain nor entirely valley bred, though retaining something of each locality, and something of the struggle between nature and civilisation seemed to have entered into them, giving them that strenuousness which all transition must bring with it . . . Such were the two communities living close together on the borders of two nations, nominally one since the middle ages, but in reality only amalgamated down to a very few inches below the surface. (pp. 3–4, 7)

The tensions to which Jacob draws attention here between the Welsh 'hill people' and the English 'valley dwellers' are from the first very apparent in the history of her central protagonist, the hill-born Rhys Walters. *The Sheep-Stealers* is a historical novel set in the 'earlier half of the nineteenth century': typically for a Welsh woman of that period, Rhys's mother Anne has undergone a Calvinist conversion to Welsh Methodism. Soon after the sudden death in childhood of Rhys's older brother, an 'earnest preacher . . . came to hold meetings among the Methodists of the mountain district', and Anne assauged her grief by becoming his convert; according to the text, 'she threw herself wholly into the sea of his relentless Christianity, for there were no half-measures with her' (p. 15). Her husband Eli, a comparatively weak and irresolute character, does not join her in her new faith, but does not oppose her either. The expected gender pattern in terms of the power relation between husband and wife is thus reversed; it is the female who becomes, through her Calvinist faith, single-minded and dominant, and the male who vacillates, providing an atypical paternal role model for the son. The narrator emphasizes that 'Eli stood in awe of his wife, and young Rhys knew it'.

This knowledge weakens Rhys's sympathy for both his parents, from whom he is further alienated by being reared largely in England. The Walters are sufficiently well-off sheep-farmers to send Rhys, now their only child, over the border to be educated, to the grammar school at Hereford where he must be a boarder. In early youth, Rhys thus 'found himself one morning on the top of the Hereford coach with a Bible given him by Anne in one pocket and half-a-sovereign given him by Eli in the other. He was very much pleased with the half-sovereign' (p. 18). But not with the Bible: he rebels against his mother's attempts to draw him into her faith, and has apparently no difficulty in repressing any tendency to bond with her. The cowed father provides little, however, in terms of an alternative role model. Nor does Rhys take anything from his schooling, apart from acquiring an upper-class accent in his pronunciation of English and learning to enjoy fighting. This makes him all the more eager, once schooldays are over and he returns home to the farm, to take part in the local agitations against the proliferating toll gates in the area. The account of the so-called Rebecca riots in this novel is faithful to the historical records of the attacks upon the toll gates of rural Wales, in the late 1830s and early 1840s, by small farmers and farm labourers exacerbated at having to pay extortionate fees for taking their animals and goods to market. Disguised as women, the rioters destroyed the toll gates, acting under the guidance of leaders they called Rebecca. In Jacob's novel, the local group asks Rhys to lead them, telling him: '[U]s have thought . . . that Rebecca bein' a Bible person and a leading woman of power and glory in this job, we will be proud if you be she . . . [We] were saying . . . just before you come in, sir, what a beautiful female you would be' (pp. 21–2). Though the local toll-gate keeper's daughter is at the time with child by him, Rhys accepts the challenge, but the whole affair is 'more of a piece of out-of-the-way amusement to him than anything affecting his opinions' (p. 23). The keeper is killed during the attack and Rhys flees, finding a hiding place in a sheep-stealer's cottage; soon he has taken up that profession himself. Yet at the beginning of the story he was himself heir to a rich sheep farm; his landed neighbours had assumed that he would join their ranks and fight to maintain law and order against the Rebecca rioters. Not only did Rhys cross gender boundaries in accepting the Rebecca role but he also switched sides in class terms. As his motivation was simply to provide himself with wayward amusement rather than support the oppressed, it is convincing that he should subsequently take what entertainment he can from his new role as outlaw and, as a sheep-stealer, start preying upon the property of the group into which he was born.

Before the close of the novel, though still in hiding in the hills, he also once more crosses national boundaries. He becomes obsessed with an English gentlewoman visiting the area; in order to win her favour, and with the help of his upper-class, Hereford school English-speaking accent, he manages to persuade her that he is an English spy, sent to Wales to gather information for the English authorities on the activities of the Rebeccaites. Rhys in effect hollows himself out in terms of identity by keeping on changing sides, or masquerading as if he belonged to different sides, throughout the novel, throwing himself with increasing emotional desperateness across the borders of class, gender and legality as well as nation. Finally, after the English woman has fled from him, having discovered his actual role in the riots, he creeps back like the Prodigal Son to the parental farm, only to find his mother in the midst of a Methodist prayer meeting and deeply unresponsive to him. His immediate reaction is to throw himself over the last border, committing suicide by leaping off a local mountain top.

Jacob's story could be said to endorse the Freudian theory that subjects without strong single-minded and goal-focused superegos will waste their resources and make no useful contribution to their culture, while those with an unbending capacity to dedicate themselves entirely to a single cultural or religious cause will not necessarily make good-enough child-carers. Anne Walters is depicted as a destructive mother because she is single-minded in her devotion to her creed, and will not compromise with her son, nor put his needs before her own, which she identifies wholly with the demands of her religion. Unwilling to side with his mother, and finding no alternative strong role model in his father, Rhys lives for pleasure alone, unguided by any form of superego except, presumably, the final punitive self-destructive impulse which kills him. Yet, in another sense, Jacob's novel can be said consistently to query Freudian models in that it goes out of its way to emphasize that traditional notions of gender differences are not grounded in biology or essence. As well as the complete reversal of traditional gender roles evident in the characters of Rhys's parents, minor characters also bear witness to the absurdity of gender expectations. During the Rebecca riots, for example, the only person to stand up to the rioters is the wife of the toll-gate keeper, 'a brave woman and a much better man than her husband' (p. 24). Later, her pregnant daughter's damaged life is healed by a male neighbour for whom there exists no stronger compulsion than the 'longing to protect a poor stricken creature' (p. 135). As for Rhys's bizarre career, the text suggests that it is his border condition, rather than any lack of forcefulness on his part, which in part gives rise to it. Rhys is as single-minded as his mother in the pursuit of his pleasures and obsessions; that he veers wildly from object to object, acting out a variety of parts, is an indicator of his uprootedness, born in one culture but educated in another and without an abiding loyalty to either. His case suggests the narrowness of those psychoanalytic theories which do not in their formulation of identity construction take into account such social and cultural specificities as class, ethnicity, epoch and location, as well as gender and familial relations.

Gender and conflict in Hilda Vaughan's and Dorothy Edwards's border narratives

The Welsh border country also provided the setting for *The Battle to the Weak* (1925), the first novel of another Welsh woman writer of the early twentieth century, Hilda Vaughan. Born in 1892, in Builth Wells, Breconshire, to a successful country solicitor and his wife, Vaughan settled in London after her 1923 marriage to the novelist Charles Morgan who encouraged her to develop her own writing career. From the first, however, her fictions tended to be located in the border counties of Breconshire or Radnorshire (today's Powys), and were characteristically concerned with rural characters caught up in intense familial or community divisions. Her first novel focuses on two warring border families, the Welsh-speaking, chapel-going Lloyds and the English-speaking, church-going Bevans. In *Romeo and Juliet* fashion, two of the younger members of this divided community, Rhys Lloyd and Esther Bevan, become strongly attracted to one another, but their families refuse to countenance their marriage. In anger Rhys emigrates to make a fortune for the two of them in Canada, only to be much frustrated and antagonized by Esther's repeated refusals to join him. She stays to nurse first her sister Gladys, then her mother, both of whom have been physically and mentally damaged by her brutal father. Years later Rhys returns home, and Esther manages to articulate to him the reasons behind her apparently unloving behaviour. She compares her own domestic struggle with his aspirations to work with the newly formed League of Nations and play some part in the post-First World War attempts to realign power on a global scale. She asks him:

> 'Isn't it because you can't bear as small little nations should be oppressed that you are wantin' the Great Powers to protect the weak? You are not holdin' as might is right, but as strength did ought to be showin' mercy . . . Well, that is what I have been feelin' all my life too; only . . . I have not been seein' it large like . . . All I was able to think on was them as was near at hand . . . I don't think as it 'ould have made no manner of difference had poor Mother and Gladys been no kin o' mine.

> Terrible weak they was. That is why I was havin' to help them rather nor you as was so strong and brave.' (Vaughan, 1925: 287)

The exercise of force on a global scale, and the survivors' reaction to it, are here compared to familial conflict in the microcosm of the domestic setting, the traditional 'woman's sphere'. And the suggestion is that in both cases the battle is not necessarily to the strong, for those who survive are not necessarily going to identify with the conqueror. Conquest here defeats its own aims because it can strengthen a subject's sympathetic attachment to the conquered; to be a defender of the weak can prove a more compelling role than to be a follower of the strong. *The Battle to the Weak* is the only one of the fictions discussed in this chapter not to end tragically, because Rhys, the strong all-conquering male, who has acquired enough wealth in Canada to buy out both the rival families' farms, accepts Esther's argument, and appreciates the connection between her domestic stand for the weak and his own political ideals. Interestingly, he also associates this underlying bond between them with the border country in which they have both been reared: '"She's of the land," he thought . . . "My nature is rooted in hers like, same as 'tis rooted in the soil from which the both of us was springin".' (p. 285) That is, it is 'of the land' – and specifically it is of that border land – to nourish and strengthen the weak and keep replenishing their underground roots, in the face of those tensions, particularly apparent in border locations, which may threaten the fragile balance by which both sides survive. Esther's and Rhys's protective qualities are pronounced; their permeable egos can embrace both strong and weak, but they devote their strength to helping the weak, thus maintaining the balance between the two.

Like *The Sheep-Stealers*, this text also exposes the hollowness of the traditional concepts of gender difference. When Rhys towards the beginning of the novel studies 'the pleasant rugged lines of Esther's profile' as she sits 'gazing straight ahead of her with that expression of steady contemplative and latent strength which had at first attracted his attention', he notes the masculinity of her features, in particular her 'strong, almost masculine chin' (pp. 54–5). But, as soon becomes evident in the battle of wills between them, Esther's strength, for all its 'masculine' aspect, is dedicated to the needs of the oppressed and the subordinated – that is, in her experience, the needs of women – and resists identification with the male until assured that he too is willing to devote himself to maintaining the fragile balance of power between the two sides. In this respect, Vaughan's heroine contrasts strikingly with the central female figure in another text by a Welsh woman writer published two years later.

Dorothy Edwards's 'The Conquered', one of the short stories included in her collection *Rhapsody* (1927), reads at first like a deliberate critique of *The Battle to the Weak*, intent upon representing a very different type of female response to invading power. Born in the south Wales industrial village of Ogmore Vale in 1903, the daughter of a strongly committed socialist whose politics she endorsed, Edwards's first-person fictions commonly employ unreliable narrators from social circles alien to her own: her narrators are nearly always male, middle class and English, who often inadvertently expose their blinkered vision as they tell their tales (see Flay, 2007). The narrator of 'The Conquered' is a young Englishman, Frederick Trenier, who, on a visit to the Wales–England border, is initially gratified to meet the alluring and sophisticated Gwyneth. One day, however, as they walk together along an old Roman road, under the shadow of 'a hill where the ancient Britons made a great stand against the Romans, and were defeated', he is taken aback to discover that she identifies with the conquerors:

> 'Did you know this was a Roman road?' she asked. 'Just think of the charming Romans who must have walked here! . . . Does it shock you to know that I like the Romans better than the Greeks?'
>
> I said 'No,' but now, when I think of it, I believe I *was* a little shocked. (Edwards, 1927: 52)

Later, Frederick is excited to find amongst the music sheets on Gwyneth's piano a favourite piece of his, the *Polnische Lieder*, Chopin's lament for conquered Poland, and he begs her to sing it. The work evokes strong memories for him of another occasion when he heard a woman perform it with intense sympathy. But when Gwyneth laughs at his excitement and refuses, saying 'I can't sing it. It does not suit me at all', he recalls with bitterness her earlier expressed partiality for imperialists: 'I thought to myself quite angrily, 'No, of course she could not sing that song. She would have been on the side of the conquerors!' The incident permanently changes his view of her: 'when I looked at Gwyneth again it seemed to me that some of her beauty had gone,' he says (pp. 55–6). Gwyneth has repelled him by not fulfilling his preconceptions that women in general, and Welsh women perhaps in particular, will empathize with the conquered; a woman who appears to find it as easy as the Freudian male to repress all tendencies to identify with any group except the most dominant is to him antagonistic.

However, Frederick does not allow his dismay at coming across such an anomaly to take him much further into an understanding of his own position in relation to border tensions and the power balance between contending peoples. He does not ask himself why it is that he should be 'suddenly disappointed' when the Welsh songs Gwyneth does choose to perform are not, as he had expected, 'melancholy' (p. 54). From his point of view, as a visiting Englishman in Wales, it is the role of the native to lament, and his to applaud the performance and enjoy its melancholia vicariously. It does not occur to him that what he is asking for is in effect a virtual repetition of the experience of conquest; he is deaf to the manner in which his narration exposes his own conventional thinking, laden with gendered and racial preconceptions. But, while Dorothy Edwards's narrator in this subtle tale may be no more enlightened or sympathetic a figure than the woman whose character he critiques, the portrayal of both characters serves to undermine any notion of essentialist gender or ethnic difference.

Both these 1920s texts, then, like *The Sheep-Stealers*, make use of their border locations to probe the relation between the social constructions of gender and ethnicity. While *The Battle to the Weak* features a heroine of rugged 'masculine' strength who wins her lover over to the side of the oppressed, 'The Conquered' suggests that there is nothing essentially female about the capacity to identify with more than one side, for Gwyneth finds it completely impossible to do so. She cannot sing a melancholy note, but is single-mindedly on the side of the conquerors.

Margiad Evans's border identity

The same cannot be said of the central protagonist of the last text to be discussed in this chapter. The title page of the first edition of *Country Dance* highlighted from the outset, for those in the know, the fragmented identity of its author: the book was presented as written by Margiad Evans with illustrations by Peggy Whistler. In fact Peggy Whistler and Margiad Evans were one and the same person: 'Margiad Evans' is the very Welsh-sounding pseudonym Peggy Whistler chose when she constructed for herself a border identity. Born in Uxbridge in south-east England in 1909, in reality Peggy Whistler's only connection with Wales was one great-grandfather, a Lancashire clergyman called Evans who was believed to be of Welsh extraction. In early adulthood, however, she opted for a Welsh or, rather, a border identity: she lived on the border, married a Welsh man, published under a Welsh pseudonym, but insisted to one correspondent in 1946, 'I'm *not* Welsh . . . *I am the border* – a very different thing' (quoted in Morgan, 1998: 32). Her early life in Uxbridge was marred by her father's alcoholism and her family's financial insecurity: in a recent article Tony Brown suggests that Wales and the border countryside must have answered Evans's need for 'stability and rootedness in a life which provided her with no permanent sense of home' (Brown, 2004: 23). But what is striking about Margiad Evans's deliberately constructed identity is its internal divisions, its instability as much as its stability. She does not opt for joining another ethnic identity, and creating a clear break between herself and her unhappy childhood; rather, she very insistently chooses a border identity, and opts to live on that liminal margin between two sides. That she herself saw the Welsh border as constituting as much of a special zone as any other international border, for all the supposed 'unity' of the kingdom to which England and Wales belong, is indicated in one of the key sentences from *Country Dance*, in which the narrator claims that the history of her central protagonist in this novella set on the Wales–England border represents 'the entire history of the Border', 'that history which belongs to all border lands and tells of incessant warfare' (Evans, 2006 [1932]: 103). Deliberately to choose a site 'of incessant warfare' as one's spiritual as well as geographical home does not suggest so much a need for stability as a desire to place oneself in the midst of duality and persistently feel the pull of contending loyalties. In a recent discussion of *Country Dance*, Diana Wallace suggests that Evans 'found in the Welsh border an imaginative space which fired her creativity as a writer, partly because it connected with her concern with insecure identities' (Wallace, 2007: 177). Through putting herself in a position which foregrounded division, forcing it to consciousness, Evans may have hoped to arrive at a greater understanding of that divided condition which according to Freud is of the essence of the female mind, and of those permeable ego boundaries which according to Chodorow are the consequence for women of the gendered pattern of child-rearing.

At any rate *Country Dance* focuses on the endless dance between two countries and two cultures which characterize border territories.

According to its narrative frame, the novel's twentieth-century narrator 'Margiad Evans' has supposedly discovered a mid-nineteenth-century journal penned by a young woman living on the Welsh borders, who, though she is herself of mixed Welsh and English heritage, has to choose between two suitors, both determinedly mono-cultural and at bitter odds with one another. Thus the diarist, Ann Goodman, herself becomes symbolic of the border country, and the reader is informed of her representative status in no uncertain terms. The first sentence of Margiad Evans's introduction reads, 'The struggle for supremacy in her mixed blood is the unconscious theme of Ann Goodman's book' (p. 3), and at its close, after the 'End of Ann's Book', she reminds the reader that Ann's diary is 'the record of a mind rather than actions, a mind which though clear in itself was never conscious of the two nations at war within it' (pp. 102–3). For most of the course of her history, Ann veers between Welsh and English identifications. When her diary-writing commences, her primary loyalty is to her English suitor, Gabriel, and she appears to share his views of the Welsh, which are not ameliorated by the fact that he is living and working amongst them on the Welsh side of the border where Ann met him. But the illness of her Welsh mother Myfanwy has just brought Ann back across the border to the home of her English father, the shepherd John Goodman, where she meets the farmer who employs him, the Welshman Evan ap Evans. For all the importance of national difference for this novel's characters it is often difficult for the reader to be clear as to on which side of the border they actually are at any given time: this is part of the teasing 'dance' element of the text. Evans is drawn to Ann initially by virtue of her half-Welshness, isolated as he is on the English side of the border. But at first he meets with little sympathy from Ann: 'I tell him, "I am English. I was with English folk in Wales, and I hate the Welsh and all their shifty ways of dealing."' He responds: 'Thou hatest the Welsh, dost thou? Is Myfanwy an English name?' 'For once I cannot answer', she confesses, halted in the unthinking repetition of racial prejudice by the sound of her mother's name and what it means in terms of her own divided loyalties (p. 30).

This is the start of her dance between the two men, to and fro across geographical and linguistic borders, and the changing borders of her own identity. That dance comes to an abrupt close, however, when the developing enmity of the men virtually forces her to choose one or the other: she accepts Evan ap Evans, but is murdered before her wedding, probably by Gabriel. The suggestion is that to choose one side is to choose death, the end of the 'dance'; neither of the two males is going to allow her to express or appreciate that side of herself which they do not share. The greater capacity of women to sustain a border identity has been suggested earlier in the tale, in a tense scene that takes place with Gabriel in a farmhouse on the Welsh side of the border:

> Gwen has put out her blackberry wine; it sets the men to singing reckless words from 'Men of Harlech' . . .
>
> One of them jumps up from his place shouting: 'I drink to Wales!' Gabriel roars: 'And I to England!' and stands facing the other across the table . . .
>
> Mary looks serious. 'There'll be trouble in a minute, the men are hot as coals,' she whispers.
>
> Gwen purses her lips. 'I give the Border,' she says, very quiet. (pp. 66–7)

Gwen's toast quietens the antagonists: they accept, temporarily at least, the way her term, 'the Border', locates them in a zone other than that of the two contending nations. It would appear that the 'border country' does not after all always and inevitably entail a site of warfare. It can be a place in which both cultures exist side by side, without taking sides.

Country Dance, then, ultimately suggests that sanity resides in being of the border, rather than of either of its sides, and that women are more likely than men to appreciate that fact and tolerate the tensions of the border condition. A subject capable of appreciating diverse identifications, without having to 'take sides' and act them out, is precisely the type of subject needed in a border zone, and likely to contribute richly to its culture; and of course, given the postmodern spread of global cultures, few areas remain which are not in a sense border zones. Freud's ideal male, with his strong superego and his single-minded forcefulness, belongs to a discredited past, and what becomes an ideal for both sexes is the 'multi-layered female psyche' with its 'more permeable ego boundaries'. Nevertheless, as texts like 'The Conquered' indicate, to posit the capacity for multiple identifications as an essentially female characteristic is misconceived; rather, it needs to serve for both sexes as an ideal, a 'feminine' ideal perhaps, but only in a context in which that appellation is no longer perceived as denoting secondary status.

Bibliography

Brown, Tony (2004). 'Stories from foreign countries: the short stories of Kate Roberts and Margiad Evans', in Alyce von Rothkirch and Daniel Williams (eds), *Beyond the Difference: Welsh Literature in Comparative Contexts*, Cardiff: University of Wales Press, pp. 21–37.

Chodorow, Nancy (1978). *The Reproduction of Mothering: Psychoanalysis and the Sociology of Genre*, Berkeley: University of California Press.

DuPlessis, Rachel Blau (1986 [1979]). 'For the Etruscans', reprinted in Elaine Showalter (ed.), *The New Feminist Criticism*, London: Virago.

Edwards, Dorothy (2007 [1927]). 'The Conquered', in *Rhapsody*, Library of Wales edn, Cardigan: Parthian.

Evans, Margiad (2006 [1932]). *Country Dance*, Library of Wales edn, Cardigan: Parthian.

Flay, Claire (2007). 'Conquering convention', *New Welsh Review*, 77, 60–6.

Freud, Sigmund (1973 [1933]). 'Femininity', *New Introductory Lectures on Psychoanalysis*, trans. James Strachey, Pelican Freud Libary, ii, Harmondsworth: Penguin.

Jacob, Violet (1902). *The Sheep-Stealers*, London: Heinemann.

Morgan, Ceridwen Lloyd (1998). *Margiad Evans*, Bridgend: Seren Books.

Richardson, Dorothy (1929). 'Leadership in Marriage', *New Adelphi*, 2, 4, 345–8.

Ross, Anne (1967). *Pagan Celtic Britain: Studies in Iconography and Tradition*, London and New York: Routledge and Kegan Paul and Columbia University Press.

Vaughan, Hilda (1925). *The Battle to the Weak*, London: Heinemann.

Wallace, Diana (2007). '"Mixed marriages": three Welsh historical novels in English by women writers', in Christopher Meredith (ed.), *Moment of Earth: Poems and Essays in Honour of Jeremy Hooker*, Aberystwyth: Celtic Studies Publications, pp. 171–84.

7

'Those Blue Remembered Hills': Gender in Twentieth-century Welsh Border Writing by Men

KATIE GRAMICH

'Wild Wales' has frequently featured in English literature from at least the early modern period as an imagined space of Otherness, which has also been marked by gender peculiarity or difference. Equally, Welsh writers have tended to emphasize cultural, linguistic and gender features which differentiate Wales from its more politically and economically powerful neighbour, England. The Welsh–English border has, therefore, become a potent signifier of difference, though the borderland itself has a distinct literary personality of its own – in both Welsh and English the traditional noun used to designate the border is in the plural: '*Y Gororau*', or 'the Marches', indicating borderlands.[1] This chapter explores the representation of the Welsh borderlands in the work of a range of twentieth-century male writers, examining the ways in which cultural, linguistic, religious and even temperamental differences are often seen as inextricably linked with gender. It discusses to what extent the traditional feminization of Wales as a place of quasi-colonial Otherness continues into the twentieth century and whether differences are distinguishable between literary representations of the gendered border at the turn of the century and at its close.

Moira Dearnley has demonstrated that Wales is depicted in eighteenth-century fictions by male and female authors as a place of retreat, remote and Edenic, a pastoral idyll which is the site of primitive virtue, set against the vice and corruption of English cities (Dearnley, 2001).[2] Yet, while the landscape of Wales is praised by writers who admire the country's picturesque potential, in general the indigenous population are seen as barbarians from whom delicate heroines must escape with decorous speed. In the nineteenth century, as Jane Aaron has shown, women novelists use a romance formula to dramatize the seduction of a female Wales by her dashing English neighbour, thus offering a feminized political narrative of the inclusion of Wales within the British Empire. This polarized use of Wales and England to define national and gender identity is, not unsurprisingly, particularly acute in literary texts which are actually set in the borderlands between the two countries. Moreover, male and female authors, though they use certain common tropes in juxtaposing Welsh and English national and cultural traits, tend to explore gender issues on the border in interestingly distinct ways.[3]

A Shropshire Lad (1918 [1896]) by A. E. Housman may be regarded as a classic English male text of the Welsh Marches at the turn of the century. In gender terms, it is achingly masculine, chronicling in a sequence of lyrical, elegiac poems the loss of male youth, a theme that would make this slim volume extremely popular among soldiers during the First World War. Despite the insistently masculine focus of the volume, when the poet turns his attention specifically to the border and to the distinction between England and Wales, his poetic language becomes tellingly gendered. In poem XXVIII, 'The Welsh Marches', the river Severn in Shrewsbury is seen as the dividing line between England and Wales; the emphasis, however, is not on disjunction but on the often painful connections between the two lands. Wales is seen as the 'vanquished' territory, while England is the 'conqueror's state' (Housman, 1918 [1896]: 41). Hand in hand with this characterization is the identification of Wales with evening darkness, England with the light of 'morn'. The speaker's mother is identified as Welsh and, in a passage deliberately reminiscent of the ninth-century Welsh elegy of *Canu Heledd*[4] which is actually set in Shrewsbury (then a Welsh territory), is described as the victim of rape by her Saxon conquerors. The speaker himself is the fruit of that violent union: 'The Saxon got me on the slave.' Thus, Wales is seen as the female victim, England as the aggressive male conqueror and rapist. Exacerbating the atrocity, the act of rape occurs upon the grave of the woman's dead brother (reminiscent of both the Welsh Heledd, mourning for her dead brother, and of Antigone). Although this act is seen as an 'ancient wrong', the speaker himself is still tormented by this history, his divided loyalties and allegiances figured as continuing to do battle 'on the marches of my breast' (p. 42). This striking internalization of the border state will, as we shall see, be repeated in many later writings. Although he was born in Worcestershire, Housman actually wrote the poems of *A Shropshire Lad* while living in Highgate, north London, in the 1890s and, in this regard, his nostalgia for a lost western land can be seen in context with works such as W. B. Yeats's 'Lake Isle of Innisfree' or the contemporary writings of Arthur Machen, which situate the lost land in Gwent. However, Housman's poems dramatize an internal division in sexual terms, too, since they are complicated by a homoerotic subtext which many critics have seen as a lament for the 'lost loves' proscribed by a repressive British society which was savage in its punishment of sexual transgression, as the trial of Oscar Wilde had recently shown (see Jebb, 1992). In a later poem in the sequence, the exiled first-person speaker longs for 'those blue remembered hills' in 'yon far country', identifying Wales with the country of lost youth, 'the land of lost content' (Housman, 1918 [1896]: 57). As we shall see, this identification of Wales with the female and with childhood and lost innocence, is common among male border writers of the earlier twentieth century. Moreover, the explicitly gendered characterization of the border is a continuation of much earlier literary representations, which cannot be explored further here; for instance, Daniel Defoe's *Tour through the Whole Island of Great Britain* (1724–6) figures the river Severn itself as masculine, and the borderland through which it flows as female: 'the Severn . . . impregnates the valleys, and when it overflows leaves a virtue behind it, particular to itself' (quoted in Roberts, 1998: 88–9). This repeated representation of the relationship between Wales and England at the border as one of sexual intercourse, either violent or intimate, but in both cases fruitful, suggest strongly that English male authors gender the Welsh Marches so as to produce a metaphor of the political union between England and Wales.

If English writers as diverse as Housman and Defoe figure the Welsh borderlands in these gendered terms, we might speculate that Welsh authors see the region somewhat differently. However, we find that the Anglo-Welsh authors who are the main subject of this chapter tend to represent and to gender the border in quite similar terms to their English neighbours. The aforementioned Arthur Machen, for instance, a Welsh-born writer who became an important and influential English man of letters in the early decades of the twentieth century, tends, like Housman, to yearn for those 'blue remembered hills' and to identify the lost Welsh territory as a pristine, virginal, quasi-holy land, as we find, for example, in his poem 'The Remembrance of the Bard'. Here, 'the land of Gwent' is seen as preserving a 'treasure . . . glorious and deeply concealed'; the bardic speaker concludes: 'Better a grave on Twyn Bwrlwm than a throne in the palace of the Saxons at Caer-ludd' (see Geraint Eirug Davies, 1999: 187). 'Twyn Bwrlwm', a hill outside Newport in what was then Monmouthshire, a notoriously ambivalent county, never securely Welsh or English, is seen as a quasi-divine land, greatly preferred to the materialistic pleasures of the English border town of Ludlow (Caer-ludd). Both Machen and his successor, the Newport-born poet W. H. Davies, tellingly resurrect the ancient Welsh name of 'Gwent' for their home territory, long before local governments revived the old names, endowing their native borderlands with a mythic reverberance, somewhat similar to the way in which Hardy resurrected and in a sense recreated the land of 'Wessex'.

W. H. Davies is an important border poet in many senses; born in Newport, Monmouthshire in 1871, he was of mixed Welsh and English ancestry. He spent most of the 1890s in America as a tramp, losing part of his leg in an accident jumping off a train in Canada. Thanks to the support of Edward Thomas, another Anglo-Welsh writer who at the time had yet to begin writing the poems on which his reputation now rests, Davies gradually extricated himself from the peripatetic life of the homeless he had been living in London and began to make a name for himself as a 'Georgian' poet in the early years of the twentieth century. Davies, like Machen, frequently writes of his native 'Gwent' in nostalgic terms, juxtaposing its unspoilt countryside with the poverty, injustice and suffering of London. In fact, though Davies tends to be remembered as a poet of gentle Romantic rural lyrics, much of his early work focuses on the often brutal lives of the tramps, prostitutes and drunks with whom he had spent his early manhood. He does not gloss over the squalor of their lives but treats them with an empathy and tenderness rare in English poetry; nevertheless, the spiritual core of Davies's writing remains in the south Welsh rural borderlands. An early poem such as 'Music' juxtaposes 'this smoky capital' (London) with a rural Wales which is also associated with the past, childhood and innocence (W. H. Davies, 1946: 61).[5] 'Days that Have Been' specifically longs for 'the hills of Gwent', mentioning places in the borderlands such as the Usk, Caerleon Castle, Llantarnam, Magor, Malpas and Alteryn. The river Severn appears, as it frequently does in Davies's verse, and is associated with the duality of the border: 'I saw the earth burned into two / By Severn's silver flood' (p. 142). In some poems, nature is conceived of in female terms, a woman 'burst[ing] her full bodice', revealing 'her fair white body' (p. 275). In another poem which contrasts London and Gwent, 'The Mind's Liberty', the hill outside Newport known as 'Twm Barlum' (an alternative spelling to Machen's) is seen as 'that green pap in Gwent, / With its dark nipple in a cloud' (p. 205). Wales here is the lost mother but, simultaneously, an eroticized figure associated with sexual desire and longing. In this regard it is interesting to note that Davies's early writings were heavily censored by editors and friends because of their explicit sexual content: the first draft of Davies's *Autobiography of a Supertramp*, for instance, was considered by his friend Edward Thomas, himself no prude, to be unpublishable for this reason (see Normand, 2003). In later life Davies settled in Nailsworth, Gloucestershire, on the English side of the border, calling his house 'Glendower'; from here he could still see the river he calls 'my lovely Severn', personified as male (p. 451). Davies remained very much an outsider all his life, defying convention by marrying, happily, late in life, a young woman whom he had picked up on the streets. He hob-nobbed with the English literati and upper classes but felt a real affinity with tramps and vagabonds; a gentle, dreamy, physically disabled person, he was at the same time capable of projecting an aggressively masculine and sexually voracious persona at times. He chose not to return to Wales but to remain within sight of it, as a friend reported because 'he wanted freedom and not to be haunted by any sort of trail from his past' (quoted in Stonesifer, 1963: 150). Interestingly, when Davies went tramping in west Wales, he found himself regarded with suspicion by those he calls 'real Welsh people' with 'their own language' (quoted in Normand, 2003: 18). Thus, the Welsh Marches, with their ambiguous identity, suited Davies perfectly, not only as a spiritual and poetic homeland but as an appropriate lodging for a man whose ambiguities – in class, national and moral terms – remained unresolved until his death in 1940.

If W. H. Davies's allegiances remained hazy, those of his fellow Monmouthshire poet, Idris Davies, were quite categorical. In a poem entitled 'Monmouthshire', the Rhymney-born Davies dismisses the current debates in Parliament over the future designation of Monmouthshire as being in Wales or England, asserting

> . . . those who know her people
> Among the smoking vales

Proclaim with pride that they were born
In Monmouthshire, Wales.
(Geraint Eirug Davies, 1999: 29)

Here, the borderland territory is unambiguously both Welsh and female. A later Welsh poet, Harri Webb, though, flatly contradicts Idris Davies's Romantic Welsh nationalism in his satirical poem, 'From Risca with Love', in which a 'citizen of Mummersher' rails against the Welsh language and proclaims an English identity:

I ates their orrid language
Wot I can't understand,
It should be a crime to speak it,
I'd like to see it banned! . . .

Just ark at em jabbering at it
Like monkeys in a zoo!
Talk English tidy we gotto, innit
Like wot ew and me do do.
(Geraint Eirug Davies, 1999: 77)

Here Webb mischievously undermines the speaker's claim to be 'as English as the Queen' by couching the poem in distinctive south Welsh dialect. Webb's poem is thus as nationalistic as Idris Davies's but he represents the borderland as a site of linguistic and cultural conflict, as we see elaborated memorably in women's border writing, such as Margiad Evans's *Country Dance* and Dorothy Edwards's 'The Conquered' (see chapter 6).

The antagonism between Welsh and English is further exemplified in the English writer John Moore's 1933 travel book, *The Welsh Marches*. Moore's narrative consistently positions the Welsh as Other and exotic, sometimes in an attractive way but more often as threatening and barbaric. He compares the border towns to 'forts on the Khyber Pass, looking into Afghanistan', while, at Talgarth, he imagines he is 'in some fragrant Persian garden through which the Caliph has caused a stream to flow for the delight of his ears and the delectation of his eyes when he walks with the veiled ladies of the harem at evening' (Moore, 1993: 62, 90). The persona Moore adopts is that of the opinionated English bon viveur who rails against Welsh Nonconformity and Sunday closing and claims to be shocked that some young people in a remote Welsh valley had never been to a cinema: 'I felt as if I were visiting some strange, lost tribe of . . . African savages' (p. 163). He diagnoses the Welsh as 'suffer[ing] from a sort of persecution mania . . . which manifests itself as hysteria' (p. 174). Even a tramp he meets is actually running out of Wales towards the English border because of the alleged meanness of the Welsh. Moore also treats his readers to his literary judgements of border writers, approving of A. E. Housman and condemning the Shropshire writer, Mary Webb, whose male characters are, he claims, unconvincing: 'How they can satisfy any male reader I cannot imagine; nor . . . any intelligent woman other than a middle-aged virgin who has been segregated in a convent since the age of fifteen' (pp. 128–9). Moore's book, objectionable though it is in its misogyny and racist contempt for the Welsh, is nevertheless interesting in its gendering of the border territories. He certainly sees the division between Wales and England – 'this England which we love so much' (p. 143) – as absolute, the border itself as a 'prohibitory line', as the eighteenth-century travel writer Thomas Pennant called it (quoted in Roberts, 1998: 71) On the English side is masculine good taste and civilization; on the Welsh is feminized barbarism, fanaticism and hysteria.

Another writer of the 1930s, Geraint Goodwin, presents a much more positive view of Wales and a more nuanced exploration of gender and the borderlands. Goodwin was born in the border country near Newtown in Montgomeryshire, which provides the setting for much of his fiction. His 1936 novel, *The Heyday in the Blood*, concerns a passionate love triangle not dissimilar to that found in Margiad Evans's 1932 novella, *Country Dance*. However, Goodwin's novel is set in modern times and centres upon the Welsh village of Tanygraig, which is 'off the beaten track' (Goodwin, 1970 [1936]: 14). The novel concerns itself centrally with gender, class, religious, town/country and national borders, focusing on a female central character, Beti, who early on perceives a difference between the worlds of her father and mother: 'Her mother's world was finite and brittle – the house trim and orderly like herself. But her father, vulgar as he was, inhabited some other place. There were no boundaries to his world – wherever it was' (p. 35). The pub kept by her father is visited by 'jentlemens' from England who come for the shooting and fishing; the class divide between them and the Welsh who serve them and regard them with considerable disdain is absolute.

Goodwin draws an interesting distinction between Wales proper and the border country, suggesting that the inhabitants of the border towns are always trying to ape English mores, while the Welsh are more genuinely cultured:

> While in the border towns the dramatic companies rehearsed their second-rate farces . . . in the Welsh villages there was Ibsen and Strindberg; and while the Border townspeople were busy with the *Cingalee* and dressing up for the occasion, the Welsh choirs had Bach and *Elijah*. (p. 49)

This characterization of the Welsh is a direct contradiction of the portrait painted by John Moore of a race of benighted barbarians. Wales is, moreover, associated with tradition and stability, while England connotes modernity and movement. Nevertheless, Beti is conscious of living at a temporal border:

> The old way of things was ending; she [Beti] had come at the end of one age and the beginning of another. Wales would be the last to go – but it was going. Even the old tweed mills no longer relied on the farmers around, but on foreign royalties and the English . . . (p. 92)

The characters are aware of these changes and frequently debate them in the pub, where contradictory attitudes are expressed: Wales is seen as the 'best place in the world to get out of!' by one drinker, while another laments '*Yr hen wlad*! [The old country] Forty years and there is no Wales. House empty, call next door.' Another chips in with 'Wales wass Wales before ever England wass England', only to be corrected by another pub-goer who shouts 'Wrong man . . . Wales wass Wales when Wales wass England' (p. 117). The apparent contradiction of the final remark refers to an historical period before the fixing of the Welsh border, when the ancient Welsh inhabited much of Britain. Yet the contemporary world is afflicted by multiple borders, not just between Wales and England but also internal borders within Wales. Some 'shonihois' from south Wales come to Tanygraig and the inhabitants find 'their ways, their talk, their dress . . . all different. "Down South" was another world' (p. 122). Religious divisions are also present: 'in Wales you were either church or chapel . . . the gulf was as wide as the grave' (p. 126). Yet, the focus of the novel is not on either side of the border but, precisely, on the border territory itself. The border town where one of Beti's suitors, Llew, lives is described as:

> like a signpost between two worlds . . . It belonged to neither . . . In its heyday the mills were throbbing . . . then the prosperity had suddenly gone, receded as a tide recedes, leaving this little town . . . like a piece of flotsam on the drying beach. It had gone back into itself, its people . . . never belonged . . . to anything but themselves. (p. 137)

The narrative describes the people from both sides of the border coming to the town on fair and market days, mingling but never meeting. With regard to gender, Goodwin strongly echoes Margiad Evans's work, positioning Beti between the rival masculinities of her cousin Llew and the bankrupt miller, Evan. At the end of the novel Beti leaves for London with an ailing Evan and the main road comes to the village, literally bisecting it. Goodwin's heroine takes charge of her future, unlike the tragic victim, Ann Goodman, in Margiad Evans's work, but in so doing she chooses England and modernity, turning her back on a traditional Wales which is being destroyed and emptied of people.

Goodwin's 1937 collection of short fiction, *The White Farm and Other Stories*, continues his exploration of gender and national borders. Fittingly, the book is divided into two sections, the first containing stories about Wales and the second stories about the borderlands. All are concerned with gender relations and very often with 'mixed marriages' between English men and Welsh women. Such is the case in the title story, where the English husband has difficulty in fathoming his Welsh wife. The couple return to 'Pant-y-Pistyll', the 'white farm' which is the woman's ancestral home, where the fire in the grate 'had never been out for two hundred years' (Goodwin, 1937: 25). She sadly remembers a youthful expedition with her cousin, Morlais, to find the source of the river (evidently the Severn) but 'they never found it. They never would find it. It had no beginning as it had no end' (p. 28). The symbolism here is deeply gendered: the Severn appears to be the border marker, between Wales and England, the past and present, and male and female, while the continuing impossibility of finding its source suggests the intractability of the gulfs it portrays. Many of Goodwin's stories represent this conflict between genders in a quasi-Lawrentian manner, suggesting that men and women inhabit different countries, and this is often figured symbolically as a difference in nationality and sometimes of class. This is true of one of the strongest stories in the volume, 'Saturday Night', in which Len, the affected dandy from the border town (clearly modelled on Newtown) and his Welsh girlfriend, Megan, are separated by their inability to bridge the gender, national and cultural gap between them. The couple meet at a lamp-post on the edge of town, beyond which 'the road trailed away into Wales' (p. 34). The same lamp-post figures in the story entitled 'Into the Dark', where, again, it is a lovers' meeting place, a boundary marker between town and country, Wales and the border, male and female. Alys, the female protagonist who lives in the border town, longs to be united with her Welsh lover, Emrys, who represents for her another 'world – so remote, so distant, with no boundaries to it' (p. 120). Yet the union between them is thwarted because of class differences and Alys's fear of the unknown.

A temporal dimension is also present in Goodwin's exploration of borders in these stories. In 'The Flying Hours Are Gone', unusually a first-person narrative, the narrator associates Wales both with a lost love, Ceri, and with the past and a different self. Now a successful London lawyer and journalist, the narrator remembers his younger self as an idealistic Welsh nationalist, believing in the possibility of 'a new Wales' (p. 187). But the past is irrecoverable, the union with lost lover, lost self, impossible; only an old ruined circle of Druidic stones remains to mark the place of the last meeting with the beloved. The symbolism here is familiar: Wales is associated with the female, the past, traditional ways of life, natural beauty, contrasting with the aggressive world of masculine, worldly success and wealth available in London. The tone of the story, though, is delicate and heartfelt, suggesting an unfulfilled desire to heal the borders between the separate territories. But this desire for what we might call a 'third space' can never in Goodwin's work, unlike Margiad Evans's, be met by an identification with the border for, as we have seen, the border for Goodwin is a negative territory, a limbo world where there can be no belonging, no authentic being.

The accuracy of Goodwin's representation of the social and cultural relations of the border is suggested in the anthropologist Ronald Frankenberg's classic 1957 study, *Village on the Border*. Many of Frankenberg's dispassionate observations of the society of 'Pentrediwaith', the fictional name he gives to the Welsh borderland town in which he lived for a year in 1953, and which is riven by multiple divisions, directly echo Goodwin's fiction. Interestingly, Frankenberg's 'outsider' study shows that the most obvious division between England and Wales is perhaps one of the least culturally absolute of the rifts observed; as he observes, 'national schisms . . . are bridged across by innumerable formal and informal ties' (Frankenberg, 1957: 14). Conversely, class divisions run very deep and tend to coincide with linguistic differences: JPs are English-speaking Anglicans with no kinship connections in the village, whereas parish councillors are Welsh speaking, Nonconformist and intricately related by kinship within the village (pp. 11–13). Even more striking is the internal gender split which afflicts the village: owing to the demise of traditional employment in the village (quarries, textile mills, and farming) the men travel to work in urban centres across the border in England, whereas the women stay at home and uphold the culture and kinship relations of the village, leading to Frankenberg's rather gloomy, Disraelian conclusion that 'there seem to be two villages, one of men and one of women which rarely mingle' (p. 51). The closing of the mills and the economic decline are chronicled in Goodwin's fiction, too, while his repeated trope of men and women inhabiting different worlds is actually borne out by the more scientific, sociological study of Frankenberg's text.

During the period studied in *Village on the Border*, the Welsh poet R. S. Thomas was living in the border region, first at Chirk and then Hanmer in Flintshire and later at Manafon, Montgomeryshire; arguably, it was his experiences here which made him into a poet or, at least, into the kind of poet that he was. Thomas has written about the powerful influence of the landscape of the Marches upon his imagination at this time:

> from there, some fifteen miles away, I saw at dusk the hills of Wales rising, telling as before of enchanting and mysterious things. I realized what I had done. That was not my place, on the plain amongst Welshmen with English accents and attitudes. I set about learning Welsh, in order to be able to return to the true Wales of my imagination. (Thomas, 1997: 10)

Thomas's positioning in border territory – between the English language, his mother tongue, and the Welsh language he admired and was beginning to learn; between his flock and the unknowable God he served; between Wales and England; between the lush landscape of Shropshire and Herefordshire and the bare hillsides of Wales – clearly created within him tensions which were personally tormenting yet poetically fruitful. In the poem 'Border Blues' (1958) he establishes the border as a site of continual crossing and migration, lamenting the contemporary exodus eastwards to England, leaving the Welsh hill country bereft and depopulated. He figures Wales as a mythologized landscape, referring to the characters of the medieval tale, *Culhwch ac Olwen*, and suggesting that those characters still inhabit the landscape, but in degenerate form: 'Olwen in nylons' and 'the old mother', whose 'cunning' easily exceeds that of the evil giant, Ysbaddaden Penkawr. Yet most have simply left, so that many of the inhabitants are immigrants from England,

> ladies from the council houses:
> Blue eyes and Birmingham yellow
> Hair, and the ritual murder of vowels
> (Thomas, 1993: 69)

In this mood of misogyny and misanthropy, the speaker takes refuge on the Welsh 'high moors', remembering an 'evicted people' (p. 70). The poem enacts further border crossings and border skirmishes: a trip to Shrewsbury to see the pantomime, the memory of a father who crossed the border with his scythe on his shoulder to help with the harvest on the other side of the border before returning home to mow his own fields. A reference to the ninth-century Welsh poem, *Canu Heledd*, reminds the reader that Shrewsbury (Amwythig) was once in Wales and that centuries of slaughter took place in these Marches. The countryside is seen as haunted by this past, the ghosts of the ancestors, yet the poem does not end despairingly. The Welsh border dwellers assert that 'Despite our speech we are not English', and the poem underlines this statement of continuity with the image of the 'delyn aur' (golden harp):

> Though the strings are broken, and time sets
> The barbed wire in their place,
> The tune endures. (p. 72)

Barbed wire suggests an enforced frontier – danger, violence, mutilation, reminiscent of a war zone or, perhaps, the penning in of animals. Violence is also suggested by the image of the border people's 'wit . . . sharp as an axe', penetrating through 'skin' and 'bone' to the 'marrow'. Thomas's representation of the borderlands in the mid-twentieth century is, thus, extremely disturbing and threatening; it is as if the whole history of violence and conflict has soaked into the very fabric of the land, making its inhabitants edgy and wary. The poem is suffused with images of duality: night and day, past and present, shadows and light. Far from being reconciled, these troubling dualities remain, harassing the land and making it an uncomfortable habitation. The gendering of the border here is overtly misogynistic: women are seen as grasping, tyrannical mothers or young tarts; even a vixen is viewed in distasteful sexual terms, 'fretting her lust/To rawness on the unchristened grass' (p. 72). Only in the ancient past or mythology are Welsh females seen in positive terms, in the figures of the virginal Olwen or Heledd; Welsh men, too, are degenerate or absent but at least the young farmer on his tractor is singing a Welsh folk song, suggesting a connection with Welsh heritage which Welsh women have lost.

Thus, Thomas's gendering of the border here is very different from the idealization of Welsh women seen in the work of Geraint Goodwin. The disturbing image of the vixen and the 'unchristened grass', together with the references to Shropshire in Thomas's poem, call to mind Mary Webb's 1917 novel, *Gone to Earth*, where the protagonist Hazel Woodus's Welsh gypsy mother is not buried in 'Chrissen-ground' (Webb, 1999 [1917]: 12). Moreover, Hazel herself and her pet 'Foxy' are literally hounded by a cruel, narrow-minded, patriarchal society which eventually destroys them both. This is the representation of oppressive gender relations condemned by John Moore, where the female victim is associated with Wales, outsider identity, wildness, while the men are on the whole vicious pack animals. Thomas seems to be revising Mary Webb's border vision, and at the same time correcting his own over-idealized dream of an 'enchanting and mysterious' Wales.

Tony Brown suggests that in 'Border Blues' Thomas 'utilizes the fragmented, multi-voiced technique of Eliot's *The Waste Land*' (Brown, 2006: 60), and, I would add, appears to share the misogynistic vision of Eliot in that poem of urban deracination. Thomas returns again to the Welsh border in the poem of that name (1963); more laconic and much more succinct than 'Border Blues', the later poem again reiterates a sense of internal division: 'Cars pass on the road, / Their light dissects me' (Thomas, 1963: 9). The speaker reflects, morosely, on the battles of the past fought here but concludes that 'the real fight goes on / In the mind; protect me, / Spirits, from myself'. Only the 'men' who died in the past are invoked; the negative female harridans of 'Border Blues' have now disappeared, leaving the speaker alone to try to heal his internal rift.

The border is also experienced as an abiding internal condition or 'structure of feeling' in Raymond Williams's autobiographical novel, *Border Country* (1960). Matthew Price, a university lecturer in history, returns to his native Wales when he hears of his father's serious illness. Matthew's experience is one of disjunction: he is attempting to research population movements in Wales in the mid-nineteenth century, yet finding that the statistical evidence and his own lived experience as a migrant do not match up. He can make no progress because there is always within him the split between 'Matthew', the English academic, and 'Will', the name by which he is always known at home, the Welsh migrant. Yet Glynmawr, his home town, based on Pandy, the Welsh border village in which Raymond Williams was born and raised, is not a static bastion of Welshness; on the contrary, it is a place of interchange and movement, symbolized by the coming and going of trains: Matthew's father, like Williams's own, is a railway signalman. When Matthew returns he realizes that 'This was not anybody's valley to make into a landscape. Work had changed and was still changing it, though the main shape held' (Williams, 1988 [1960]: 76). Matthew has to relearn his identity as Will and remember the complex interrelationships (very similar to those described by Frankenberg in *Village on the Border*) which hold the society together. At the local eisteddfod, for instance, 'Illtyd Morgan identified [each] family, and recalled older members of the same family, who had come as children to this platform . . . [Will] knew how much this ceremony of identification and memory meant to the silent and apparently unresponsive listeners' (p. 201). At the eisteddfod, both English and Welsh national anthems are sung, with the latter kept for the end, 'when they were really involved'. When this happens and the choirs begin to sing, 'it was no use at all even trying to stay separate . . . the border had been crossed' (pp. 206–7). In a trope typical of Welsh fiction, Matthew climbs the hill and looks down on Glynmawr, trying again to understand its, and his own, history: 'his country . . . not just the valley and the village, but the meeting of valleys, and England blue in the distance . . . On the high ground to the east the Norman castles . . . Glynmawr, below them, was the disputed land, held by neither side, raided by both' (p. 292). *Border Country* is one of the most intense representations of the lived experience of the border, rendered both spatially and temporally. The father–son relationship is central (as it is in the poetry of Owen Sheers, a later border writer, discussed below) and is used in the novel to reach a sense of synthesis, an understanding of the relationship between the generations, the inevitability of change, the dichotomy and the fluid interaction between the two sides of the Welsh border. Williams's representation of gender relations is much more muted and kept in the background; women occupy important roles in family structures but they are emphatically subordinate to the strong father figures. Nor is this represented as an exclusively Welsh trait but, rather, as one which exists on both sides of the border, though there are signs that the younger generation of women – such as Will's cousin, Glynis – are beginning to question traditional social structures.

If Raymond Williams's novel is intensely personal, the English writer Bruce Chatwin's novel of the Welsh Marches, *On The Black Hill* (1982), is characterized by a cool detachment. It has been dismissed by one Welsh critic, Stephen Knight, as mere 'touristic sentimentality' (Knight, 2000: 176), but another, English, critic asserts that 'if it is legitimate to talk of a literature of the Welsh borders then *On the Black Hill* is one of its canonical texts' (Murray, 1993: 9). Certainly, the novel is a tour de force of the imagination, conjuring up twin brothers, Lewis and Benjamin Jones, living 'on the black hill' and chronicling their lives, which span most of the twentieth century. Chatwin was, rather like W. H. Davies, a writer who drew upon his own peripatetic life, though Chatwin's background was solidly English upper middle class. Nevertheless, like A. E. Housman, Chatwin was a sexually ambiguous character temperamentally drawn to people who lived on the peripheries. *On the Black Hill* explores the Welsh borderland as a place of national and gender ambiguity, often encapsulated in the lives of the twins themselves, who embody many of the contradictions inherent in border existence. We first glimpse them in the opening pages of the novel as old men sharing an ancient double bed covered with a patchwork quilt sewn by their dead mother, whose memory they cherish. Immediately, the contradictory concepts of duality and unity are conjured up by the text, both in the identical twin brothers sharing one bed and in the views available from their farmhouse, The Vision, one of Wales and one of England; indeed, 'the border of Radnor and Hereford was said to run right through the middle of the staircase' (Chatwin, 1983 [1982]: 10). The novel focuses initially, however, on the lives of their parents, the cultured, well-travelled English vicar's daughter, Mary Latimer and the passionate, rough Welsh farmer, Amos Jones. This duality reverses the usual pattern in border fictions, in which Wales is associated with the female and nature, while England is linked with the male and culture. In the figures of their offspring, the twins, Chatwin appears to be attempting an elaboration of the 'third space' of reconciliation, where Welsh and English, nature and culture, male and female, are reconciled and form one indissoluble being. For the twins, separately, seem to embody male and female traits but form a single identity, where one feels the other's pain and neither can really differentiate between their separate selves: 'Mary tried to drill into their heads the difference between "yours" and "mine" [but] . . . they persisted in sharing everything' (p. 44). Their grandfather, Sam, instils into them a sense of Welsh identity, illustrated both topographically in the contrasts between the 'Welsh walk' and the 'English walk' which they take with him and also in the allegorical painting of 'The Broad and Narrow Path' which hangs in The Vision and which they identify in local, border terms: 'the Road to Hell was the road to Hereford, whereas the Road to Heaven led up to the Radnor Hills' (p. 96). Nevertheless, they identify emotionally with their English mother, Mary, though they cannot share in her class privileges nor understand her connection, despite her 'unfortunate' marriage, to the odious Bickertons, the English squires, who enjoy a wealth derived from the euphemistically described 'West India trade' (p. 27). Chatwin himself eschewed the idea of Englishness which he inherited from his background, consistently satirizing ideas of empire, and preferring instead a nomadic life, which, he theorized, was the natural state of human beings (see Murray, 1993). His novel is particularly interesting because it is non-partisan: it views Welsh and English rivalries with an unwonted detachment. Here, if anywhere in Welsh border writing by men, is a covert advocacy of a distinct border identity, embracing the sexual and cultural ambivalences which such an identity allows.

Turning now to contemporary border writing, Owen Sheers's second volume of poetry, *Skirrid Hill* (2006), signals its concern with borders and rifts from the title onwards. The author's note explains that the name of the hill near Abergavenny which gives the book its title derives from the Welsh work *Ysgariad*, meaning divorce or separation. However, this is an exploration of gender, linguistic, temporal and cultural borders which virtually ignores the stereotyped polarity between Wales and England. Instead, the landscape around Abergavenny, where Sheers was brought up, is viewed as being 'on the edge of the world' – almost as if there is a void on the other side of the border (Sheers, 2006: 12). Possibly this may be accounted for by the fact that Sheers (like Raymond Williams) appears to be primarily concerned with temporal borders: the past and the present. The past turns up in the landscape of the present, often literally, as in 'Mametz Wood', where the farmers of today are still ploughing up the skeletons of dead Welsh soldiers from the First World War. The earth, throughout these sensuous poems, is seen through strikingly corporeal imagery as a living entity, a scarred body:

> And even now the earth stands sentinel,
> reaching back into itself for reminders of what happened
> like a wound working a foreign body to the surface of the skin.
> (Sheers, 2006: 1)

Many poems are about father–son relationships, chronicling the links and gaps between the generations, as in 'Farther', where father and son are climbing Skirrid Hill together and the latter notices his father stopping to get his breath: 'again I felt the tipping of the scales of us, / the intersection of our ages' (p. 12). 'Border Country' is about multiple borders: between life and death, childhood and adulthood, past and present, focused in a single geographical space, an old quarry once filled with wrecked cars where the speaker and his friend played; but the friend died in childhood: 'Your father found at dawn – / a poppy sown in the unripe corn' (p. 11). As in the work of Raymond Williams, Owen Sheers's border country is a repository of memory, a living, dynamic history which is owned by those who inhabit the land. A number of poems concern the 'marking' of land – the planting of a tree for the birth of a child in 'Trees', the leaving of lovers' shapes in the long grass in 'Landmark' (pp. 13 and 28). Two poems at the centre of the collection are signalled as complementary by their matching titles: 'Y Gaer (*The Hill Fort*)' and 'The Hill Fort (*Y Gaer*)' which concern the mourning father revisiting the hilltop fort he had once visited with his young son (pp. 20–2). From the summit he views all the border places inhabited by 'the fathers and sons before them: / Tretower, Raglan, Bredwardine'. The place gives solace; the ruined walls of the fort now 'protect as much as they defend'. As well as the father–son relationship, gender relations, especially sexual liaisons, are addressed, often in sensual, erotic terms, in the collection. Lovers are seen as complementary, a 'double heart of a secret fruit' (p. 31). The last poem in the collection, 'Skirrid Fawr', is perhaps the most eloquent exploration of the border state. The mountain itself is seen in female terms, almost goddess- or prophetess-like: 'I am still drawn to her back for the answers / to every question I have ever known' (p. 52). The mountain is an 'edge', 'a lonely hulk / adrift through Wales', speaking a 'vernacular of borders', revealing one 'dark' and one 'sunlit' side. She is freighted with 'the unspoken words / of an unlearned tongue', suggestive of the language split which underlies the Welsh experience in the twentieth century. Sheers uses the border experience partly to explore the nature and limits of Welshness; as anthropological studies have suggested, allegedly 'peripheral' zones around the border may paradoxically be even more important in the definition of national and cultural identity than the so-called 'core' areas of the nation-state (Donnan and Wilson, 1994: 1–14). Sheers demonstrates this in his poem 'Flag' which describes a journey westwards by train from the border country into Wales, looking at the increasingly numerous examples of the Welsh flag fluttering in unexpected places. The border speaker has a poignant, tender attitude towards these markers of national identity, the flag 'wrapped up in itself . . . a bandage tight on the wound / staunching the dreams of what might have been' (p. 25).

The anthropologists Hastings Donnan and Thomas M. Wilson have remarked on the paradoxical nature of state borders: intended to be definitive, absolute, 'there to be defended . . . markers of the limits of national . . . sovereignty', they have nevertheless frequently become both 'the focus of . . . social, economic, political and cultural transformations which threaten the future of the nation-state' and territories characterized by 'dynamic dialectical relationships' (Donnan and Wilson, 1994: 1–2). While borders are necessarily used to differentiate self from Other, the native from the foreign, borders are at the same time places of continual interaction and interchange between self and Other, the native and the foreign. Given that paradox appears to be inherent in the concept of the border, then, it is unsurprising to find male writers of the Welsh border representing these paradoxical qualities and doing so in explicitly gendered terms. For the male–female polarity which is ensconced in biology and reinforced by societal gender constructions is surely an obvious parallel for the paradox of the border: just as men and women are expected to define themselves as separate sovereign states so, in practice, the interactions between them are always dynamic and dialectical. As Donnan and Wilson observe, 'limits . . . [are] continuously negotiated and reinterpreted through the dialectics of everyday life among all people who live at them' (p. 10). The twentieth century has been a century of the most radical renegotiation and reinterpretation of gender roles in much of the Western world, including Wales and England; border writers such as those discussed here frequently combine an engagement with this historical revolution in gender relations with an exploration of the political, social, cultural and economic meanings of borderland identity. While some might argue that the very existence of the Welsh–English border in the twentieth century has become increasingly tenuous, anthropologists such as A. P. Cohen convincingly argue that 'the diminution of the geographical bases of community boundaries has led to their renewed assertion in symbolic terms' (Cohen, 1985: 50). Offa's Dyke may be little more than a long-distance footpath today, but it is clear that the frontier which it marks between Wales and England continues to retain great symbolic resonance.[6]

Notes

1 'Marches' derives from the Old French *marche*, meaning 'edge, or boundary'. It is cognate with, for example, Latin *margo* ('margin') and Old Irish *mruig* ('borderland'). See *New Shorter Oxford English Dictionary*, i, 1695.

2 Among the male-authored texts Dearnley discusses are: James Parry's *The True Anti-Pamela* (1741), Tobias Smollett's *The Expedition of Humphrey Clinker* (1771), Richard Graves's *The Spiritual Quixote* (1773) and *Eugenius* (1785), and William Godwin's *Fleetwood, or The New Man of Feeling* (1805).

3 See Aaron, 2007. This chapter should be read alongside that of Jane Aaron in the present volume (chapter 6), which explores in more detail and from a psychoanalytical perspective, the work of early twentieth-century Welsh women writers of the border.

4 For an English translation of this work, see Conran, 1986: 127.

5 Poems dealing with tramps and doss-houses include 'Saints and Lodgers' (Davies, 1946: 38–41), 'Facts' (p. 62), and 'The Jolly Tramp' (pp. 65–6).

6 Offa's Dyke is the earthwork built by the eighth-century Mercian King Offa to protect his territory and mark it off from that of the Welsh to the west. The line of Offa's Dyke is still visible for much of the present-day border between England and Wales.

Bibliography

Aaron, Jane (2007). *Nineteenth-Century Women's Writing in Wales*, Cardiff: University of Wales Press.

Borrow, George (1995 [1862]). *Wild Wales: Its People, Language and Scenery*, Llandysul: Gomer Press.

Brown, Tony (2006). *R. S. Thomas*, Cardiff: University of Wales Press.

Chatwin, Bruce (1983 [1982]). *On the Black Hill*, London: Picador.

Cohen, A. P. (1985). *The Symbolic Construction of Community*, London: Tavistock.

Conran, Tony (1986). *Welsh Verse*, Bridgend: Poetry Wales Press.

Davies, Geraint Eirug (ed.) (1999). *Border Voices: Poems of Gwent and Monmouthshire*, Llandysul: Gomer.

Davies, W. H. (1946). *Collected Poems*, London: Jonathan Cape.

Dearnley, Moira (2001). *Distant Fields: Eighteenth-Century Fictions of Wales*, Cardiff: University of Wales Press.

Donnan, Hastings and Thomas M. Wilson (eds) (1994). *Border Approaches: Anthropological Perspectives on Frontiers*, Lanham: University Press of America.

Evans, Margiad (2006 [1932]). *Country Dance*, Cardigan: Parthian.

Frankenberg, Ronald (1957). *Village on the Border*, London: Cohen and West.

Goodwin, Geraint (1937). *The White Farm and Other Stories*, London: Jonathan Cape.

—— (1970 [1936]). *The Heyday in the Blood*, Bath: Cedric Chivers.

Housman, A. E. (1918 [1896]). *A Shropshire Lad*, London: Grant Richards.

Jebb, Keith (1992). *A. E. Housman*, Bridgend: Seren.

Knight, Stephen (2000). *A Hundred Years of Fiction*, Cardiff: University of Wales Press.

Moore, John C. (1933). *The Welsh Marches*, London: Chapman and Hall.

Murray, Nicholas (1993). *Bruce Chatwin*, Bridgend: Seren.

New Statesman (1992). Borderlands Supplement, 19 June.

Normand, Lawrence (2003). *W. H. Davies*, Bridgend: Seren.

Roberts, Dewi (ed.) (1998). *Both Sides of the Border: An Anthology of Writing on the Welsh Border Region*, Llanrwst: Carreg Gwalch.

Sheers, Owen (2006). *Skirrid Hill*, Bridgend: Seren.

Stonesifer, Richard J. (1963). *W. H. Davies: A Critical Biography*, London: Jonathan Cape.

Thomas, R. S. (1963). *The Bread of Truth*, London: Rupert Hart-Davis.

——(1993). *Collected Poems*, London: Dent.

——(1995). *Selected Prose*, ed. Sandra Anstey, Bridgend: Seren.

——(1997). *Autobiographies,* trans. and ed. Jason Walford Davies, London: Dent.

Webb, Mary (1999 [1917]). *Gone to Earth*, London: Virago.

Williams, Raymond (1988 [1960]). *Border Country,* London: Hogarth.

——(2003). *Who Speaks for Wales? Nation, Culture and Identity*, ed. Daniel Williams, Cardiff: University of Wales Press.

III

GENDER AND THE DRAWING OF INTERNAL BORDERS

8

Crossing Intimate Borders: Gender, Settler Colonialism and the Home

MARGARET D. JACOBS

Introduction

The project of colonialism has always involved a transgression and reconstruction of borders – from the initial penetration of established boundaries to the erection of new ones. The not-so-subtle sexual metaphors in the previous sentence are no Freudian slip. Historians of colonialism have noticed for many decades that imperial discourse is saturated with sexual and gendered imagery. The recognition that colonial powers often gendered themselves as masculine and colonized groups as feminine represented a point of entry for studying gender and colonialism. Thereafter, two other questions have dominated the scholarship on gender and colonialism: sexual liaisons between colonizing men and colonized women (and the resulting ambiguous status of their offspring) and the role that white women played in empire. Of late, scholars have turned their attention to what Ann Laura Stoler calls the 'intimacies of empire' and what I refer to here as 'intimate borders'; that is, fluid sites of affective and emotional cross-cultural encounters where colonial relations played out on an often daily basis. Moreover, rather than studying these intimacies of empire primarily in extractive overseas colonies of European powers, many more historians are turning their attention to how these intimate relations played out in settler colonies, such as those in North America, Australia, New Zealand and South Africa. In fact, in an influential essay and subsequent edited collection, Stoler called for a new kind of comparative colonial history linking North American history and (post)colonial studies (Stoler, 2001: 830).[1]

The study of the intricate relationships that developed along and across these intimate borders provokes new inquiries into gender and colonialism and calls for a re-examination of white women's role in empire. While an obvious intimacy of empire refers to cross-cultural sex, my essay focuses on three different types of intimate relationships that took place in one settler colonial context at the turn of the twentieth century. One of these relationships involved white women's efforts to transform the homes of American Indian women in the American West, another centred on white women becoming surrogate mothers to Indian children within Indian boarding schools and a third entailed young Indian women's domestic service within white women's households. Many of the white women on whom I focus here were members of a reform organization, the Women's National Indian Association (WNIA). The WNIA's journal, *The Indian's Friend*, and annual reports comprise the majority of source material for this chapter.

The WNIA and a few other reform organizations at the turn of the twentieth century set out to solve the so-called 'Indian problem', that is, the concern that Indian people were dependent on the federal government and unincorporated into the nation as a whole. Believing that it was within the most intimate circle of Indian families that the root of both 'the Indian problem' and its solution lay, many white women missionaries, reformers, matrons and schoolteachers went to live among native communities in the late nineteenth and twentieth centuries. Here, they sought to establish intimacy with Indian women in an attempt to reconstruct Indian homes and family relationships within them. However, some white women reformers (and male authorities) believed Indian women's homes so incorrigible that the only way to solve the 'Indian problem' was to transgress another intimate border: to remove Indian children from their families and place them in Indian boarding schools. In these institutional homes many white women sought to take the place of the children's Indian mothers and establish new intimacies with Indian children. Despite their rhetoric of uplifting Indian children, the boarding schools also prepared Indian children, particularly girls, to be transferred to another intimate setting – white families' homes, where they would work as domestic servants and manual labourers (see Jacobs, 2009). Thus 'the home' and the intimate borders around and within it became a key theatre of settler colonial power relations. However, this was a truly mobile home and these intimate borders did not remain fixed and static, but were constantly shifting.

Settler colonialism and the Indian problem in the American West

My use of the term 'colonialism' to refer to the American West at the turn of the twentieth century may be jarring to those of us accustomed to thinking of colonialism in terms of European imperialism in Asia and Africa. When American historians use the term 'colonial', we usually are referring to an era before the American Revolution in which English settlers in America still were a colony of England (see Stoler, 2006). I use the term here instead to refer to a particular kind of colonial intervention – settler colonialism – a type of European expansion that resulted not in overseas empires but in 'societies in which Europeans have settled, where their descendants have [become and] remained politically dominant over indigenous peoples, and where a heterogeneous society has developed in class, ethnic and racial terms'. As Daiva Stasiulis and Nira Yuval-Davis explain it, 'colonies of exploitation' or extractive colonies rested on the 'appropriation of land, natural resources and labour' through 'indirect control by colonial power through a small group of primarily male administrators, merchants, soldiers, and missionaries. In contrast, settler [colonies] were characterized by a much larger settler European population of both sexes for permanent settlement' (Stasiulis and Yuval-Davis, 1995: 3). In extractive colonies, European colonizers appropriated natural resources through enlisting the local indigenous population to labour on plantations, in mines and on railroads. By contrast, in settler colonies, where the ultimate goal was the acquisition and control of land (and therefore the elimination or removal of indigenous people), colonizers relied on importing labour – often slaves or indentured workers (Stasiulis and Yuval-Davis, 1995: 3; see also Evans et al., 2003; Russell, 2001; Denoon, 1983; and Wolfe, 2001). Thus, in the American West in the late nineteenth century, where American Indians still retained some land (upon which many valuable minerals and oil had been discovered), settler colonial relationships were alive and well, if obscured and masked as 'the Indian problem', a term government administrators used to refer to unsettled colonial dynamics.

By the late nineteenth century in the US, a century of treaty-making with and military actions against Indian peoples had led to the conquest and control of vast tracts of Indian territory. Still, to officials and reformers with the Bureau of Indian Affairs (BIA), a so-called 'Indian problem' persisted, especially in the American West. Some recalcitrant Indians continued to hunt outside the borders of their designated territories and, in the eyes of government authorities and reformers, clung to outmoded land tenure systems. Christian missionaries complained that many Indians continued to perform heathen rituals and worship false gods. Moreover, due to the loss of their land, most Indian peoples had become dependent on government rations and reduced to a state of impoverishment (for overviews of Indian colonization, see Calloway, 1999; Utley, 1984; and Weeks, 1990).

To address this 'Indian problem', an influential reform movement prodded the federal government to initiate a new assimilation policy towards American Indians in the last decades of the nineteenth century. This policy included the Dawes Severalty Act of 1887 – to allot communally held Indian land to individual Indians – and the Religious Crimes Code of 1883 – to criminalize Indian religious practices (see Hoxie, 1984; Bolt, 1987; and Calloway, 1999). In order truly to transform Indians, however, policy-makers and reformers believed that it was also necessary to reach Indians in their homes and, moreover, to reorder and uplift their homes. Thus, in the late nineteenth century, the US government sought to breach and then reconstruct the most intimate of borders to complete the process of colonizing indigenous Americans. Prior to this era, Indian affairs had been the province of white men. In their dealings with Indian peoples, government officials often, in fact, called themselves 'The Great White Father'. In this new era of crossing intimate borders to enter Indian homes, white women – keepers and guardians of the home – now had an important new role to play as 'The Great White Mother' (the title derives from an article in the WNIA journal, *The Indian's Friend*, 1904, 16/5: 5).

This new assault on indigenous homes and intimacies in the American West was not unique. In the same period, native-born reformers in many urban areas also targeted the home life of many immigrant families, particularly Jewish and Catholic immigrants from eastern and southern Europe (see Hawes, 1991; Tiffin, 1982; and Platt, 1969). Moreover, in other colonial contexts in this era, many missionaries, reformers and state officials identified the homes of indigenous peoples as the root of resistance to colonialism and the key to resolving the persistent 'problem' with indigenes. Since both white women reformers and male colonial authorities designated the home as a woman's domain, they deemed it white women's proper role to carry out what they called 'women's work for women'; that is, the task of crossing intimate borders to clean up and bring order to indigenous homes and to rescue indigenous women from the allegedly oppressive relationships they suffered within their homes (see Pascoe, 1990; see also, for 'women's work for women' globally, Welter, 1978; Brumberg, 1982; Flemming, 1989; Hunter, 1984; Burton, 1994; and Jayawardena, 1995).

Overall, white women reformers were not unwilling recruits into this new colonial endeavour. In fact, in the US such reformers agitated for a greater role to play within setting and implementing Indian policy. In the late nineteenth century, many white, Protestant and middle-class American women transferred their interest in reform from abolitionism and temperance to the 'Indian problem'. In 1879, a group of veteran white women reformers established the WNIA to address the ongoing violence between white settlers and Indians, the prevalence of poverty among native groups and the need for the 'civilization' of supposedly backward and savage peoples living within the territorial borders of the United States. The WNIA began by petitioning the government to respect the treaty rights of American Indians, but once a comparable men's organization – the Indian Rights Association (IRA) – started in 1882, the women quickly deferred to the men on questions of political and civil rights. Soon, the WNIA came to devote itself almost entirely 'to uplifting Indian homes; to aiding the vastly needed work within Indian hearts, minds and souls' (WNIA Report, 1883: 10, 11; see also Mathes, 1990a, 1990b; and Wanken, 1981).

The WNIA can properly be seen as part of a widespread maternalist movement that swept across North America, western Europe and other modernizing nations at the turn of the twentieth century. Maternalists believed that women's traditional associations with motherhood and the home should be infused into political and public life and that women's unique perspectives and contributions could solve some of the problems that beset modern, industrializing nations. Maternalists, themselves usually from a middle-class and upper-middle-class background, concentrated on addressing the problems of poorer women, casting themselves as benevolent and guiding mothers to other women who were like children in relation to them. Maternalists also believed that the root of other women's problems – in fact, society's problems – could be found in the home and thus the solution they posed was to rescue other women and uplift them through transforming their homes. Much maternalist effort in the early twentieth century resulted in the apparatus of the modern welfare state (see Gordon, 1994; Michel, 1999; Mink, 1995; Ladd-Taylor, 1994; and Skocpol, 1992).

Like other maternalists, WNIA members identified the home as the cradle of civilization. According to them, it was within the intimate borders of the Indian home that the heart of the 'Indian problem' lay and where it had to be solved. For example, a Mrs Mead declared to the Lake Mohonk conference of Friends of the Indian in 1898: 'I have been intensely interested in the Indian home question, because it is the woman that makes the home and exalts the family.' She added: 'Until we reach the Indian woman in her tepee, until we rouse her aesthetic and moral nature, and develop her mental power, we shall never have an Indian civilization worthy of the name of humanity' (Lake Mohonk Proceedings, 1898: 94).[2] The WNIA pursued several different strategies for transforming the Indian home, beginning with on-site white women missionaries, who would move to reservations and teach Indian women how to make proper homes. Over time, many WNIA members and other white women reformers came to assert that it was only through removing Indian girls from their homes and bringing them up 'properly' within boarding schools and white women's households that Indian homes would eventually be transformed.

Transforming Indian women's homes

The WNIA began its efforts towards 'reach[ing] the Indian woman in her tepee' through establishing a number of missions throughout the West, beginning with an outpost at the Ponca Agency in Nebraska for Poncas, Otoes and Pawnees in 1884, another at Round Valley in California in 1885 and an additional fifteen missions by 1889 (WNIA Report, 1884: 20–1; and 1885: 32). Unlike missionary organizations in an earlier era, the WNIA particularly stressed the need for white and often single women to carry out their missionary and reform work. Mrs Dorchester, for example, a regular contributor to *The Indian's Friend*, asserted that middle-aged Christian women were needed to serve as field matrons on Indian reservations. These women 'should have motherly hearts so warm and big that every red sister who wished, or ought to wish, for a better life, would find in them the needed helper' (WNIA journal, 1890, 2/10: 1). As Mrs Dorchester's comment reveals, to maternalists, all middle-class, native-born Protestant women – whether they had actually given birth to and reared children themselves – possessed a maternal instinct that would qualify them to uplift Indian women. Ironically, given the dominant view that women should stay within the home as wives and mothers, the WNIA's philosophy and programme empowered women to forgo marriage and motherhood, leave their homes and move to Indian communities, where they were to establish model homes, inspect native homes and teach Indian women new domestic skills in order to reorder their homes (see Bannan, 1984; Emmerich, 1987; Jacobs, 1997, 1999).

Through the pages of their monthly journal and during their annual conference, WNIA members routinely bemoaned the state of the Indian home. One woman declared that 'The suffering of Indian women and their desolate abodes are waiting for our help' (WNIA journal, 1888, 1/4: 1). Commonly, white women reformers asserted that many Indian groups had no word for 'home' in their language. Sue McBeth, a Presbyterian missionary among the Nez Perce, claimed in 1884 that there was 'no word for "family" in the language – only . . . a "band" – and no word for "home" – only . . . an "abode" – tent or house – and . . . a place of dwelling'. McBeth asserted that the 'permanent success of missions among them' depended on establishing 'Christian and civilized homes . . . among a people so lately out of heathen barbarism' (quoted in Coleman, 1985: 89). Clearly, to white women reformers like McBeth, the home signified more than a shelter or a place to enact domesticity and was a concept saturated with significance.

Some of white women's concerns with the home revolved around a particular conception of order and cleanliness that was intimately tied to Indian women's bodies and their conformity to white women's hygienic and sexual standards. Mrs Frye spoke of 'the constant suffering among the women from the want of hygienic knowledge and of the unlimited service which could be rendered by Christian women among them' (WNIA Report, 1890: 19). One matron, Sybil Carter, testified to the Lake Mohonk conference in 1894, 'I began with the mothers, teaching them in their homes', she declared.

> My special work is to clean up the home, . . . I go after the women, . . . I put it to [them] plainly that it is their duty to work, that I have spent money and time and a great many prayers that they may learn to be industrious, and to be clean and sweet and pure. (Carter, 1894: 23–4)

Here, we see that 'clean[ing] up the home' entailed not only housekeeping but also disciplining Indian women and purifying their bodies.

To white women reformers, a proper Christian home also connoted a place in which women supposedly enjoyed an elevated status. In the late nineteenth century, especially within the US, white women repeatedly invoked the ideal of the 'Christian home', which Peggy Pascoe has described as being 'identified with the moral authority of women rather than the patriarchal control of men'. Here, nineteenth-century middle-class women 'gained affection and moral influence at the cost of legal and economic powerlessness'. Husbands in the Christian home were expected to carry full economic responsibility for their family but to defer to their dependent wives' 'gentle moral guidance' within the home (Pascoe, 1990: 33 and 36). Thus, white women often connected Indian women's lack of a proper home with their supposed degradation at the hands of men. In 1898, Mrs Egerton Young asserted that

> in their wild pagan state, the condition of [Indian] women [to the west of Hudson's Bay] was most deplorable, and the fact that there was no word for 'home' among them shows their degradation. The wives and daughters were considered the absolute property of their husbands and fathers, to be treated just as they in their whims desired. (Young, 1898, 10/6: 9)

In the second part of her article, she claimed that 'these [Indian] men were magnificent hunters and fishermen, . . . showed great skill, strength, and endurance, yet whenever possible they left the heavy work and drudgery to the women', including carrying back to camp the game they had killed. Young even claimed that Indian men in this area killed older women who were no longer able to perform such duties. She asserted that those Indian men who converted to Christianity developed a new-found respect for women, and no longer abused, neglected, or required them to carry out such heavy work (Young, 1898, 10/7: 9 and 10).

Other white women also made such connections between the absence of permanent dwellings in many Indian cultures and Indian women's allegedly lower status. Helen Gibson Stockdell, a missionary for the Trinity Mission at Lemhi Indian Agency in Idaho, believed that Indian women

> make slaves of themselves for the men, and when child-birth comes the poor squaw is obliged, by the custom of her tribe, to go off into a wretched hovel made of willow boughs [a wickiup], and stay there through her time of greatest need. There must be fierce warfare waged against the cruel *wickiup* . . . The *wickiup* and all that it stands for in the debased idea of woman, must go. (Stockdell, 1902: 53–4)

Indigenous women must have found white women's efforts baffling, as they did not regard their homes as unclean or their home-keeping as disorderly and inadequate. The Navajos (or Diné), for example, prescribed specific ways that women were to keep their homes. Their religious beliefs, as expressed in the creation story of Changing Woman, endowed tasks such as making and keeping fires, preparing food, caring for pots and arranging bedding with a sacred dimension (Stewart, 1980: 41; Roessel, 1981: 72 and 74).[3] Many American Indian women would also have been surprised to find that white women considered them to be degraded. Among the Navajos, for example, although women at the turn of the twentieth century did engage in agricultural labour and tended livestock, they also owned their own sheep, a sign of wealth and status in Navajo society. Countering white women's beliefs – up to our own time – that Indian women have been the 'squaw drudges' of their men, Navajo Ruth Roessel, who herself had attended boarding schools, writes that, both in the past and present,

> Navajo women do not feel that the work and labor required is something that is too much or too hard, but, rather, they feel that it is something that is right, necessary and good. Their work in the fields gives them meaning and pleasure as well as allowing the close identification of these women with Changing Woman [a Creator] and with the Holy People who . . . gave to the Navajos corn and the other crops.

Roessel asserts: 'The Navajos always have said that as long as they have cornfields and *Kinaaldá* [a puberty ceremony for girls] they have nothing to worry about . . . . in both elements the women play the primary role' (Roessel, 1981: 105; see also Smits, 1982).

Although scholars today largely share Roessel's view that Indian women actually enjoyed a high status within their groups, most white women reformers at the turn of the twentieth century were bound – at least in theory – to a sexual division of labour based on a nineteenth-century model of middle-class, Christian, white gender norms. In this model, 'true women' oversaw domestic duties and guided affective relationships within the home while their husbands worked outside the home for pay.[4] Ironically, of course, in their work on behalf of Indian women, most WNIA members strayed far from this ideal.

Given their negative assessment of Indian homes, some white women began to believe that attempts to transform Indian women's homes were futile. In 1902, Loulie Taylor, a missionary at the Fort Hall Reservation in Idaho, contrasted the model home in which she lived at the mission with the home of an Indian woman:

> we had . . . the advantage of seeing just how the Indian lives in his tepee, and what had been the life of these children before coming to the mission. What a contrast! The smoking fire in the centre of the tepee, and on it the pot of soup stirred by the not over-clean squaw, whose black hair fell in as she stirred; men, women, and children lolling on the ground, a few blankets the only furnishing of the tepee; and then to think of the neat, comfortable home at the mission, with the uplifting of its daily prayer offered to their Great Spirit, our Heavenly Father. We realized what a blessed work these faithful missionaries . . . were doing in giving to these poor, neglected children . . . some of the light and blessing that had been given to them. (Taylor, 1902: 208–9)

Linked to notions that Indian women did not keep their homes clean was an equally ubiquitous complaint from white women that Indian mothers did not properly care for their children. Mrs Weinland, a missionary in southern California, accused Indian women of neglecting to provide their children with the finer things in life. 'How dull and uninteresting is the life of these children', she told the WNIA.

> No comfortable home; no toys of any kind; the little girls have no dolls; no picture-books; no music excepting at their dances, and nothing that can make childhood bright and happy. Is it any wonder that so many of them grow up hard, wicked and immoral. (WNIA Report, 1889: 18)

Such sentiments were echoed continually by WNIA members. The WNIA journal declared, for instance, in 1902 that 'the homes of the little Washoes and Paiutes children who come to the Kindergarten at the Carson Indian Boarding School are surely not planned for the best development of young minds' and 'the majority of them are nothing more than guerny sacks and old rags fastened around sticks to imitate tents and are called Wickiups, having no furniture, no decorations, no sign of cleanliness or thrift around' (p. 10).

White women and Indian children within institutional homes

A number of white women had come to see the Indian home as incorrigibly resistant to their efforts and came to believe that the only way to effect absolute change was to take Indian girls (as well as boys) away from the deficient home environment in which they lived. Here white women concerned with Indian affairs diverged from the path of other maternalists. Whereas other maternalists worked to ensure that poor women could stay in the home – through mother's pensions or allowances – many WNIA women instead undermined Indian women's roles as mothers. Thus the WNIA became a major supporter of a new and vast network of Indian boarding schools that were established beginning in 1879. Estelle Reel, who held the influential position of superintendent of Indian education from 1898 to 1910, asserted that 'the Indian child must be placed in school before the habits of barbarous life have become fixed, and there he must be kept until contact with our life has taught him to abandon his savage ways and walk in the path of Christian civilization' (Reel, n.d.).

Reel often implied that Indian mothers were a lost cause. She asserted, for example, in 1901 that

> one of the greatest obstacles in the elevation of the Indian race is the difficulty of overcoming the prejudices of the mothers of the tribe. The men, from constant contact with the white people, have their ideas broadened and absorb many of the ways of civilization, but the women, remaining in the camps, cling with tenacity to their old-time superstitions. (Reel, 1901)

Certainly, it is not possible to generalize that Indian men more readily assimilated to white society than Indian women, but whether they did so or not, Reel's remark suggests that Indian women resisted white women's attempts to trespass across intimate borders and to reorder their homes.

Given the concern that Indian women were still successful in socializing their daughters into Indian ways, Reel and other reformers came to believe that, truly to transform Indian homes, Indian girls must be removed and trained properly in the boarding schools. 'The homes of the camp Indians are to be reached mostly through our school girls', Reel declared, 'who are to be the future wives and mothers of the race, and on their advancement will depend largely the future condition of the Indian'. Appealing to maternalist visions of the home as the foundation of society and to the idea of women as essential to human advancement, Reel continued: 'All history has proven that as the mother is so is the home, and that a race will not rise above the home standard' (Reel, 1901).

Reel and other reformers believed that the boarding schools could transform gender roles and elevate Indian women. Commissioner of Indian Affairs Thomas J. Morgan (1889–93) declared, for example, that

> co-education of the sexes is the surest and perhaps only way in which the Indian women can be lifted out of that position of servility and degradation which most of them now occupy, on to a plane where their husbands and the men generally will treat them with the same gallantry and respect which is accorded to their more favored white sisters. (Morgan, n.d.)

To bring Indian children to the boarding schools, government authorities resorted to a variety of means ranging from cajolery to military force; in turn, Indian people responded in many different ways to this new pressure to give up their children. Some Indian parents thought their children might gain valuable skills and knowledge in the schools that would help their tribes keep their land and sovereignty. Other Indian families suffered from economic hardship – much of it brought on by colonization – and came to depend on the schools to provide their children with some degree of food, clothing and shelter. For other Indian people, especially women, attempts to trespass across the intimate borders of Indian homes were deeply alarming. Many Indian women fiercely resisted efforts to remove their children. Among the Mescalero Apaches, 'every possible expedient was resorted to by [the women] to keep their children from school'. Agent V. E. Stottler claimed that Mescalero women

> would brazenly deny having children despite the evidence of the accurate census rolls and the ticket on which they had for years drawn rations. Children were hidden out in the bushes; drugs were given them to unfit them for school; bodily infirmities were simulated, and some parents absolutely refused to bring their children in.

To overcome such resistance among the Mescaleros, Stottler resorted to 'the deprivation of supplies [food rations, which had been guaranteed by treaty] and the arrest of the old women'. Stottler boasted that his efforts 'soon worked a change. Willing or unwilling every child five years of age was forced into school' (WNIA journal, 1897, 10/1: 10; for more on the practice of Indian child removal, see also Jacobs, 2004 and 2009).

Despite their support for assimilation and the boarding schools, such use of coercion did not sit well with reformers who, after all, touted assimilation policy as a humane and benevolent alternative to the prior 'century of dishonour'; that is, an era of brutal violence against Indian peoples. Thus, where possible BIA officials preferred to use persuasion to bring Indian children to the schools. Some agents, along with many white women reformers themselves, deemed white women 'gentle tamers', who could easily persuade Indian women to part with their children. Reel, in fact, presented herself as having a special talent – because she was a woman – for convincing Indian women to give up their children. In one of her press releases, reprinted verbatim by a newspaper in 1903, she asserted:

> No man superintendent of Indian schools could have done what Miss Reel is doing. Her strongest hold is to go into the wigwams of the Indian women, gain their confidence and liking and make them see how much better it is to trust their children to the training of civilization . . . these wild women trust Miss Reel utterly when she goes into their wigwams and tells them that their children will have power to cope with the white man and get their own back again if they learn to use the white man's own weapons. As woman to woman she appeals to them, and they listen and acquiesce. (Gray, 1903)

Though Reel actually had little to do with the day-to-day implementation of removing Indian children to boarding school, many white women did become 'recruiters' of Indian children, travelling far from home to breach intimate borders yet again and convince Indian families to send their children to distant boarding schools (see Jacobs, 2005). In 1884, for example, Cora Folsom, a teacher at Hampton Institute in Virginia, went to a Minniconjou Sioux community in the Dakota Territory to recruit children for her school. The council of elders told Folsom that 'they have taken away our tobacco and we will give up our rations; we will not give up our children'. Folsom recounted that, when they came out of their council,

> crowds of men and women had collected around the tipi and when we came out feeling like chastened children we had to pass down a long line

> of blanketed Indians, some of whom responded to our smiling 'How' while others looked pained and grieved to see women so young and so apparently innocent ready to tear little children from the loving arms of their parents. They had seen to it, however, that there was nothing to fear, for not a child of the five hundred appeared in sight to tempt us. Where so many could have hidden in tipis so devoid of hiding places we shall never know, but the children must have been in the game for no sound of them reached our ears. (Quoted in Buffalohead and Molin, 1996: 5–6)

When recruiting efforts like those of Folsom failed, as they often did, the government often sent in the military or police to compel parents to send their children to boarding school. Many white women reformers and male authorities believed that such drastic action was necessary and that, by moving the Indian children to a new well-ordered home, the 'Indian problem' could be solved. From their inception in the late nineteenth century up until the 1930s, when the government turned to more day schools for Indian children under commissioner of Indian affairs John Collier's so-called 'Indian New Deal', tens of thousands of Indian children attended the boarding schools.[5]

Within the new setting of the boarding school, white women sought to reconstitute intimate borders. As both white women reformers and government officials deemed it women's proper role to teach and care for children within the institutions, a majority of employees within the boarding schools were white women. Historian Cathleen Cahill has found that the proportion of women employees in the Indian School Service averaged between 55 and 62 per cent from 1890 until well into the twentieth century (Cahill, 2004: 161 and 387; see also Adams, 1995: 82–3). As a kind of surrogate mother to Indian children within the boarding schools, white women were to create alternative spheres of intimacy that were designed to undermine and replace Indian children's previous intimacies within their own families and communities.

Just as they had emphasized the significance of the home in their work with Indian women on reservations, many white women in the boarding schools invested their work with a similar radical potential. Miss Worden of the Santee School, for instance, told the Lake Mohonk conference in 1893:

> We cannot lay too much emphasis on the value to these girls of learning cooking and nursing. When they learn to understand these things, their home life will be revolutionized. The telling work must be done in the homes, and the women have the most important part of the home life to see to. When you get a woman to understand that it is her highest duty in this world to take care of her family and home in a Christian and intelligent manner, you have got near the heart of the matter. (Lake Mohonk Proceedings, 1893: 28–9)

White women teachers and matrons like Worden sought to introduce Indian girls and boys to new types of clothing, housing and food and to instil in them new standards of conduct within their intimate relations.

White women teachers and matrons in the schools linked clean homes with clean bodies; training in domesticity went hand in hand with promoting white women's standards of sexual morality. To contain young Indian women's sexuality, white women crossed intimate borders yet again. They instituted a system of inspection and surveillance of the intimate lives of girls in their care. Navajo Ruth Roessel remembered that at the dormitory at Fort Wingate boarding school,

> the matrons had a book with every girl's name in it, so that when each girl had her period they would mark it down. In this way they kept track of each girl's period, and if one missed her period they would know about it and they would call the girl in and ask what happened. (Roessel, 1981: 170)

Here we see a particularly profound transformation of girls' intimate lives. Signs of a girl's period went from being a source of pride and cause for celebration (the Navajos and many other indigenous groups in North America mark the onset of a girl's menses with a rigorous and sacred puberty ceremony) to becoming a source of shame and mystery that had to be closely controlled and monitored (see also Stewart, 1980: 19–20; and Frisbie, 1967).

Indian girls negotiated these new intimate borders in myriad different ways. Some, like Elizabeth Bender at the Carlisle Institute in Pennsylvania, seemed wholly to embrace white women's view that the 'unkempt homes [of Indian families] are breeding places for filth and disease.' She asked readers of the Carlisle publication, *The Redman*, in 1916, whether we can 'expect to develop great, strong Christian leaders in spite of such home conditions'. She herself firmly believe that it could happen:

> We can take our youth away from home, send them off to such [Indian boarding] schools as Haskell, Carlisle, or Hampton for a period of years, . . . and have them associate with high minded instructors who shall teach that the home is the very core of any civilization, that the ideal home shall permeate its environment and bring it into keeping with that of their school. (Bender, 1916: 154–5)

It is unlikely, however, that the boarding school newspaper would have published the views of the many children who failed to embrace this particular view.

Other young Indian women contested – sometimes forcefully, at other times subtly – portrayals of their original homes as 'breeding places for filth and disease' and of Indian women as immoral and impure. At Hampton Institute's commencement, graduating senior Lucy Conger presented a positive view of the Indian home as a place where 'a child is always welcome and enters life the possessor of the most passionate love of its parents'. Rather than focusing on the material condition of Indian homes, Conger emphasized the quality of human relationships that Indian families valued. She stressed the importance of 'the intricate line of relationships' and the 'social obligations of an Indian', declaring that 'from babyhood the children were taught to respect their elders . . . They must always be patient, truthful, self-controlled.' Moreover, 'hospitality too must both be offered and accepted without a question' (Conger, 1903: 2 and 11). Through such home environments, Conger suggested, Indian children learned proper ways to behave; that is, their own codes of morality. Countering the commonly held belief that Indian girls grew up without morals, Conger asserted that 'to be modest and industrious were the virtues' set before Indian girls and that this 'produced an energetic and a very feminine type of woman' (Conger, 1903: 2 and 11). Having been taught in the boarding schools that Indian home life was inferior to that of white, middle-class Christian women, then, Conger used her speaking opportunity to hold up Indian home life as a viable, but misunderstood, alternative.

Indian girls as domestic servants in white women's homes

While the schools routinely claimed that they were training Indian girls in order to transform Indian homes, ultimately they prepared the girls to take up residence in yet another intimate setting. Through the so-called 'outing program', boarding schools placed Indian children – the girls as domestic servants, the boys as field and/or manual labourers – with white families for part of each day, over summer vacations and even after leaving school. Many other impoverished American women, most of whom were black or recent immigrants, also laboured in domestic service, and some industrial homes and schools in urban areas also sought to train young immigrant women for such service (see Rollins, 1985; Dudden, 1983; Sutherland 1981). For Indian girls, however, white policy-makers and authorities did not characterize domestic service as merely a job to earn money or as a means of filling a shortage of domestic labour, but as a necessary part of their curriculum in being 'uplifted' from savagery to civilization. Or, as Reel put it, the outing system

> places the student under the influence of the daily life of a good home, where his inherited weaknesses and tendencies are overcome by the civilized habits which he forms – habits of order, of personal cleanliness and neatness, and of industry and thrift, which displace the old habits of aimless living, unambition, and shiftlessness. (Reel, 1901: 189)

Thus white women reformers ennobled domestic service and invested white women employers with an important role to play in 'civilizing' Indian girls and young women within their private households. Ironically, Indian girls from homes that were deemed so dirty were now charged with keeping white women's homes up to middle-class standards of cleanliness.

Although this home proved to be less controlled than the boarding school environment, the contours of its intimate borders were equally shaped by power relations. Some schools hired 'outing matrons' to maintain close supervision over outed Indian girls. Records kept by these matrons in the San Francisco Bay Area capture the dissonance that seemed inherent to the relationship between the girls and their employers. On the outing form of a girl named Iris (a pseudonym), for example, the matron wrote, that she was a 'good girl – slow. Very impudent to Mrs. Lester. Mrs. Maurice says not clean or good worker.' And it was mentioned that Louisa 'did not make good at first place.

Stayed out nights left Mrs. Wilson's. Mrs. Moore let her go because out all night and saucy.'[6]

White women employers wanted obedient and dedicated servants who would work long hours for low wages. Dorris Taft of San Mateo wrote to the matron to request a new servant: 'I would like awfully to get a good girl, but one who will stay, this changing and training is a very hard thing both on the girl and on me.'[7] Moreover, white women employers sought to control their servants' leisure time as well, seeing themselves as both employers and surrogate mothers, who needed to protect their charges. Mrs Parlier of Berkeley, for instance, was annoyed when her servant Sylvia went with her girlfriends to San Francisco in a taxi cab. She was 'indignant that people who did household employment should spend their [money] in that way'.[8]

For their part, the Indian girls sought employment with reasonable hours and decent wages and full control over their leisure time. They also objected to certain types of work. Opal (a Pomo Indian) lamented that when Mrs David

> did let me go to Oakland for the dances she always wanted me to go up to the house to mow the land and kill fleas. The house was just infested with them. That is a terrible job by itself. That meant scrubbing all the ten rooms.[9]

Indian girls also chafed at the restrictions their employers placed on their social lives. One girl's intercepted letter to her boyfriend is revealing in this regard. After staying out late with him, Myra wrote to him that 'I was locked out so I couldn't come in, I sure wished I stayed with you then. I am here at the YWCA now writing you these few lines.'[10]

Despite the watchful eyes of both their employers and the outing matron, many young Indian women who were outed in the San Francisco Bay Area forged their own intimate relationships, seeming to relish the company of other young Indian women and the chance to socialize with men. As a result, like many other domestic servants elsewhere, about a quarter of the young Indian women in the case files of the San Francisco Bay Area outing matron became pregnant while in service. These women in turn confronted new challenges on the intimate borders of their lives. One wonders, for example, how the unmarried Jane, who bore a baby on 13 December 1928, cared for him after she began work again on 30 January 1929.[11] If she was typical, she boarded her child with a care-giver while she worked in another woman's home or sent her child home to live with a grandmother or aunt. In such cases, outing matrons still policed the intimate borders of Indian women's lives, often putting pressure on young Indian women to give their children up for adoption or to put them in boarding schools.

Thus we have come full circle. Beginning in the late nineteenth century, white women's breaching of intimate borders created a cycle of intervention into indigenous families that reproduced itself over many generations. Insistent that transforming the Indian home and the Indian woman's role within it was central to solving 'the Indian problem', white women reformers first set out to live in Indian communities. There they hoped to set up model homes and train Indian women in domesticity. Some white women reformers found Indian women resistant to their ministrations and turned instead to removing Indian girls to distant boarding schools, where they planned to raise them according to their Christian, middle-class standards. The boarding school's domestic curriculum ultimately prepared Indian girls more for domestic service in white women's homes than for setting up their own homes on the middle-class, Christian model within their Indian communities. As many Indian girls became mothers while employed as domestic servants, they faced another round of condemnation from white women. Working to support themselves rather than ensconced within a proper home, these young Indian women appeared to white women as unfit mothers. White women often advocated that their children, too, should be separated from them and be more appropriately reared in an institution or a white family. This intervention into Indian families serves as a powerful example of the significance of intimate borders to an understanding of the ongoing nature of settler colonialism's deepest workings. We see that the home, far from being a private refuge or haven from larger social forces, also came to operate as yet another permeable and contested site of settler colonialism.

Notes

1 Albert Hurtado uses another variation of the phrase in his book *Intimate Frontiers* (Hurtado, 1999). For an overview of early scholarship on gender and colonialism, see Strobel, 1994. For recent works on interracial relationships, see Stoler, 2002; and Perry, 2001. For more on white women and empire, see Burton, 1994; Chaudhuri and Strobel, 1992; and Jayawardena, 1995.

2 Beginning in 1883, reformers from the WNIA, the IRA and other organizations convened annually in Lake Mohonk, New York, to discuss and coordinate their efforts to address 'the Indian problem'.

3 In the Diné people's telling of their own creation, when the Holy People had come into the Fourth 'Glittering' World from the lower world, First Man and First Woman discovered an orphan baby girl in a cloud resting on top of a small mountain. They brought the child into their home and together with other Holy People decided how to nurture her. First, they determined that they must name the little girl before she was four days old and then pierce her ears. When the infant laughed for the first time, the Holy People decreed it to be a time of rejoicing and happiness. After the girl had her first menstrual period, the Holy People honoured her passage to womanhood through holding a *kinaaldá* or puberty ceremony. Changing Woman soon became impregnated by the Sun as she lay by a pool of water and subsequently gave birth to twin boys – Monster Slayer and Child-Born-of-Water – who were put on the earth to destroy all its monsters so as to make a safe place for humans to reside. After the twins had killed the monsters, Changing Woman moved to her home in the West, where she created the four clans of the Navajo people from different parts of her own body. Changing Woman put life into each of the humans she created; when they matured, she then instructed the people to go to their original home, a high desert region bounded by four sacred peaks and carved with rocky canyons (in today's south-western United States), where they were to live and raise corn. The teachings the Holy People passed on to First Man and First Woman about how to raise Changing Woman became the Blessing Way, which, according to Ruth Roessel, 'remains even today the core of Navajo life and a primary source for teachings by the Holy People' (Roessel, 1981: 42). The version above comes from: Roessel, 1981; Frank Mitchell, a Blessingway singer, quoted in Frisbie, 1967: 12; and Frisbie and McAllester, 1978: 180–1.

4 For more on recent scholarship regarding the complementarity of American Indian gender roles, see Klein and Ackerman, 1995; Ackerman, 2003; and Perdue, 1998. For the classic essay on the 'true womanhood' ideal, see Welter, 1966.

5 For some statistics on Indian enrolments in boarding schools, see Peairs, 1911; Adams, 1995. John Collier's Indian New Deal put a halt to many

features of the earlier assimilation policy, including allotment and the criminalization of Indian religious ceremonies. Part of a new generation of reformers who favoured Indian cultural preservation, Collier sought to replace boarding schools with day schools and to teach Indian languages, histories and cultures within them (see Philp, 1977; Kelly, 1983; and Jacobs, 1999).

6 File of V. G., Box 2, and D. L., Box 3, Relocation, Training, and Employment Assistance Case Records, 1933–1946, Outing Girls, RG 75, BIA California Sacramento Agency, National Archives and Records Administration, Pacific Region, San Bruno, CA. These case files include sensitive material and, therefore, I have used pseudonyms in the text to conceal the identity of the Indian women in the files. See also, for a more extensive account of Indian women's domestic service in the San Francisco Bay Area, Jacobs, 2007.

7 Taft to Traxler, 13 November 1933, H. E. file, Box 2, Relocation, Training, and Employment Assistance Case Records.

8 File of I. S., Box 4, Relocation, Training, and Employment Assistance Case Records.

9 P. Ar. to Van Every, 30 October 1934, P. Ar. file, Box 1, Relocation, Training, and Employment Assistance Case Records.

10 V. F. to 'Dearie', 3 May 1928, V. F. file, Box 2, Relocation, Training, and Employment Assistance Case Records.

11 Ev. A. file, Box 1, Relocation, Training, and Employment Assistance Case Records.

Bibliography

Ackerman, Lillian (2003). *A Necessary Balance: Gender and Power among Indians of the Columbia Plateau*, Norman: University of Oklahoma Press.

Adams, David Wallace (1995). *Education for Extinction: American Indians and the Boarding School Experience, 1875–1928*, Lawrence: University Press of Kansas.

Bannan, Helen M. (1984). *'True Womanhood' on the Reservation: Field Matrons in the U.S. Indian Service*, Southwest Institute for Research on Women, working paper no. 18, Tucson: Women's Studies.

Bender, Elizabeth G. (1916). 'Training Indian girls for efficient home makers', *The Redman*, 8, 5, 154–5.

Bolt, Christine (1987). *American Indian Policy and American Reform: Case Studies of the Campaign to Assimilate the American Indians*, Boston: Allen & Unwin.

Brumberg, Joan Jacobs (1982). 'Zenanas and girlless villages: the ethnology of American evangelical women, 1870–1910', *Journal of American History*, 69, 347–70.

Buffalohead, Roger W. and Paulette Fairbanks Molin (1996). '"A nucleus of civilization": American Indian families at Hampton Institute in the late nineteenth century', *Journal of American Indian Education*, 35, 3, 59–94.

Burton, Antoinette (1994). *Burdens of History: British Feminists, Indian Women, and Imperial Culture*, Chapel Hill: University of North Carolina Press.

Cahill, Cathleen (2004). '"Only the home can found a state": gender, labor, and the United States Indian Service, 1869–1928', Ph.D. thesis, University of Chicago.

Calloway, Colin (1999). *First Peoples: A Documentary Survey of American Indian History* Boston: Bedford/St. Martin's Press.

Carter, Sybil (1894). 'Work for Indian women', Lake Mohonk Proceedings.

Chaudhuri, Nupur and Margaret Strobel (eds) (1992). *Western Women and Imperialism: Complicity and Resistance*, Bloomington: Indiana University Press.

Coleman, Michael C. (1985). *Presbyterian Missionary Attitudes toward American Indians, 1837–1893*, Jackson: University Press of Mississippi.

Conger, Lucy (1903). 'Indian childhood', Hampton commencement address, *The Indian's Friend*, 16/1.

Course of Study of the Indian Schools of the United States, Industrial and Literary (1901). Washington, DC: US Government Printing Office.

Denoon, Donald (1983). *Settler Capitalism: The Dynamics of Dependent Development in the Southern Hemisphere*, Oxford: Clarendon Press.

Dudden, Faye (1983). *Serving Women: Household Service in Nineteenth-Century America*, Middletown, CT: Wesleyan University Press.

Emmerich, Lisa (1987). '"To respect and love and seek the ways of white women": field matrons, the Office of Indian Affairs, and civilization policy, 1890–1938', Ph.D. thesis, University of Maryland.

Evans, Julie, Patricia Grimshaw, David Philips and Shurlee Swain (2003). *Equal Subjects, Unequal Rights: Indigenous Peoples in British Settler Colonies, 1830–1910*, Manchester and New York: Manchester University Press.

Flemming, Leslie A. (ed.) (1989). *Women's Work for Women: Missionaries and Social Change in Asia*, Boulder, CO: Westview Press.

Frisbie, Charlotte Johnson (1967). *Kinaaldá: A Study of the Navaho Girl's Puberty Ceremony,* Middletown, CT: Wesleyan University Press.

Frisbie, Charlotte J. and David P. McAllester (1978). *Navajo Blessingway Singer: The Autobiography of Frank Mitchell, 1881–1967*, Tucson: University of Arizona Press.

Gordon, Linda (1994). *Pitied But Not Entitled: Single Mothers and the History of Welfare*, Cambridge, MA: Harvard University Press.

Gray, Lillian (1903). 'Estelle Reel: Superintendent of Indian schools', *The New Orleans Item*, Box 1, 'Articles' folder, Estelle Reel papers, H6–110, Wyoming State Archives.

Hawes, Joseph (1991). *The Children's Rights Movement: A History of Advocacy and Protection*, Boston: Twayne Publishers.

Hoxie, Frederick (1984). *A Final Promise: The Campaign to Assimilate the Indians, 1880–1920*, New York: Cambridge University Press.

Hunter, Jane (1984). *The Gospel of Gentility: American Women Missionaries in Turn-of-the-Century China*, New Haven, CT: Yale University Press.

Hurtado, Albert (1999). *Intimate Frontiers: Sex, Gender, and Culture in Old California*, Albuquerque: University of New Mexico Press.

Jacobs, Margaret D. (1997). 'Resistance to rescue: the Indians of Bahapki and Mrs. Annie E. K. Bidwell', in Elizabeth Jameson and Susan Armitage (eds), *Writing the Range: Race, Class, and Culture in the Women's West*, Norman: University of Oklahoma Press, 230–51.

——(1999). *Engendered Encounters: Feminism and Pueblo Cultures, 1879–1934*, Lincoln: University of Nebraska Press.

——(2004). 'A battle for the children: American Indian child removal in Arizona in the era of assimilation', *Journal of Arizona History*, 45, 1, 31–62.

——(2005). 'Maternal colonialism: white women and indigenous child removal in the American West and Australia, 1880–1940', *Western Historical Quarterly*, 36, 453–76.

——(2007). 'Working on the domestic frontier: American Indian servants in white women's households in the San Francisco Bay Area, 1920–1940', *Frontiers: A Journal of Women Studies*, 28, 1 and 2, 165–99.

——(2009). *White Mother to a Dark Race: Settler Colonialism, Maternalism, and Indigenous Child Removal in the American West and Australia, 1880–1940*, Lincoln: University of Nebraska Press.

Jayawardena, Kumari (1995). *The White Woman's Other Burden: Western Women and South Asia during British Colonial Rule*, New York: Routledge.

Kelly, Lawrence C. (1983). *The Assault on Assimilation: John Collier and the Origins of Indian Policy Reform*, Albuquerque: University of New Mexico Press.

Klein, Laura and Lillian Ackerman (eds) (1995). *Women and Power in Native North America*, Norman: University of Oklahoma Press.

Ladd-Taylor, Molly (1994). *Mother-Work: Women, Child Welfare, and the State, 1890–1930*, Urbana: University of Illinois Press.

Lake Mohonk Proceedings (1893, 1898). *Proceedings of the Annual Meeting of the Lake Mohonk Conference*, Lake Mohonk, NY: Lake Mohonk conference.

Mathes, Valerie (1990a). *Helen Hunt Jackson and her Indian Reform Legacy*, Austin: University of Texas Press.

——(1990b). 'Nineteenth-century women and reform: the Women's National Indian Association', *American Indian Quarterly*, 14, 1–18.

Michel, Sonya (1999). *Children's Interests/Mother's Rights: The Shaping of America's Child Care Policy*, New Haven, CT: Yale University Press.

Mink, Gwendolyn (1995). *The Wages of Motherhood: Inequality in the Welfare State, 1917–1942*, Ithaca, NY: Cornell University Press.

Morgan, Thomas (n.d). 'The education of American Indians', paper read before the Mohonk Conference, Box 160, Folder 005/810, Records of the Bureau of Indian Affairs (BIA), National Archives and Records Administration, Rocky Mountain Region, Denver, Colorado (NARA-DEN).

Pascoe, Peggy (1990). *Relations of Rescue: The Search for Female Moral Authority in the American West, 1874–1939*, New York: Oxford University Press.

Peairs, H. B. (1911). 'Location, capacity, enrollment, and average attendance, United States Indian schools', Box 160, Folder 005/860, Correspondence with Supervisor of Schools, Records of the BIA, NARA–DEN.

——(1910–13). Consolidated Ute Agency Decimal Files, 1879–1952, RG 75, Records of the BIA, NARA–DEN.

Perdue, Theda (1998). *Cherokee Women: Gender and Culture Change, 1700–1835*, Lincoln: University of Nebraska Press.

Perry, Adele (2001). *On the Edge of Empire: Gender, Race, and the Making of British Columbia, 1849–1871*, Toronto: University of Toronto Press.

Philp, Kenneth R. (1977). *John Collier's Crusade for Indian Reform, 1920–1954*, Tucson: University of Arizona Press.

Platt, Anthony M. (1969). *The Child Savers: The Invention of Delinquency*, Chicago: University of Chicago Press.

Reel, Estelle (n.d.). 'Her work for the Indians: Miss Estelle Reel, Genl Supt of Indian Schools, talks interestingly regarding Indian matters, Favors compulsory education and industrial training', Estelle Reel papers, H6–110, Box 1, 'Articles' folder, Wyoming State Archives, Cheyenne.

——(1901). 'Education for Indian girls', *The Woman's Journal*, 19 January, Box 2, Folder 1, Reel papers, Eastern Washington State Historical Society, Northwest Museum of Arts and Culture, Spokane, Washington (EWSHS).

Relocation, Training, and Employment Assistance Case Records (1933– 1946). Outing Girls, RG 75, BIA California Sacramento Agency, National Archives and Records Administration, Pacific Region, San Bruno, CA.

Roessel, Ruth (1981). *Women in Navajo Society*, Rough Rock, Navajo Nation, AZ: Navajo Resource Center, Rough Rock Demonstration School.

Rollins, Judith (1985). *Between Women: Domestics and their Employers*, Philadelphia: Temple University Press.

Russell, Lynette (ed.) (2001). *Colonial Frontiers: Indigenous–European Encounters in Settler Societies*, Manchester and New York: Manchester University Press.

Skocpol, Theda (1992). *Protecting Soldiers and Mothers: The Political Origins of Social Policy in the United States*, Cambridge, MA: Belknap Press of Harvard University Press.

Smits, David D. (1982). 'The "squaw drudge": a prime index of savagism', *Ethnohistory*, 29, 281–306.

Stasiulis, Daiva and Nira Yuval-Davis (1995). 'Introduction: beyond dichotomies – gender, race, ethnicity and class in settler societies', in Daiva Stasiulis and Nira Yuval-Davis (eds), *Unsettling Settler Societies: Articulations of Gender, Race, Ethnicity and Class*, London: Sage Publications.

Stewart, Irene (1980). *A Voice in Her Tribe: A Navajo Woman's Own Story*, ed. Doris Ostrander Dawdy, Socorro, NM: Ballena Press.

Stockdell, Helen Gibson (1902). 'Woman's work for women on the Lemhi Reservation', *The Woman's Auxiliary*, 67, 1, 53–4.

Stoler, Ann Laura (2001). 'Tense and tender ties: the politics of comparison in North American history and (post) colonial studies', *Journal of American History*, 88; reprinted in Stoler (2006).

——(2002). *Carnal Knowledge and Imperial Power: Race and the Intimate in Colonial Rule*, Berkeley, CA: University of California Press.

——(2006). *Haunted by Empire: Geographies of Intimacy in North American History*, Durham: Duke University Press.

Strobel, Margaret (1994). *Gender, Sex, and Empire*, Washington, DC: American Historical Association.

Sutherland, Daniel E. (1981). *Americans and their Servants: Domestic Service in the United States from 1800 to 1920*, Baton Rouge: Louisiana State University Press.

Taylor, Loulie (1902). 'What a diocesan officer saw on an Indian reservation', *The Woman's Auxiliary*, 67, 3, 208–9.

Tiffin, Susan (1982). *In Whose Best Interest?: Child Welfare Reform in the Progressive Era*, Westport, CT: Greenwood Press.

Utley, Robert (1984). *The Indian Frontier of the American West, 1847–1890*, Albuquerque: University of New Mexico Press.

Wanken, Helen (1981). '"Woman's sphere" and Indian reform: the Women's National Indian Association, 1879–1901', Ph.D. thesis, Marquette University.

Weeks, Philip (1990). *Farewell My Nation: The American Indian and the United States, 1820–1890*, Arlington Heights, IL: Harlan Davidson.

Welter, Barbara (1966). 'The cult of true womanhood: 1820–1860', *American Quarterly*, 16, 151–74.

——(1978). 'She hath done what she could: Protestant women's missionary careers in the nineteenth century', *American Quarterly*, 30, 624–30.

WNIA journal (1888, 1890). *The Indian's Friend*, 1, 4 and 2, 10.

——(1902). 'Indian children in kindergarten', *The Indian's Friend*, 14, 11, 10.

WNIA Report (1883, 1884, 1885, 1890). *Annual Meeting and Report of the Women's National Indian Association*, Philadelphia: Women's National Indian Association.

——(1889). *Report of the Missionary Committee of the WNIA* (November), Philadelphia: Women's National Indian Association.

Wolfe, Patrick (2001). 'Land, labor, and difference: elementary structures of race', *American Historical Review*, 106, 3, 866–1006.

Young, Mrs Egerton (1898). 'The transformed Indian woman', *The Indian's Friend*, 10, 6 and 7.

9

Scottishness and Gender History in a Cross-border/International Context: Reinventing the Border?

SIÂN REYNOLDS

Introduction

To consider the question of borders from a Scottish perspective is to be faced with an immediate paradox. Geographically, Scotland's frontiers are largely maritime, but it is the disputed landward border with England, the scene of bitter struggles for hundreds of years, which dominates thinking about borders. In much historical writing produced in Scotland, this border has been primarily associated with invasion, warfare and bloodshed, and Scottish identity has most often been asserted as difference from the neighbour to the south. To introduce gender to the equation forces us to consider other kinds of difference: the extent to which gender has been a part of this disputed past and the ways in which, in recent years, it has been written into a disputed history. It is a story of hidden inclusions and exclusions, of a discourse of identity constructed until recently around a masculine version of Scottishness. This chapter is particularly concerned with the writing of Scottish history, but seeks to place it in a wider cultural and political context, viewed from a feminist perspective, that is, one which uses gender as an analytical concept, recognizing that any national history is composed of the actions, thought and words of both men and women, whatever the differences of their experience.

An illustration from Scottish history

Let me take as a starting point a set of four examples from *The Biographical Dictionary of Scottish Women* (Ewan et al., 2006), to indicate the dynastic role of royal women in Scottish history. Queens appear in the dictionary under their given names, and the reader who opens it at the name 'Margaret', will find entries for several Queen Margarets from the eleventh to the sixteenth century. The earliest is Saint Margaret (*c.*1046–93). Probably born in Castle Reka, Hungary, she was the daughter of Edward the Exile, English prince and possible heir, and his wife Agatha of West Friesland, neither of them Scottish. Threatened by the Norman conquest, the family fled north to find protection with Malcolm III Canmore of Scotland, who was resisting the Normans. In *c.*1070, he married Margaret as his second wife. Of their eight or more children, three became kings of Scots, while their daughter became Matilda, queen of England. Queen Margaret's influence on Scottish religious and cultural life was marked, and she was later canonized. (Her fame is the reason why so many Scottish girls are called Margaret.)

The second Margaret (1282–90) died as a child and never became queen: the daughter of Erik II of Norway and his wife Margaret, daughter of Alexander III of Scotland, Margaret, the 'Maid of Norway', was probably born in Bergen. As Alexander's granddaughter, she was sole direct heir to the Scottish throne, her right to inherit having been passed by Parliament in 1284. The little girl was due to marry the son of Edward I, king of England in 1286, to promote friendship between the kingdoms. But her death in Orkney, on the voyage over, led to a dynastic crisis, precipitating decades of Anglo-Scottish warfare, today usually known as the Wars of Independence (fought by Wallace and Bruce).

The third princess, Margaret of Denmark (1457–86), was the daughter of Christian I and Dorothea of Brandenburg. She married James III of Scotland in 1469, aged twelve. One aspect of her role was that she brought Orkney and Shetland under the Scots crown, because her Danish father defaulted on the dowry. Later a key player as guardian to the Scottish heir while her husband was imprisoned, her political acumen is credited with a relatively peaceful solution to the 1482 crisis.

The final example is Margaret Tudor, born in 1489 in Westminster, daughter of Henry VII and Elizabeth of York and thus sister of Henry VIII of England. She married James IV of Scotland, who in 1509 joined with the French against Henry and was killed at Flodden Field in 1513. Margaret Tudor's own life was full of incident, but for our purposes, we may note that soon after her own death in 1541, her brother, Henry VIII, and her son, James V, were at war, in what is known as the 'Rough Wooing'. The Scottish border region, where 'war had been an almost daily fact of life since the Wars of Independence . . . was now repeatedly savaged, tens of thousands were killed, many homes were burned and razed to the ground' (Lynch, 2001: 533). Margaret Tudor's granddaughter, James V's daughter, Mary, queen of Scots, became queen of Scotland within a week of her birth in 1542. Through Margaret Tudor, she had a potential claim to the English throne, hence her trouble with her cousin, Elizabeth I.

From these four examples, several observations suggest themselves. First, the obvious point that the course of early Scottish history, affecting many lives – both men and women were killed in large numbers – often depended on dynastic politics, which is another term for *gendered* politics or, more plainly put, marriage, sex and procreation. Dynastic politics, viewed as necessary both to cement international alliances and to provide any heir with a convincing pedigree, influenced European history for many centuries.

Secondly, and particularly pertinently for our subject, all these royal women, whatever their role and influence, were born *outwith* Scotland. Their birthplaces were elsewhere in Europe, but they became Scottish, thus indicating the fluid nature of nationality compared to marriage, where women were concerned (something only rarely true of men). Some of these women had Scottish ancestry, some had none, but all had to cross borders to become absorbed into Scottishness by marriage.[1]

A third point that can be noted from their stories is that cross-border warfare was explicitly seen at the time, and has often been described by historians since, in terms of sexual imagery. 'Rough wooing', after all, is more or less a euphemism for rape. Many wars are described in terms of *border crossing*, seen as stepping over a threshold, invading, penetrating, taking by force. 'Independence' can be seen as freeing oneself from the aggressor/rapist. Similarly, alliances between countries or groups are often described in metaphors of sexuality and/or marriage: flirtation, consummation, divorce. Gender is metaphorically built into the language of borders.

Fourthly, from these fairly random examples one can see that a major feature of medieval and early modern Scotland was the key importance of the previously mentioned border, the one with England (today fixed but *internal*). This stormy relationship with England has given its present-day name to the region south of Edinburgh and

Glasgow, still commonly called 'The Borders' (in institutions like Lothian and Borders Police for instance). Dynastic, that is, gendered, preoccupations marked the relationship for hundreds of years. Even at times when English and Scots were at war, their royal families were blood relations: marriage, childbirth and consanguinity were at the centre of their relations.

The borders region has been much fought over and the actual line of the border varied in the early Middle Ages, with both formal and informal violence continuing in the fifteenth and sixteenth centuries, sporadically revived in later years. The crowns were united in the person of James VI and I in 1603, and the Act of Union was signed under Queen Anne in 1707, but neither union meant unbroken peace. Warfare might reflect a desire to eliminate the border (Cromwell) or to reinstate it (the Jacobite risings). Nevertheless, once the Jacobite risings were over in 1746, the union went more or less unchallenged for the next couple of hundred years. The Scots had retained significant elements of their society – their church, education and legal system – but were otherwise integrated into Britishness, and in particular to the nineteenth-century expansion of the British Empire. Border questions ceased to be of pressing concern.[2]

At this point, at the risk of sounding incongruous, I could add to the list of Margarets a fifth woman, to bring the story into the present. Born in Grantham, England, in 1925, she was remarkable for many things, among them breaching the centuries-old male monopoly of prime ministerial office. It has plausibly been argued that Margaret Thatcher's government of the 1980s accentuated Scottish irritation with Westminster. The poll tax, for instance, was tried out first in Scotland, to much protest, and arguably contributed to Mrs Thatcher's downfall, certainly to her unpopularity north of the border, where the Labour party was dominant. Her policies can undoubtedly be said to have precipitated the increased appeal of devolution, and thus in part the renewed sense of separateness of Scotland and the revival of a border which during the previous two centuries or so had come to be quite a low wall (rather like the unremarkable Antonine Roman wall). After all, in 1979, there had apparently been no huge enthusiasm for Scottish devolution, since the referendum of that year failed to get the requisite majority. But the late 1990s saw general approval of the proposals for a separate Scottish Parliament, with Labour leaders such as Donald Dewar, later the first first minister, voicing their enthusiasm. To some extent, this move could be described as 'rebuilding the border', something which did not happen in isolation.

Rebuilding the border?

What is notable about the last few decades in Scotland, pre-dating but also accompanying the Scottish Parliament first elected in 1999, has been the emergence of a revived national culture, which sees itself as Scottish, rather than British.[3] It is perhaps most evident in the cultural field, in the arts, in publishing and in academia, where a wealth of books about Scottish history and national identity has appeared. A glance at any large city bookstore in Scotland provides overwhelming evidence of this 'renaissance' which has gathered pace in the years since devolution. It could be argued that the shift has contributed in a sense to rebuilding the border, in other words identifying what is specifically Scottish within a history and culture where 'Britishness' was sometimes taken for granted in the past. It might mean reclaiming as Scottish some famous cultural creators who had previously been assimilated to British culture, often because they had left Scotland: Thomas Carlyle, Conan Doyle, Robert Louis Stevenson, John Grierson and Muriel Spark, for example. It might mean the raised saleroom prices for paintings by the 'Glasgow Boys' and the 'Scottish colourists' and of contemporary Scottish artists, or claiming a new national prominence for writers who remained in Scotland, rather than moving south, such as Alasdair Gray, Liz Lochhead, Iain Banks, Kathleen Jamie, Ian Rankin and A. L. Kennedy. In popular culture, the success of the Hollywood film *Braveheart* (1985) led to a well-publicized rediscovery of William Wallace and Robert Bruce, while debates over the film's accuracy gave the Wars of Independence a much higher profile and renewed emphasis in history syllabuses. Nationhood and national identity became, in the 1990s, a fashionable subject, and the Scottish 'renaissance' fitted the context, with a determined effort to fight the 'cultural cringe' (a term originally invented in Australia). Of course, there was a great deal of selectivity in this literary-historical-cultural rebuilding of the border, including a variable degree of hostility to England.

This brings us back to the subject of gender. Where, if anywhere, was gender as a component in this revival? While far more of the new creative artists were women than in the past, gender-blindness had been for many years a feature both of popular culture and of mainstream historical works. Not so very long ago, in 1980, Clifford Hanley could describe the stereotypical portrait of the Scots as follows:

> The Scots are tall, rugged people who live in the mountain fastness of their native land, on a diet of oatmeal, porridge and whisky. They wear kilts of a tartan weave, play a deafening instrument called the bagpipes, are immediately hospitable but cautious with money . . . They are sparing with words, but when they speak they speak the truth. When they leave their native land they immediately rise to the top in other people's industries and professions. (Quoted in Houston and Knox, 2001: xv)

Scots are familiar with 'tartanry', as it is sometimes called, of which this is a caricatured example. Could any comparable caricature of Scottish women be composed – or were they supposed to be like women everywhere else? On display in every souvenir shop in Scotland, tartanry has a set of symbols which, when looked at seriously, turn out to be male icons: Burns suppers, malt whiskies, the kilt, the bagpipes, Harry Lauder, Sean Connery. This picture is often mocked, but its masculinist character is less often remarked on. The *Braveheart* phenomenon gave another but equally masculine depiction of Scottishness, as too did Irvine Welsh's novel *Trainspotting* (1993). Similarly, Scottish history was long characterized by a stress on what is sometimes called *l'histoire-bataille*, the history of war. In the past, this was routinely discussed as if it had no gender implications. The Flower of Scotland, its manhood, was lost at various battles, mostly with the English, and if women were mentioned it was as bystanders, lamenting the loss of their menfolk. Warfare was what Marilyne Frye in 1983 described as the male-imagined foreground:

> I imagine phallocratic reality to be the space and figures and motion which constitute the foreground and the constant repetitive activities of women to constitute and maintain the *background against which the foreground plays*. It is essential to the maintenance of the foreground reality that nothing within it refer in any way to anything in the background, and yet it depends absolutely on the existence of the background. (Quoted in Rose, 1993: 5; my italics)

Or, as Michèle Le Doeuff writes, 'work which, while claiming to be exhaustive, forgets about women's existence and concerns itself only with men' (quoted in Rose, 1993: 4). Other favourite historical subjects concerned areas of Scottish life which were – or were seen as – male preserves are trade unions and politics, the Covenanters, religious conflict and the Enlightenment. Women were not entirely absent from such accounts – in the early modern period, dynastic politics and elite women, as described above, played an important role – but they were only fleetingly glimpsed, except, significantly perhaps, in studies of witch-hunting. Until the 1990s, comparatively few books were published specifically on gender or women, unlike the situation south of the border.[4] Whether coincidentally or not, few women had posts in Scottish university history departments in the twentieth century. Various reasons for the neglect can be suggested. It is not really satisfactory to suggest that Scottish male historians were more intolerant of the early moves in women's history than historians elsewhere, although anecdotal accounts sometimes claim this. It could be argued perhaps that Scottish women/ feminist historians were not numerous enough, or confident enough, to overcome a certain institutional weight of inertia; or that it needed the higher profile of Scottish studies generally to stimulate the emergence of new thinking. But it would not be inaccurate to call *most* twentieth-century Scottish historiography 'masculinist' in the sense used by Gillian Rose, in that 'it falsely assumes that the experience of men can represent all experiences' (1993: 53).

Whatever the reason, gender has in recent years had a higher profile in the reassertion of Scottish identity, but to what extent? It has to be conceded that the newest Scottish history is not as gender-blind as the old, though references to it have sometimes taken the form of a bad conscience rather than analysis. With a dearth of serious empirical studies, there was a tendency among writers of the new Scottish history (say, post-1990) to recognize the omission by issuing a disclaimer: 'one of the main features of Scottish culture in the twentieth century is . . . that it has been male-dominated, arguably to a greater extent than most modern societies'; 'Scotland was a male-dominated culture'; 'the overwhelmingly male-dominated nature of Scottish society'; '[there are ways in which] Scottish history and culture have been crudely phallocentric'.[5]

One approach, often well intentioned, is the chapter on women or gender in a survey – and there are plenty of examples in recent works (see, for example, Devine, 1999). But this strategy, which ignores 'men' and 'masculinity', remains open to the objection that it corrals 'women' inside a kind of internal border, rather than allowing gender to be universally relevant. All those border wars, religious disputes, the Enlightenment, the Disruption, have yet to be seriously analysed from the point of view of gender. But there is another problem. In some ways, a nationalist approach, pursued with passion, has worked against notions of inclusiveness, of which gender-encompassing is one. In 1995, Christopher Whyte edited an essay collection, largely on literary topics, *Gendering the Nation*, which set out to disprove the proposition that 'Nationalism is always bad news for women' – recognizing that it sometimes has been.[6]

An example that well illustrated nationalist gender-blindness was a collective book, *Scotland: A Concise Cultural History* (1993), intended to 'mark the start of a new subject in its own right, Scotland as a great creative force in European civilization' (P. H. Scott, 1993). Its jacket lists thirty-three cultural heroes, from Duns Scotus to John Grierson and Sorley MacLean, by way of Burns, Hogg, Telford, Kelvin, Stevenson, MacDiarmid and others, to enforce the claim that 'No nation of its size has contributed so much to world culture'. It is an impressive list for a small nation with a history of emigration. But none of those mentioned was a woman, nor did women feature more than minimally in its pages. In that case, as in others, the nationalist agenda has apparently occupied the foreground, pushing gender to the side.

This can still happen, although the years since 1999 in particular have witnessed more moves towards gender-awareness in Scottish society, with the greater prominence of women in public life (politics, the law and the kirk), the publication of more books on women, and gendered analyses of Scottish history, the appointment of more feminists to academic positions, and more Ph.D. theses tackling the primary research on gender. In terms of public life, the new Scottish Parliament, like the new Welsh Assembly, was radically different from Westminster in one respect: the deliberate policy aim of having more women representatives. The Scottish Trades Union Congress (STUC) women's committee and other bodies lobbied effectively, and the Constitutional Convention of 1994 recommended a voluntary target of 40 per cent women in any future parliament. The Labour party explicitly, and the Scottish National Party (SNP) de facto, operated a policy of placing more women both in winnable seats and in good positions on the regional lists. The result was that of the 129 members of the Scottish Parliament (MSPs) in 1999, 48 or 37.2 per cent were women in the first legislature, a remarkably high proportion in European politics (28 of them were Labour, 15 SNP; see below for present situation). Several women embarked on careers as ministers, and various family-friendly rules were introduced to the new Parliament (see Reynolds, 2002). The Parliament also commissioned an artwork celebrating Scottish women's rights: a ceramic wall designed by Shauna McMullan to feature 100 women, famous or obscure, which was inaugurated in 2006. More women were also present in local politics and a woman provost was no longer a complete rarity.

In terms of historical research, the Scottish Women's History Network (operating since the 1990s and renamed Women's History Scotland in 2006) has provided a focus for research and regular conferences, and Scottish history departments now have more graduate students writing theses on gendered subjects, to an extent that would have been unlikely only a decade or two ago. Two recent publication projects in particular were collective endeavours: the *Biographical Dictionary*, and the collection of essays *Gender in Scottish History since 1700*, following an earlier book on women in medieval and early modern Scotland.[7] Masculinity has become a regular topic for conference papers, if not yet many full-length works. So it can be argued that, at least to some extent, gender has been part of the revival of Scottish history and Scottishness has been part of the feminist agenda. That still leaves us with some questions of a broader nature about gender and frontiers in a context of nationalism, in particular with the much remarked revival of the fortunes of the Scottish National Party in 2007. Is nationalism really bad news for women or not?

State of the union: gender as the last frontier?

By an irony that will not have gone unnoticed, exactly 300 years after the 1707 Act of Union, the pro-independence Scottish National Party emerged from the elections held on 3 May 2007 as the single party with the most seats in the Scottish Parliament – if only just: 47 seats to Labour's 46. It captured a substantial share of the popular vote and also scored highly in the local elections held on the same day.

In anticipation of the tercentenary of 1707, several works looking at the state of the union had appeared shortly before this. In particular, Chris Whatley in his 2006 study looked in detail at the debates of 1707, nuancing judgements about the reasons behind the union. He concluded that 'the long-held and popular notion that the Scots were bought and sold for English gold seems not to stand up to close scrutiny. On its own, neither does the argument that Scots bargained away their parliament for free trade and access to England's colonies' (p. xiv). He went on to refer, like Linda Colley, to the period of apparent satisfaction with the union in the nineteenth century, when 'unionist nationalism' reflected the greater equity and parity of esteem for Scotland in the union, at a time when it was both benefiting from and contributing to the imperial venture' (p. 17). During the twentieth century, he conceded, 'as Britain's wings were clipped . . . the benefits of the unionist partnership became less apparent to the Scots'. Nevertheless, 'there is a belief amongst historians that, economically as well as socially, Scotland has benefited greatly from its position within the United Kingdom for much of the twentieth century and continues to do so'. Whatley argued that after devolution, 'the union was shaken but remains intact', and that 'the *Braveheart* effect . . . seems to have worn off . . . those Scots who call for independence are in a minority' (p. 19).

In 2007, despite the election result, repeated opinion polling seemed to show that this assumption was correct. Only a minority of Scots appeared to be in favour of independence from the rest of Britain. It seemed likely that disenchantment with the Labour government in Westminster and lack of enthusiasm for it north of the border was more of a factor in the election result than a great surge for independence. At the time of going to press, the hostility of most other parties at Holyrood to a referendum on independence and the absence of an overall majority has obliged the SNP-led government to compromise on this and other issues for the time being. Nevertheless, public opinion has already shown signs of more sympathy to various aspects of going it alone, and Scottish independence does not seem quite as unthinkable today as it has so far been in our lifetimes. (Since a UK general election will be held between going to press and publication, all bets are off for the evolution of Scottish public opinion over the next few years.)

When I gave this paper at the Glamorgan conference in 2005, I ended it by remarking that the greater confidence assumed by Scottish culture was arguably making the border with England bulk less large as a preoccupation, and that Scotland was becoming a more open society and culture, in ways that could be seen as promising at all levels, including gender. Does the recent surge in support for the SNP suggest any nuances to this picture?

In one respect, and perhaps surprisingly, the SNP leader has gone out of his way to tone down hostility to England, by repeatedly saying that Scotland would be 'best pals' with England (and Wales presumably) if it were independent. On the other hand, where at one time 'independence within Europe' was a prominent SNP slogan, more wariness has crept in and a greater instrumentalism and defensiveness towards the European Union can be seen in the 2007 manifesto:

> In the EU we will press for Scotland to *take the lead* in negotiations on fisheries . . . The SNP wants a *stronger voice for Scotland in the EU* and we will seek to improve direct contacts with the Commission, reform Scottish Parliamentary scrutiny of EU legislative proposals and seek closer relations with other parliaments. We propose enhanced procedures for implementing European legislation in Scotland and *better* post-implementation monitoring to reduce the burden and free Ministers to introduce *legislation that suits Scotland.* (SNP manifesto (2007); my italics)

In other words, and despite references to international aid, the rhetoric of twenty-first-century Scottish nationalism could be seen as rather more defensive of Scotland's primary interests than outward looking, at least in the world of politics where, after all, electoral considerations count. Fisheries loom large, for example, but there was nothing specific in the SNP manifesto about immigration into Scotland.

Nor is there more than an extremely brief mention of gender, which was indeed conspicuously absent from most parties' election literature. (The exception was the Scottish Socialist Party, which won no seats.) The SNP manifesto has a short section on approving anti-discrimination legislation of all kinds. Despite the still-strong showing of women politicians, gender as a hot issue appeared to have moved virtually out of sight by the 2007 elections. In terms of the representation of women, all the same, the figures were strong by comparison with Westminster, though slightly lower than in the past. The SNP contingent was not notable for gender balance, despite having been led until recently at Holyrood by a woman, Nicola Sturgeon (now Deputy First Minister and Cabinet Secretary for Health). However, there are currently 5 women ministers out of 17 including some in senior posts. Of the 129 new MSPs elected in 2007, there are now 42 women: 23 Labour out of 46, 14 SNP out of 47, 2 Liberal Democrat out of 16, 5 Conservative out of 16 and 1 independent. Labour MSPs at Holyrood were briefly led by a woman, Wendy Alexander, and Annabel Goldie is currently the Conservatives' leader.[8]

Despite what may be seen as shifts in emphasis in the political context, I would still argue that Scotland is today culturally a much more confident place, with little need to be defensive: the Edinburgh Festival is very far from being the only international event of the year, and is much less of an alien body than in the past, and both Edinburgh and Glasgow can claim to be among the many active poles of European culture. Certainly in the last few years there has been much more immigration into Scotland, especially from eastern Europe, and this was explicitly welcomed by a former first minister, Jack McConnell, as a bonus for an ageing nation (although the newcomers have sometimes met a mixed reception, here as elsewhere in the UK). And Scotland's culture is arguably no longer as aggressively masculine as when Carol Anderson and Glenda Norquay wrote passionately about the 'male monopoly on Scottish culture' in the magazine *Cencrastus* in 1984.

In academic terms, greater openness and less inward-looking preoccupations can be seen in the now fashionable subjects of study: a renewed interest in what is known today as 'the Scottish diaspora', worldwide. As a country of massive emigration, Scotland's identity has been sometimes as visible outside Scotland as inside. Some of the 'Scottish identity' writing specifically centres on the British Empire or indeed 'the Scottish Empire',[9] arguing that much of what made it British was its Scottish contingent of soldiers, administrators and missionaries. This impact could be for good or ill, and today's analysis tends to put it in a postcolonial framework. New studies are also more gender conscious than in the past. The missionary world was one in which women were particularly concerned and they can be studied more dispassionately than when the hagiographical model was current. One of the benefits of gender analysis means rescuing women from condescending views of their 'achievements' and allowing them to have negative or disputed qualities (see Breitenbach, 2005). Another possible new focus is the participation of Scots in international organizations: Lady Aberdeen (Ishbel Gordon) figures in the index of no general histories of Scotland, for example, yet she was president of the International Council of Women for many years between 1900 and the 1930s, and internationally highly visible.[10]

There is some evidence, then, that the diaspora, immigration, gender and a less narrow vision are going to shape Scottish historiography in the next ten years much more than in the past. 'It is perhaps only in this present generation that a more inclusive vision of Scottish culture has begun to be formulated', Michael Lynch wrote in 1993 (P. H. Scott, 1993: 37). Such a formula has several possibilities, relating to crossing of borders in both directions, whether immigration from Ireland in the nineteenth century, the place within Scottish culture of expatriates from England and Wales in the twentieth century, or the increasing numbers of new Scots from further afield (the Commonwealth, eastern Europe). In an optimistic view (and it remains unfulfilled at present), Scotland would be able to move on from some rather one-dimensional stereotypes towards the 'polyphonic' culture Robert Crawford wishfully imagines, with many voices, differing in region, ethnic origin, language, sex, class and religion (Crawford, 1997: 93).

More fluid ideas about borders would undoubtedly fit better with feminist analyses of nationalism and national identity. Virginia Woolf's remark in *Three Guineas*, is often quoted in this context: 'As a woman, I have no country, as a woman I want no country. As a woman, my country is the whole world' (Woolf, 1977 [1938]: 125). She was writing in a particular historical context in 1938, when women, especially married women, were still excluded from certain civil and civic rights and were effectively absent from property owning and most powerful institutions. They had no stake (as New Labour would say) in the nation. At that time, women were deemed to take the nationality of their husbands in many countries (like medieval queens) and could often not easily travel abroad unaccompanied; as late as the 1960s a woman who got married was obliged to change the name on her British passport. In this, as in many other ways, international politics like national politics 'has, in a sense, been enacted on a field of gender', as Joan Scott put it (Scott, 1999: 49). Is nationalism, in however benign a form, still a threat when looked at from a gendered perspective?

A strong current in feminist thought certainly thinks so. Doreen Massey has argued that 'All attempts to institute horizons, to establish boundaries, to secure the identity of places can . . . be seen to be attempts to stabilise the meaning of particular envelopes of space-time', which she calls a 'culturally masculine need'. She goes on to quote Chantal Mouffe's remark that communities are only 'precariously and temporarily sutured', and argues that this can be seen in positive terms (Massey, 1994: 5). Or, as Rosi Braidotti has written, using different imagery from that of marriage or rape with which this chapter started, in a postmodern world, the feminist can be seen as a nomad. Turning Virginia Woolf's words round, Braidotti suggests that the feminist thinker is not so much a homeless person as 'one who has abandoned the idea of fixity, and is happy to look outwards, regularly crossing and recrossing borders, settling in more than one place in a life'. She sees the nomadic subject as a myth that enables one to think across established categories and has come up with this much-quoted formulation, on which I will end: 'blurring boundaries without burning bridges' (1994: 4).[11] It is an individual rather than a collective formula, but an attractive one.

Notes

1 This pattern of international marriages was the norm: Margaret Logie (1330–73), who was Scottish born, was the first Scotswoman since the eleventh century to marry a reigning king of Scots. But there were many more foreign queens to come. Note that for illustrative purposes, I am largely setting aside questions of queenship and the relative power of queens. For a recent discussion of these topics, see Earenfight, 2007.

2 Not that it was always an easy relation: an uneasy sense of being overshadowed by their large neighbour is common to many countries living in close proximity to a powerful state. (The term 'sleeping with an elephant' was coined in Canada to describe the border with the United States, and has been used of Scotland too.) Nevertheless, as Linda Colley writes, 'by 1837, Scotland [while it] still retained many of the characteristics of a distinct nation . . . was comfortably contained within a bigger nation. It was British as well as Scottish' (Colley, 1992: 373).

3 Both Scotland and Wales have experienced such cultural renaissances during the twentieth century with rather different chronologies, and the reader will not need chapter and verse. Note that Colley (1992: 373), remarks that Welsh culture, in part because of its language dimension, was always more distinctly 'foreign' to the English, though that remark begs some questions. Note too that the situation of Gaelic in Scotland, although much favoured lately, does not approach that of Welsh in Wales.

4 Although T. C. Smout commented in 1986 that 'the history of the family and of child upbringing and the place of the woman within and without the home is so neglected in Scotland as to verge on becoming a historiographical disgrace' (292; the terminology here is itself rather telling).

5 For full references to these quotations from recent histories, all by well-intentioned male historians, see my chapter in Abrams et al., 2006: 171 and notes. The protestations seem to me to be exaggerated. Scottish society in the past was arguably no more male dominated than that of many of its neighbours. Its historiography is another matter.

6 It is perhaps not surprising that this is a collection of literary criticism, since gender has been more present analytically in this field than in history.

7 For references to the large (and expanding) number of publications on women and gender in Scotland since the 1990s, as well as the pioneering works before that and discussions of 'the gender agenda', see, Ewan et al., 2006: introduction; Abrams et al., 2006: especially chapters 1 and 2; and Ewan and Meikle, 1999. For the purposes of exposition, I have generalized about the earlier period, but Rosalind Marshall, Rosalind Mitchison, Leah Leneman and Elspeth King, among others, published trail-blazing books in the 1980s.

8 Alexander resigned after a few months over an infringement of campaign rules. For slightly different overall figures see *The Scotsman*, 5 May 2007; latest figures from the Scottish Parliament website, consulted 11 November 2009 (*www.scottish.parliament.uk*). The press did not immediately remark much on this point. Perhaps it could be said that women MSPs are now so well accepted that it seems normal.

9 The title of a (controversial) book by Michael Frye; cf. also, T. M. Devine, *Scotland's Empire* and many publications by Marjory Harper.

10 See the entry on her in the *Biographical Dictionary of Scottish Women*. International women's organizations have lately been the object of more sustained study generally than in the past.

11 Braidotti's formula is particularly attractive to me as a Welsh woman living in Scotland, with a family that includes French, Russian, American and Finnish members. The previous quotation is also by Braidotti, from an essay which could not be located, but the introduction to *Nomadic Subjects* (1994) gives a comprehensive explanation of this stimulating idea, of capital importance in any consideration of gender and borders.

Bibliography

Abrams, Lynn, Eleanor Gordon, Deborah Simonton and Eileen Yeo (eds) (2006). *Gender in Scottish History since 1700*, Edinburgh: Edinburgh University Press.

Anderson, Carol and Glenda Norquay (1984). 'Superiorism', *Cencrastus*, 15, 8–10.

Braidotti, Rosi (1994). *Nomadic Subjects: Embodiment and Sexual Difference in Contemporary Feminist Theory*, New York: Columbia University Press.

Breitenbach, Esther (2005). 'Empire, religion and national identity: Scottish Christian imperialism in the 19th and early 20th centuries', Ph.D. thesis, University of Edinburgh.

Colley, Linda (1992). *Britons: Forging the Nation 1707–1837*, London: Pimlico.

Crawford, Robert (1997). 'Dedefining Scotland', in S. Bassnett (ed.), *Studying British Cultures*, London: Routledge.

Devine, T. M. (1999). *The Scottish Nation 1700–2000*, London: Allen Lane.

——(2003). *Scotland's Empire*, London: Allen Lane.

Earenfight, Theresa (2007). 'Without the persona of the prince: kings, queens and the idea of monarchy in medieval Europe', *Gender and History*, 19, 1, 1–21.

Ewan, Elizabeth and Mauren Meikle (eds) (1999). *Women in Scotland c.1100–1750*, East Linton: Tuckwell.

Ewan, Elizabeth, Sue Innes, Rose Pipes and Siân Reynolds (eds) (2006). *The Biographical Dictionary of Scottish Women*, Edinburgh: Edinburgh University Press.

Frye, Michael (2001). *The Scottish Empire*, East Linton: Tuckwell.

Houston, R. A. and W. W. J. Knox (eds) (2001). *The New Penguin History of Scotland*, London: Allen Lane.

Lynch, Michael (ed.) (2001). *The Oxford Companion to Scottish History*, Oxford: Oxford University Press.

Massey, Doreen (1994). *Space, Place and Gender*, Cambridge: Polity.

Rose, Gillian (1993). *Feminism and Geography*, Cambridge: Polity.

Reynolds, Siân (2002). 'Lateness, amnesia and unfinished business: gender and democracy in twentieth-century Europe', *European History Quarterly*, 32, 1, 85–110.

Scott, Joan (1999). *Gender and the Politics of History*, rev. edn, New York: Columbia University Press.

Scott, P. H. (1993). *Scotland: A Concise Cultural History*, Edinburgh: Mainstream.

Smout, T. C. (1986). *A Century of the Scottish People*, London: Collins.

SNP manifesto (2007), *www.snp.org*.

Whatley, C. A. with Derek Patrick (2006). *The Scots and the Union*, Edinburgh: Edinburgh University Press.

Whyte, Christopher (ed.) (1995). *Gendering the Nation: Studies in Modern Scottish Literature*, Edinburgh: Edinburgh University Press.

Woolf, Virginia (1977 [1938]). *Three Guineas*, London: Hogarth (Penguin edn).

10

Sexual/Cultural Hybridity in the 'New' South Africa: Emergent Sites of Transnational Queer Politics

WILLIAM J. SPURLIN

The processes of transnational and diasporic movement have helped influence the politics of culture in South Africa in its ongoing movement towards full democracy, especially following the end of economic isolation after the collapse of apartheid. Early attempts at the ongoing deracialization of South African society and African National Congress (ANC) initiatives to bring about democratically based social change and freedom from discrimination across the social register in the years immediately following the collapse of apartheid are peculiar to South African history to the extent that, as Albie Sachs notes, South African culture is not separate from a history of political struggle and liberation (Sachs, 1998: 241). The beginning of the shift towards democratization in South Africa, along with its fuller participation in world markets, similarly helped broaden social spaces for lesbians and gay men to claim political viability and solidarity in ways that were previously not possible under the apartheid regime and the concomitant repression of human rights. While colonialism in South Africa certainly helped to lay the foundation for apartheid, as I argue elsewhere, it would be naive, or quite plainly wrong in the case of South Africa, to assume that decolonization straightforwardly and self-evidently occurred with independence from colonial control, when, in fact, the apartheid regime, in many respects, solidified the colonial legacy.[1] Indeed, the new meanings of national identity and citizenship in postcolonial nations, imagined and sustained through discourses of nationalism, often slide from operating as a site of opposition (to imperial control) to one of oppression with regard to racial, ethnic and linguistic differences, with regard to the status of women (in so far as gender equality is inhibited through appeals to 'culture' and 'tradition' that keep women in traditional roles) and with regard to lesbians and gay men (whose 'lifestyles' are often regarded as western aberrations and therefore as remnants of empire).

Yet the attempts at redressing the inequalities brought about by colonial and racist domination in South Africa cannot be products of national containment alone. Conceding that practices of resistance are tied to a specific history and to material, cultural and ideological conditions in South Africa, they are not confined or bound to that geographical space alone, but also include a reimagining of social space beyond strict national demarcations. How have new modes of self-representation and the formation of individual and collective identities in the 'New' South Africa been influenced not only by internal revisions of (South) African nationhood and citizenship, but also by the processes of cultural hybridization enabled by transnational liberation struggles and practices of resistance that may exceed a reified identification with reclaimed national identity in South Africa? Seeing culture as a site of hybridity and as circulatorial, rather than as limited only to a given territorial space, can help destabilize fixed national identities defined through essentialized categories of race, ethnicity, gender and sexuality, and thereby challenge national cultural hegemony and expose new sites of difference. Further, as Arif Dirlik argues, national cultural hegemony has resulted historically in the denial of full political and participatory citizenship for those citizens who have resisted assimilation into renewed conceptualizations of national culture (Dirlik, 2002: 94), and this would include, of course, those marked by sexual difference. Hybridity, conceived as 'in-betweenness', has particular relevance to queerness both as an intellectual strategy and as a political praxis since queerness disrupts and exceeds the coherence of normative citizenship tied to the reproduction of heteronormative social relations.[2]

Hybridity can function as a theoretical *and* political strategy to challenge nationalist discourses in postcolonial contexts that view any Western influence on local indigenous cultures as contaminating a self-contained, yet highly invented, 'pure' original state that supposedly existed prior to colonial domination. Hybridity, so conceived, helps deconstruct the West/East binary put in place by national cultural hegemony.[3] But Dirlik warns that hybridity, understood only on the level of epistemology, abstracted from its anchorings in actual socio-historical practices, runs the risk of blurring significant distinctions between various differences, masks social inequalities to the extent that one reduces to a state of hybridity all those who may be considered to be 'marginal', and fails to ask what new identities the dialogic encounters with other cultures may produce (Dirlik, 2002: 105–6). While Dirlik is correct in stating that not all marginalities can be reduced to sameness, is it possible for hybridity, read as a condition of history, to operate credibly on the level of epistemology alone, apart from socio-historical contextualization, a premise which seems to structure the shortcomings of cultural hybridity Dirlik highlights? My point is that just as the self is bound, indeed formed, by social, ideological and historical constraints, no cultural or national identity, as part of its movement through history, can exist untouched by the circulation of cultures, presently occurring at increasingly higher speeds across the globe (through increased migration and greater human mobility across vast distances, through the rapid transnational exchange of commodities, as well as through the rapid movement of culture by electronic means and the mass media). Along these lines, then, agency, especially in a collective or cultural sense, rather than in an individual one, can be produced only in the interactions, contradictions and interstitial spaces produced in the encounters between cultures rather than imposed by anti-colonial nationalism, on the one hand, or by transplanted social movements (for example, feminism and queer politics) from the West on the other.

Thinking of culture in terms of hybridization can help disrupt dichotomous thinking and operate as a site of transnational interaction and as an impetus for radical social change provided that conjunctural encounters between cultures are theorized in relation to specific historical and material conditions, and provided that social inequalities made more visible by the encounter, along with the underlying hegemonies, are articulated and exposed. South Africa's transition from apartheid to a juridical recognition of the broadest range of human rights possible has been informed by the dialogical tension between the local and the global – that is, the political transition has been mediated by the resistance to the specific historical precedent of apartheid, and its colonial antecedent, and by the influence of globalised human rights discourses and politics. This specific history of struggle against state-enforced racism and a recent cultural and political context of democratization and attempts to shed a racist past is critical to understanding queerness as a site of resistance to new (as well as to historically inherited) forms of national cultural hegemony that perpetuate heteronormativity, and to understanding queer politics and identities in South Africa as a hybrid space. Surely the democracy that has been slowly emerging in South Africa, largely through material practices struggling to become more closely aligned with what is juridically proscribed, is reducible neither to the history of internal struggles in South Africa nor to human rights discourses and politics elsewhere (how many other countries have a constitutional clause specifically making discrimination by sexual orientation unlawful?), but is influenced significantly and partially by both. The process of hybridity in this sense, according to Homi Bhabha, has enabled not only 'a turning of boundaries and limits into the *in-between* spaces through which the meanings of cultural and political authority are negotiated' (Bhabha, 2000 [1990]: 4), but similarly accounts for heterogeneity and difference, and for potential social transformation, rather than being mired only in abstract theorizing as Dirlik suggests.[4] When Bhabha speaks of hybridity as 'incorporating new "people" in relation to the body politic, generating other sites of meaning and, inevitably, in the political process, producing unmanned [*sic*] sites of political antagonism and unpredictable forces for political representation' (Bhabha, 2000 [1990]: 4), he could very well be speaking about what has emerged, and continues to emerge, in the political and social space of the 'New' South Africa to the extent that he is asking us to examine the relations, the spaces, between nations and cultures, between past and present. Since queer theoretical enquiry and political praxis are concerned largely with the proliferation of social differences, and with resistance to all normativities and fixed borders (not only sexual ones), and, since cultural hybridity functions as a site of destabilization of normative categories, and therefore as a site of queerness, they can be productively linked as modes of cultural analysis and critique.

Part of the challenge to national cultural hegemony – in so far as it attempts to fix national spheres with self-contained, historically decontextualized meanings pertaining to national identity – as well as the challenge to the imperialist tendencies of Western queer studies/activism in the West, must include the circulation of sexuality transnationally, both as a materiality and as a discourse, which can further unsettle reductive readings of homosexuality as alien to particular nations and to particular racial, ethnic, or national identities, and as having an originary, privileged status in the West. Acknowledging the potential of queer discourse as a site of cultural hybridity does not mean that global influences are reducible to the familiar trope of non-reciprocal penetration; nor does it mean that the flow of power (coming from Western queer influence or coming from national cultural hegemony in particular nation-states that view homosexuality as a Western decadence) is unidirectional. Contentious practices of resistance in South Africa historically have been intimately connected to struggles for fundamental human rights and to the resistance to fixed identities previously imposed by state-enforced racism. Queer practices in South Africa also stem from these historically and culturally specific struggles and from the building of broader coalitions for human equality and human rights for all citizens. As Michiel Heyns has clarified, historically there has been a link between queer identity and political dissent in South Africa. This has meant, as Heyns explains, that (queer) dissociation from heteropatriarchy is a disavowal of, and resistance to, the political situation which heteropatriarchy in South Africa has wrought (Heyns, 1998: 115). Queer resistance in South Africa, then, is not a simple mimicry of Western models of queer politics, as some forms of cultural nationalism may imply, but western queer discourses and political activism, which circulate through global linkages (such as the Internet and information technology), are co-opted and used strategically for local political purposes.

In spite of globalized efforts to achieve a single world economic system, not only is an opposition between Africa and the West kept in place by the continual peripherization of Africa under such a regime, which heightens the vulnerability of its local economies, but a hierarchy reminiscent of colonialism is perpetuated to the extent that a prestige is still attached to Western culture, economics and technology. At the same time, the history of hierarchical, dichotomous relations between Africa and Europe have, of course, been similarly perpetuated by the West and are relied upon in the economic financialization of the globe. Largely citing and critiquing Jürgen Habermas, Emmanuel Eze has pointed out that Africa has served paradigmatically as the 'mythical' world against which one can establish the achievements of the modern Western, 'rational' world-view; a view which, in spite of the growth of European capitalist societies, whose political and economic growth depended, from the seventeenth century onwards, on imperial domination, transatlantic slavery, colonization and ideologies of white racial supremacy, still reads Europe as scientific, socially differentiated and familiar, and Africa as animistic, socially totalistic and alien (Eze, 2002: 49–50; 58; see also Habermas, 1984: 8–74). As long as Africa is discursively and economically inscribed by the West as 'a continent apart', Africa will remain outside the reach of global investors and traders and the idea of a free market in a new, globalized order remains highly problematic and exclusionary.

The unevenness of access and development in an increasingly globalized world is especially significant for non-heteronormative sexualities in Africa with respect to HIV infection and AIDS. South Africa, in particular, has the highest HIV-positive population worldwide, presently estimated at about 5.7 million of its total population of 47 million, with the largest concentration of sufferers located in the province of KwaZulu-Natal; the government has only recently begun to provide anti-retroviral drugs to those South Africans who are HIV-positive and cannot afford them.[5] Yet, in representing AIDS in South Africa, it is important not to read a simplistic opposition between *global* understandings of AIDS (as narrated by the World Health Organization and Western medicine, for example, in terms of mapping HIV infection and tracking its movement, as well as statistics on the global distribution of drugs and education/prevention programmes) and *local* needs, economic conditions and resistances. Rather, it is important to focus on the dialogical tension between global and specifically localized spheres, acknowledging the imperialist impulses of the West in globalized discourses on the representation of AIDS worldwide, and the specificities not only of local needs and conditions in South Africa, but of resistances to Western hegemonies which, in turn, create new sites of hybridity and difference that can transform dominant narratives of AIDS globally.

Certainly the hierarchies between Africa and the West are reinscripted not only in Western narratives of the AIDS pandemic, but historically in medical discourses which attempted to locate the disease in geographic regions and track the transmission patterns of HIV infection. The use of the term 'African AIDS' has mobilized racist ideologies of unchecked, unbridled sexuality in Africa and among black people in general.[6] As with Western readings of heterosexual sex between indigenous Africans, the idea of homosexuality being a foreign, Western intrusion in postcolonial national imaginaries also has its roots in a history of Western imperialism, in so far as colonial management had an effect on local sexualities by enforcing draconian laws against homosexual practices as part of its 'civilizing' mission.

The reluctance of African nations to admit to a presence of homosexuality within their borders, and even higher rates of HIV infection than were originally assumed or predicted, is an effect of imperialism, tied to deep-seated historical anxieties by African nations about discursive appropriations of African sexuality by the West in decadent terms, appropriations which remain in discourses surrounding the global surveillance and tracking of HIV infection. The reading of homosexuality as un-African by some strands of African cultural nationalism, and the subsequent denial of the practice of anal intercourse among indigenous African men who have sex with men, produced a significant gap and subsequent delay in education and prevention programmes among groups of men who escaped the categories of the West, given that the WHO saw HIV transmission in Africa largely in heterosexual terms in the early days of the pandemic, and given that some men practised anal sex with other men but did not necessarily identify as gay. AIDS educators were not initially sensitive to the fact that anal sex has different meanings and values in other symbolic regimes that need to be addressed in helping those men, who may engage in the practice of anal sex with other men as partners, recognize that 'safer sex' applies to them as well, even if they resist taking on a gay identity as it is understood in the West.

At the same time, however, the increased participation of local queer and AIDS activists has helped create a transnational, hybrid space of queerness to question radically the nexus of sexual, racial and national inventions in general, and the global management of AIDS in particular. According to Cindy Patton, the adoption of the more descriptive phrase 'men who have sex with men', or MSM, by the World Health Organization's Global Programme on AIDS (GPA), though unwieldy and not completely divorced from Western understandings of homosexuality, enabled GPA HIV educators to work more sensitively with local homosexualities, while, in turn, individuals in South Africa shed light on their own complex sexualities which deconstructed Euro-American understandings of homosexuality as a more or less distinct identity and community. And, as local queers in South Africa began to achieve global mobility and exposure by participating in local and global AIDS politics, they broadened the sphere of international queer politics while insisting on their own cultural differences (Patton, 2002: 81–2).

Yet the rubric 'men who have sex with men' also sanitizes (anal) sex between them, and, more importantly, provides a thinly veiled screen, or closet, if you will, not only of secrecy, but of a 'safe' identity that is more legibly heterosexual and, therefore, supposedly not at risk for HIV transmission or infection. The problem with Western interpretations of homosexuality as it is practised amongst indigenous men is not so much the conflation of anal sex with homosexuality, which was a problem early in the pandemic for Western GPA education consultants, but is the conflation of sexual *practice* with sexual *identity*, which places Foucault's proposition of a shift in homosexuality in the nineteenth century from a temporary aberration (based on specific acts) to an emergent identic category *even more* firmly in the West (Foucault, 1980 [1976]: 42–3).[7]

However, this does not diminish the importance of transnational spheres of exchange, the (queer) hybrid spaces between national borders, that are produced in the dialogical tension between globalized and local homosexualities in global AIDS narratives and policies to the extent that these hybrid spaces help destabilize related fixed social epistemes pertaining to race, nationality, gender and social class *in addition to* sexuality. Resisting the attachment of local homosexualities to Western prototypes of gay identity and community has helped transform the ways in which the GPA and those involved in the global management of AIDS read same-sex desires and sexual practices in local contexts outside the Euro-American axis. Similarly, globalized versions of queer desires and social activism have been differentially appropriated by queer activists in southern Africa and reworked strategically for political gain in local contexts. Local activists in South Africa do know of Western forms of queer activism, such as Act Up and Queer Nation, are intrigued by these new fractious politics and are excited to use them to find their own ways to explore the contingency of the nation even as the governments of some developing nations have officially rejected feminism and gay liberation as unwelcome intrusions into their national imaginaries (Patton, 2002: 24–5). By producing themselves as queer, through acknowledging cultural differences between local and Western forms of homosexuality and queer activism, activists in South Africa have been able to call to the attention of health ministers and government officials forms of homosexuality practised by indigenous citizens and to challenge the stigma associated with devastating illness and death related to AIDS.

Most importantly, South African queer activism has focused international attention on the plight of AIDS in South Africa by challenging placid assumptions in the West that the availability of anti-retroviral drugs means that HIV-positive status no longer necessarily signifies eventual death when this is precisely what it signifies for the nearly one thousand South Africans dying from AIDS-related diseases each day because they cannot afford the cost of treatment and because some health officials initially believed those living in poverty were not literate enough to follow the prescribed regimen of treatment. Activist Zackie Achmat, co-founder of the Treatment Action Campaign (TAC) in South Africa in 1998, has worked to ensure access to affordable treatment for all people with HIV/AIDS in the nation. The TAC fought quite successfully against international pharmaceutical companies that were profiting at the expense of those who suffer from HIV/AIDS and against bureaucratic delays and official neglect from the South African government. Calling attention to the production and distribution of power, destabilizing institutional, social and governmental facades and making use of the international media where possible, reminiscent of the strategies of Act Up in the US in the 1980s and 1990s, but also constructed by a specific South African history of disobedience, struggle and resistance, the TAC wilfully ignored international trade agreements pertaining to the production, import and use of less costly generic versions of patented anti-retroviral drugs for the treatment of HIV infection. The TAC has also exposed the bureaucratic inefficiency of the South African government of President Thabo Mbeki to manage effectively the AIDS crisis.

This blatant and unapologetic challenge to international drug policies and distribution practices, and the attendant media attention, helped force thirty-nine major pharmaceutical companies to withdraw their legal challenges against South African laws which allow for the production and importation of generic versions of the more expensive brand-name, patented drugs to be used to fight HIV/AIDS in South Africa (*Time*, 2003: 72). The French non-governmental human rights organization in South Africa, Médecins Sans Frontières (MSF) (Doctors without Borders), which has been working in the impoverished township of Khayelitsha near Cape Town, provides anti-retroviral medication to HIV/AIDS sufferers. While breaching patent law by importing generic drugs from Brazil, the results of the MSF intervention defied globalized discourses on AIDS in Africa that presume that poor Africans are too uneducated to take the pills responsibly and follow the strict regimen required: over 90 per cent of patients in the Khayelitsha programme in 2003 followed the regime and, after six months of treatment, the average patient in the pilot project gained 8.8 kilograms and the level of HIV in the blood dropped below the rate of detection (*Observer*, 2003: 5). Moreover, Achmat himself, who is also HIV-positive, and for a time refused to take anti-retrovirals until they were available for free to everyone through the national health care system, points both to the connection to and influences of the contentious practices of queer activism in the West and to the connection of local queer politics in South Africa to a history of opposition to oppressive regimes. One can almost hear intertextual references, such as 'We're here, we're queer, get used to it!' and 'Silence equals death' in Achmat's own words with a critical difference specific to local conditions in South Africa:

> It's not about being proud to *come out* and admit that the disease is with us [revealing the preoccupation with the visibility of queerness and HIV-infection in the West]. It's about being *realistic* [countering denials of homosexuality among indigenous Africans in nationalist discourses – while acknowledging local differences – and countering related denials of the high numbers of HIV-sufferers in South Africa as well as earlier denials among health and government officials relating to the efficacy of anti-retroviral drugs in the treatment of HIV infection and AIDS-related illnesses]. That's when *fighting* it can begin. (*Time*, 2003: 72; emphasis and parentheses mine)

The decolonization of desire has not occurred in the aftermath of colonization in postcolonial nations, nor can it occur if the hegemonic underpinnings of sexual identity and sexual politics in western culture remain undeconstructed as they intersect with non-western cultures. Indeed, as Anne McClintock reminds us, 'feminism is imperialist when it puts the interests and needs of privileged women in imperialist countries above the local needs of disempowered women and men, borrowing from patriarchal privilege' (McClintock, 1995: 384); and the connections of western queer discourse and politics to imperialism can, and often do, occur along similar, though not reducible, lines. One must distinguish between the *acknowledgement* of western queer influences (as opposed to their simple imposition and reproduction elsewhere) and their *strategic redeployment* for localized needs and purposes within a history of imperial domination. In South Africa, in particular, this also means looking at queer struggles in relation to broader post-apartheid struggles for democracy and racial equality. Recognizing the conjunctural encounter of global and local spheres, but locating queer in the hybrid space between them, rather than solely within one or the other, enables not only a reimagining of public and social space, but what Diana Fuss has termed an 'imaginative enactment of sexual *re*definitions, *re*borderizations, and *re*articulations' (Fuss, 1991: 7; emphasis mine). It is within these interstitial spaces that new sites of queer difference can take shape and produce renegotiations of sexual and gender identity, race, national borders and global influence. Refiguring sexual and national borders may not signify the end of queer struggles in South Africa or elsewhere, but may bring those South Africans who articulate and/or enact same-sex desires one step closer to determining how they wish to live, one step closer to 'incorporating new "people" in relation to [a new] body politic' that is fragmented, dispersed and not reducible to national borders alone.

Notes

1 For a more detailed discussion of the ways in which British imperial policy in the early twentieth century helped to set the cornerstone for racial segregation in South Africa and eventual apartheid, see Spurlin, 2006: 82–4 ff.

2 This point is worth making since, as Dirlik notes, hybridity is most often used as a site of critique around the categories of nation, race and ethnicity rather than gender or class (Dirlik, 2002: 108); but he, too, fails to make any connection whatsoever to sexuality or to the disruptive potential of hybridity as queer.

3 This preservation of national culture from western influence is also at the heart of what Chatterjee has referred to as the spiritual domain, that inner core of national culture that must be protected from the West. See Chatterjee, 1986: 2–3, and Chatterjee, 1993: 5–6, the latter of which shows how his argument surrounding anti-colonial nationalism is contextualized in his discussion and critique of Benedict Anderson's *Imagined Communities* (1983). But it must be said that even the spiritual domain of national culture, similar to its material domain of economic, scientific and technological development, cannot remain 'pure' from the influences of other cultures and, left uncritiqued, can potentially reinvent dichotomous, binary thinking.

4 Dirlik is concerned that theories such as Bhabha's result in hybridity as disruptive of binary modes of thinking on the level of epistemology,

being abstracted from social and historical anchorings rather than functioning as an articulation of actual human conditions. I disagree as my discussion of Bhabha in the text shows, but Dirlik's concern that hybridity could blur, 'in the name of difference, significant distinctions between different differences' (Dirlik, 2002: 106) is a significant point in need of consideration, and is one which I discuss in greater detail in *Imperialism within the Margins* (Spurlin, 2006: 107–10).

5 Largely as a result of increased negative publicity, in November 2003 the South African government approved a plan to provide free AIDS medication to all who needed it within five years. The distribution of anti-retroviral drugs began at hospitals in seven of the nine provinces on 1 April 2004, including Gauteng, South Africa's richest province, which includes Johannesburg and Pretoria, with distribution in other provinces following shortly thereafter. But it is estimated that the drugs are reaching only a small percentage of the people who need them; in fact, the distribution of anti-retroviral drugs has been so slow that, according to a report of the World Health Organization, only 33 per cent of South Africans in need of receiving treatment have been reached as of the end of 2006 (WHO, 2007). It remains unclear, therefore, whether the demand for treatment will be able to match resources, and whether a diagnosis of AIDS will signify a manageable disease, as is often but not always the case now in the West, as opposed to the eventual death sentence it has signified in South Africa for so long.

6 An article on AIDS in southern Africa in a 2002 issue of *The Economist* begins with a voyeuristic narrative of sexual practices in Botswana, describing some indigenous men's preference for 'dry sex' whereby women, in order to provide more pleasure for their male partners, insert toothpaste or herbs into their vaginas in order to prevent lubrication, which can lead to tears in vaginal tissues, bleeding during penetration and more easily allow the human immunodeficiency virus to penetrate the tissue (*Economist*, 2002: 27). While the practice, provided the male partner is HIV-infected, could place the woman at risk for infection, beginning an article about AIDS in southern Africa with 'dry sex' textually (re)produces an orientalist (and thereby voyeuristic) erotics that imagines non-Western exotic Otherness as a site of sexual deviance or excess, far removed from the sexual epistemologies and practices of the West.

7 Similarly, the reduction of safe-sex practices to the condom in globalized HIV prevention discourses simply replicates the idea of western, urbanized male sexual subjects who have sex with other men (Patton, 2002: 84), yet fails to acknowledge the more fluid shifts, the more contested borders, between hetero- and homosexuality within indigenous contexts.

Bibliography

Anderson, Benedict (1983). *Imagined Communities: Reflections on the Origin and Spread of Nationalism*, London: Verso.

Bhabha, Homi K. (ed.) (2000 [1990]). *Nation and Narration*, New York: Routledge.

Chatterjee, Partha (1993). *The Nation and its Fragments: Colonial and Postcolonial Histories*, Princeton: Princeton University Press.

——(2001 [1986]). *Nationalist Thought and the Colonial World: A Derivative Discourse?*, Minneapolis: University of Minnesota Press.

Dirlik, Arif (2002). 'Bringing history back in: of diasporas, hybridities, places, and histories', in Elisabeth Mudimbe-Boyi (ed.), *Beyond Dichotomies: Histories, Identities, Cultures, and the Challenge of Globalization*, Albany: State University of New York Press, pp. 93–127.

Economist (2002). 'Fighting back. Special report: AIDS in southern Africa', 11 May, 27–9.

Eze, Emmanuel Chukwudi (2002). 'Beyond dichotomies: communicative action and cultural hegemony', in Elisabeth Mudimbe-Boyi (ed.), *Beyond Dichotomies: Histories, Identities, Cultures, and the Challenge of Globalization*, Albany: State University of New York Press, pp. 49–68.

Foucault, Michel (1980 [1976]). *The History of Sexuality*, I, trans. Robert Hurley, Harmondsworth: Penguin.

Fuss, Diana (1991). 'Inside/Out', in Diana Fuss (ed.), *Inside/Out: Lesbian Theories, Gay Theories*, New York: Routledge, pp. 1–10.

Habermas, Jürgen (1984). *The Theory of Communicative Action. I: Reason and the Rationalization of Society*, trans. Thomas McCarthy, Boston: Beacon Press.

Heyns, Michiel (1998). 'A man's world: white South African gay writing and the State of Emergency', in Derek Attridge and Rosemary Jolly (eds), *Writing South Africa: Literature, Apartheid, and Democracy, 1970–1995*, Cambridge: Cambridge University Press, pp. 108–22.

McClintock, Anne (1995). *Imperial Leather: Race, Gender and Sexuality in the Colonial Contest*, New York: Routledge.

Observer (2003). 'Aids orphans' survival offers Africa hope', 25 May, 5.

Patton, Cindy (2002). *Globalizing AIDS*, Minneapolis: University of Minnesota Press.

Sachs, Albie (1998). 'Preparing ourselves for freedom', in Derek Attridge and Rosemary Jolly (eds), *Writing South Africa: Literature, Apartheid, and Democracy, 1970–1995*, Cambridge: Cambridge University Press, pp. 239–48.

Spurlin, William J. (2006). *Imperialism within the Margins: Queer Representation and the Politics of Culture in Southern Africa*, New York: Palgrave / Macmillan.

Time (2003). 'Dying to get AIDS drugs to all', 28 April, 72.

World Health Organization (WHO) (2007). 'Towards universal access: sealing up priority HIV/AIDS interventions in the public sector', 17 April.

11

The Construction and Negotiation of Racialized Borders in Cardiff Docklands

GLENN JORDAN AND CHRIS WEEDON

Introduction

This chapter is concerned with the relationship between race, gender and class in the construction of social borders as they were lived by the inhabitants of Wales's oldest multi-ethnic community in the 1930s and 1940s and the ways in which they figure in popular memory. Known until recently as Tiger Bay, this community is located in Butetown at the heart of Cardiff docklands. When given voice, those with links to it continue to evoke positive images. Listen, for example, to the voice of Fred Daniels from Aberdare in the Welsh Valleys, who became friends with Butetown evacuee children during the Second World War:

> I tell you what, and I say to my wife now, marvellous, I say. Years ago now, when I used to go down to Tiger Bay and you could walk through the park there and there'd be all colours, all the races imaginable, and it was safe. There was no fear of anybody, you know, molesting you or that type of thing, you know, or raping you, in those days. They were all great, nice people everybody. (Daniels, 2005)

Beyond the borders of the community perceptions have often been very different. In his family and community history, *The Tiger Bay Story*, Neil Sinclair relates how

> [you would hear] disparaging, second-hand 'hearsay' remarks, such as 'you couldn't walk down the streets (in safety) in Tiger Bay!', 'It was dangerous there!', 'Harm would come to you there!', 'They carry knives

> and all kinds of weapons down the Bay!' 'It was a terrible place. People gambled openly in the street!' (1993: 3)

In this chapter we draw on examples from the oral history of Cardiff docklands to look at how racialized borders were constructed between multi-ethnic Tiger Bay and the rest of Cardiff and beyond. We examine how individual perceptions of these borders were lived and negotiated by those contained within them and how they are laid down in the collective memory of Wales's longest-established mixed-race community. The specific focus of the chapter is on different gendered accounts of this lived experience as they are retold in the individual life stories of key members of the community covering the period before and during the Second World War. We look at the interweaving of gender, class and race and argue that the thematic tropes and coping strategies that emerge from these life stories tell us as much about the present as the past.

Since 1988 Butetown History & Arts Centre (*www.bhac.org*) has been collecting the people's history of Cardiff docklands. The archive that we have assembled consists largely of oral history interviews and photographs. This collection offers a unique insight from inside into life in Butetown – it allows access to both typical and exceptional narratives of the imagined and geographical community that was Tiger Bay, of its physical, class and racialized borders and of perceptions of life beyond them. In the preface to *The Tiger Bay Story*, Sinclair, born and bred in Butetown, stresses the importance of oral traditions:

> As a youth in the Tiger Bay community of the 1940s and 1950s I was entirely fascinated with the life of the people around me . . . As to events before my time of which I have no personal experience these are recalled from the many moments spent at many a kitchen table or by a fireplace or nowadays in a pub or community centre imbibing the many tales passionately and humorously told of Old Tiger Bay from the people who knew them best. (1993: 1)

Oral testimony is particularly important to the individual and collective memory of people who grew up and lived in Tiger Bay. There are two main reasons for this: first, it defines how they saw and continue to see themselves in the face of 150 years of negative written and visual portrayals of the area. Secondly, as a working-class community, Butetown previously had no recorded history of its own that preserved alternative narratives about the people of the area and no museum to archive and show social life from below. The former Welsh Industrial and Maritime Museum (now relocated to Swansea) had numerous documents and photographs about shipping and ship owners, but little on the men who manned the ships or worked in the dockyards, or the women who married across racial and cultural boundaries, and their families and communities. It is here that oral history interviews and written life stories, collected and published by Butetown History & Arts Centre, have begun to redress the balance.

Butetown, a district on the southern tip of Cardiff bordering the Bristol Channel, developed with the growth of the docks and the coal trade and by the 1880s was the commercial hub of what had become the leading coal exporting port in the world. Canals and railways connected Cardiff Docks to the south Wales coalfield and the coal trade connected Cardiff with ports throughout the world. Geographically a small area, approximately a mile long and a quarter of a mile wide, Butetown had distinct physical borders comprising (now filled-in) canals, railway tracks and the sea. Older residents refer to the top (northern) part of the area as 'The Bay' or 'Tiger Bay' and the bottom part as 'The Docks'. Outsiders often referred to the whole district as 'Tiger Bay' and, since the redevelopment that began in the late 1980s, the area has come to be known as Cardiff Bay.

Butetown developed as a multi-ethnic, multicultural seaport, which was a product of British colonial expansion and the global economic, social and cultural changes that occurred as a result of it. It was a community peopled primarily by seamen from throughout the British Empire, by seamen and refugees from Europe and by women of Welsh, Irish and English descent, that is, by these groups along with their mixed-heritage descendants. The seamen who settled brought with them their cultural traditions, establishing diverse social and religious institutions. Positive narratives of Tiger Bay as a cosmopolitan and tolerant community remain central to both individual and collective memories and to the identities of people from the bay. This diversity also attracted large numbers of journalists, social scientists and others who have written about the area, largely in negative terms. Butetown has never been an exclusively 'coloured area' – despite the impression given by Little, Drake, Collins and many other social scientists (Little, 1942, 1943, 1972 [1948]; Drake, 1954, 1955; Collins, 1957). It has always been multinational and multi-ethnic and, from the last few decades of the nineteenth century onwards, it has had a significant non-white population (around 50 per cent when Little and Drake conducted research in the 1940s).

The long history of negative representations in the media, popular culture and by the city fathers, which extends down to the present, began soon after the seaport came into being, with its boarding houses and brothels and its ethnically and racially mixed population. For a period of 150 years, negative and romanticized constructions of the bay created and reproduced racialized borders between it and the rest of Cardiff. The negative and exotic images and stories about Tiger Bay that were recycled over many decades have become deeply engraved in popular consciousness. Depictions of the area as dirty, violent, diseased and immoral circulated alongside those that constructed it as exotic and a mecca of 'racial harmony' (see Jordan, 1988). Throughout the later nineteenth century and much of the twentieth century, Tiger Bay was the focus of a series of moral panics. Between the 1880s and the 1930s, campaigns were waged by white British seamen with the support of the local press, the police and other 'moral guardians of society' (Hall et al., 1978). They constructed Cardiff's 'coloured' seamen as aliens (despite the fact that they were British citizens and subjects) and deprived them of their livelihood (see Drake, 1954: 75–119 and 180–6; Evans, 1980; Collins, 1957). The rhetorical tropes that recurred repeatedly during these campaigns suggested that immorality and miscegenation marked Butetown residents as negatively different from the rest of Cardiff. A typical example of this ongoing media campaign was a series of long, popular feature articles entitled 'Darker Cardiff: seamy side of the great seaport' that the *South Wales Daily News* ran two or three times a week from 22 November 1893 until early January 1894. It focused on a range of perceived threats to the way of life of respectable (middle-class) society. The articles described the exploitation of seamen by avaricious boarding-house masters, the widespread presence of prostitutes on Cardiff streets at night, the subculture of bookies and gamblers, the presence of thinly disguised brothels (in some instances, in Cardiff's 'respectable' neighbourhoods), the practice of illegally capturing drunken and/or drugged labourers (so-called 'hoodlums') to 'man the ships', the existence of stray and homeless children on the streets and the difficulties of the unemployed. As for the phrase 'Darker Cardiff', it was ambiguous – pointing both to the 'low life' (gambling, drinking, prostitution, etcetera) of Cardiff's 'Sailor-Town' and to its 'coloured inhabitants'. Absent was any sense of a culturally and ethnically diverse community of ordinary people, supporting each other and living normal daily lives. This sort of construction of Tiger Bay/ Butetown as a hotbed of vice and infamy remained a dominant one in the local press until the 1970s, and it was mobilized to justify the so-called 'slum clearance' campaigns in Cardiff during the 1950s, 1960s and 1970s which replaced the old Tiger Bay with high-rise tower blocks and council houses. This mode of representing Butetown has continued to surface from time to time in press articles. For example, in 1988, during the investigation following the murder of Lynette White (a young, mixed-race prostitute who worked in the dockland area of Cardiff), one of Wales's leading police officers referred to Butetown as 'a square mile of vice'. Yet often this type of representation is combined with a sense of exoticism, danger and mystery. For example, the *South Wales Echo* ran a popular nine-part series on Tiger Bay in 1970, recycling the long-established stereotypes. Its headlines included: 'The legend of Tiger Bay: 1. Pub brawls, pimps and opium dens . . . but for many it was Utopia'; '2. The human tigers who lay in wait for seamen'; '3. Out come the knives as the tong war flares' (18 September–2 October). One hundred and fifty years of representations such as these, which are rich in sensationalism, negative stereotypes and romanticization, together with more directly negative attacks that featured forms of 'immorality' including intermarriage between people from different races, helped to construct and reaffirm racialized borders between Butetown and the rest of Cardiff that gave the actual physical borders of the area specific meanings. These meanings had specific racialized gender dimensions that reflect more widespread attitudes to acceptable modes of respectable femininity and masculinity. The repeatedly recycled outsider narratives form the backdrop against which people from the area felt and continue to feel obliged to define themselves in their own insider narratives of who they are.

Economic and social borders

It was not just the geographical location and history of negative representation that created racialized borders between Butetown and the rest of Cardiff and south Wales. It was also racist material practices, most especially in relation to employment. Various life-history interviews with local residents testify to the difficulties faced by non-white seamen and dockworkers in finding work, a situation that would only change temporarily with the outbreak of the Second World War:

> Before the war you couldn't get a job, or any job for the coloured man was very menial, and it was only the job that anybody else didn't want really. The only tidy man who had a good job down here was Mr Trottman. He was a carpenter . . . but the rest of the men had to put their couple of bob in their discharge book to get a ship. But Harold sat there one day and said: 'Hitler's our best friend, because they want us now!' (Billy Sinclair, 2004)

If non-white seamen and dockworkers found themselves subject to discrimination in employment on the basis of racialized difference, black and mixed-race women also found it difficult to gain employment beyond the borders of Butetown. Access to a gendered labour market for working-class women was racialized and even within the area, black and mixed-race women found themselves consigned to the dirtiest and least desirable jobs. In her oral history, Patti Smith (née Douglas) recounts her experience of the labour market before the Second World War and her reasons for joining the army when war broke out: 'We had some terrible jobs . . . It used to be rag stores over the dock and that was the only job you could get, terrible, terrible. When the war started, I thought it was marvellous. That's why you joined the army' (Smith, 2005).

Similarly, in describing her motivation for joining the ATS during the Second World War, Vera Johnson (née Roberts) recounts how racism was a material force that prevented access to working-class employment let alone social mobility:

> Before the war I went to Currans for a job; the labour exchange gave me a card to go to Currans, the ammunition factory. There was a lot of girls there from the Valleys, they came down by coach. And we got talking 'cause there was a queue and we had to wait and we made friends there, you know, whilst we were waiting. And when it got to my turn to go in, there was no vacancies. They put a card there saying 'no vacancies', so I came out and I waited for the girls who I was friendly with who were behind me and I asked them if they got a job and they said 'yes'. And they were from up the Valleys and I was only from up the road, and they said there were 'no vacancies'. My Father was home from sea at the time and said, 'If you go there for a job any more, I'll cut your legs off,' he said, 'Never ever work in that place again.' So that's how I joined the forces 'cause I couldn't get a job, and when, ah, I came out of the forces,

> wouldn't you know, the first job they offered me was with Currans, and I refused this, I refused to take it. She said, 'Why are you refusing to take this?' So I told her, I did, 'Well I went there in 1941 for a job, they took everyone before me and when it came to me, they signed my paper 'no vacancies'. I said, 'All the girls behind me came from the Valleys and I'm from up the road.' She said, 'Oh, I don't think so.' I said 'yes', so I refused to work there. (Johnson, 2005)

The racialized borders that marked Butetown as negatively different and cut its inhabitants off from surrounding areas were also experienced by non-white Butetown children who were evacuated to the south Wales valleys during the war. Alec Neil recalls his first experience of rejection as a six-year-old and his coping strategy of reversing its meaning:

> On the day I was evacuated we were all going up in buses and we all went to this hall and they were putting us all out. I'll have you, I'll have you. I'll have you. I was last out; no one wanted me! [laughs] I was the short straw! I wasn't frightened, but I thought, I mean, no one wants me, I'm last here, I must be the pick of the litter. (Neil, 2004)

In his life story interview, Neil describes in detail his experience of living with a white family in the Aberdare valley and of attending the local school:

> At Aman junior, that's where we went . . . That was a cracker, that was. There wasn't a day go by you wasn't in a fight. Well the people up there then, I know it sounds a bit daft, but the people up there they didn't see colour. The only thing they saw was pictures black and white, see, and they saw us and they used to look and they used to touch you to see if it was going to rub off. I know it sounds hard to believe, and of course the name-calling come and all that like. You know, we just stood up for ourselves . . . I used to have the strap as well if I was performing . . . I was six at the time, when I first went up and uh, oh, if I performed I had the strap and I was taken home from school, 'you fighting again'. We went to St Margaret's Church down over the bridge. Believe it or not, I was a choirboy. I know it's hard to believe but I was in the choir. (Neil, 2004)

This account of evacuee life points to common features in accounts of the lived experience of Butetown residents – both men and women – when they crossed the borders of Tiger Bay, which included verbal racist abuse, physical 'othering' and the need to fight back and establish a protective reputation for being hard. Whereas fighting back both physically and verbally tended to take gendered forms, its purpose for both was to establish invulnerability. Once this reputation is in place, then racialized subjects can participate in a more normal everyday life and in Neil's case even become a choirboy.

Insider narratives of Tiger Bay

While Butetown people were very much aware of the racism of wider Cardiff and the Valleys, they experienced their own community very differently and a strong nostalgia for this sense of community and belonging continues to permeate life stories from Tiger Bay. Nostalgia for a lost community has been a feature of narratives and studies of working-class life for decades. In the case of Tiger Bay, however, the intertwined stories of poverty and a community life, structured around institutions such as pubs, clubs, churches, chapels, prayer rooms and mosques, in which doors to individual homes remained unlocked and people helped each other are complexified by the multi-ethnic, multiracial nature of the area. As in other working-class docklands communities, women in particular come across as strong, forced as they were to provide for the needs of families whose men would be away at sea for many months at a time. The oral histories tell of marriages across race, culture and religion and of the participation of different groupings in the celebrations of the different cultures among which they lived. For white women, especially those from the Welsh Valleys and Cardiff, marrying non-white seamen often meant a radical and unbreachable break with their immediate and extended families. The hostility of families beyond the bay only added to the perception of racialized borders and the degree of defensive social cohesion within Tiger Bay itself. Important in individual and collective memories is the acceptance of differences within families that, outside Tiger Bay, were and are still subject to much greater degrees of negative racialization. Mabel Collette, born in 1920, recalls how

> I had two white brothers and my mother married my dad then, see, but I didn't realise I was coloured and he was white. We all got on. There were families they'd be calling you a black 'b' an' all, but I never realised he was white and I was coloured. I had a coloured brother an' all. My mother married his Dad and when he died she married my dad. And when you're growing up you don't realise you're coloured, it's only when the kids call you, you 'black nigger'. (Colette, 2005)

Mabel Collette in 2005 holding a photograph of her brother
(copyright BHAC)

A constant theme in Butetown lifestory interviews is how bay people became aware of racialized difference, discrimination and the idea that they lived somewhere undesirable only on crossing the borders of the community and leaving the area. Neil Sinclair, for example, recounts how 'It was as a child on expeditions outside the Bay that I heard remarks that Tiger Bay was thought of as a slum' (1993: 88). Many interviews detail how a scholarship to grammar school or work in wider Cardiff made Butetown children realize their difference and the negative attitudes towards it. A further theme to emerge in interviews is the importance of urban space and its effects on community. Whereas hegemonic outsider narratives saw the physical layout of old Tiger Bay as conducive to criminality, insiders saw it as important to the sense of community. Moreover, they continue to see the redevelopment of the 1960s and 1970s as the key to the economic, social and cultural decline of the area:

> The 'vast colourless estate', designed with anti-social, lacklustre streets, is the more likely reason for the loss of heart in the current younger generation in Tiger Bay. The central focus point of our community, the park in Loudoun Square, has been destroyed. And the rows of streets

> where front doors faced one another have been replaced with an architectural monstrosity that is not conducive to social harmony. Front doors now face the side of other structures and do not form conventional streets. Furthermore the anonymity of life in a block of flats adds to the disintegration of the community. Who will open their front door to an empty hallway? Who will take the time and the pride to wash the stoop? How can you associate and congregate with your neighbour? The architecture clearly has had a profound destructive influence on such a once tightly knit society. (Sinclair, 1993: 98)

Sinclair's *The Tiger Bay Story*, like most of the unpublished oral-history interviews, subscribes fully to the positive narrative of Butetown as an exceptional example of social and racial harmony. The type of representations produced by insiders in oral and written life histories take up some of the more romantic images found in mainstream representations but radically distance themselves from hegemonic negative images of poverty, crime, immorality and racial conflict. In the process the 'exotic' becomes the normal, and faceless, nameless people become named individuals with families and normal everyday lives. Much stress is laid on intermarriage and on a non-conflictual multiculturalism in which people help one another and participate in the different rituals and festivals of ethnic groups other than their own. Insider texts are characterized not only by positive images of racial and ethnic difference but by affirmative images of working-class family life and community.

The gendered experience of crossing racialized borders

We turn now to gendered examples of individual stories of negotiating the class and racialized borders between Butetown and the world beyond it in time of war. Hegemonic narratives tend to characterize the Second World War as a time when the nation was united in a common struggle, when the social borders between genders and classes became much more permeable and when the coloured citizens of the empire fought with the motherland against an evil Nazi regime. What does not emerge from such narratives is the experience of racism, as it affected either service men and women from the empire or Britain's own non-white populations. War, of necessity, led to a marked increase in the crossing of the racialized physical, social and cultural borders that constituted Tiger Bay, as both women and men were called up for war work and military service. This meant moving out into an ignorant and often hostile white world, bereft of the comfort, safety and support of the Tiger Bay community. We begin with an extract from Vera Johnson's story.

> I joined the ATS with a friend of mine called Rosette Crews and they refused her . . . so I had to go on my own. I had a compassionate posting because my mother suffered with asthma and so I didn't go far. I did my training in Wrexham. Three weeks' training. My first posting, then, from there was Chepstow, Beachley Camp and there were young boys training as officers, you know. Very rude some of them were, yes.

In her very first posting, Vera is confronted with a gendered public display of racism that forces her to establish an identity, common to both women and men from Tiger Bay, as someone who will not stand for it.

Vera Johnson in uniform
(copyright BHAC)

> I was a cook. It was nice, I liked it there, except, I was in trouble once. I was serving out the food and there were platoons of soldiers waiting to have their meal. You had to serve them, you know, and you were in all your whites, 'kerchief and everything and all of a sudden this young chap came out and got on his knee and got in front of me and he starts singing 'Mammy, Mammy, . . .' you know, and doing all that kind of . . .,

> and they were all roaring, the soldiers, laughing, you know, but I wasn't laughing. We had these big iron spoons, you know, for serving. Mind you, I didn't mean to hit to cut his head open, and he still kept on and they were saying, 'Get up from there,' you know, and I just went with the spoon like that, I just flicked it like that the top and bottom like that and I hit him across the head and split his head open. He had to go to hospital. Well, that stopped their laughter, and there was a lot of prejudice there and they took him to hospital anyhow and stitched him and I was put on a charge then, court martial. I was on a court martial for splitting his head open but I got away with it because everybody could say what the boy had done. I didn't provoke him, he came out of the crowd and he, you know, so they threw it out of Court. So I had respect after that . . . (Johnson, 2005)

Central to Vera's narrative of self, as she recalls her wartime experience, is the recognition of a pervasive racism against which the best defence is attack, that involves establishing her profile as someone not to be messed with. In doing so she locates herself firmly within an insider narrative of Tiger Bay as strong and resistant to the intimidation of wider white society:

> the Armed Forces were very prejudiced. When I first went in, they were very prejudiced and you'd get all this nonsense of 'You black so and so,' you know, 'The Nigger over there,' or something like that, you know . . . I was born and bred in Tiger Bay and I knew how to stick up for myself and I fought my own battles, I didn't go to nobody. (Johnson, 2005)

Vera sees this as setting her apart from black women from elsewhere:

> Once I sorted myself out with those people who insulted me, I got on fine with the girls, you know, wherever I went. And I was in the Forces with one girl from up the Valleys, she was black and she was very timid. I used to have to fight her battles for her because she'd let them walk over her, you know, and she wouldn't say anything to them but I could stand up for myself and her. (Johnson, 2005)

Although Vera tells of how she enjoyed army life, once she had put a stop to racist remarks, especially the company and friendships of the other women, she also states clearly that, as a black woman, she could not get promotion, pointing to the institutional racism which people from Tiger Bay continued to confront even in times of war. The forms of identity that come through in insider narratives of Tiger Bay, that stress the absence of racism and not only celebrate but normalize difference and racial and ethnic mixing, produce subjects who refuse to comply with forms of interpersonal institutional and individual racism that are encountered beyond the borders of Butetown. They are much less effective against other forms of institutional racism as it effects work, promotion and where one is posted in times of war.

If throwing a cook's ladle, putting down insults verbally and forming alliances with other women are arguably gendered modes of response to racism, men from Tiger Bay often resorted more directly to physical modes of establishing that they would not tolerate abuse. On joining the forces, black and mixed-race men from Butetown, who would otherwise have worked below deck in the Merchant Navy, found themselves in an ignorantly racist white world. John Actie, who became an air force pilot, recalls how:

> When I got called up, I had to go to Padgate. That's just outside Warrington. Up in Lancashire. They were all aircrew; there was about 200 of us and we were all aircrew. So the flight sergeant, he's telling us now where we have to go to pick particular items up and so on and so forth. So when he finished, now, he said, 'The one on the top of the list can take you around.' So naturally Actie, I'm on top of the list. So he said 'Who's Actie?' I said, 'me Sergeant.' 'Oh, we'd better not have you,' he said, 'we'd better have someone who can speak and understand English.' Of course I told him. Well, you know the intelligence of the man. To think I'm stuck there, the only black face amongst all the white ones, and I can't speak English plus the fact we've all passed an exam. We've all sat an exam to get there in the first place. (Actie, 2005)

If education could lead eventually to social mobility in rare cases, like that of John Actie, and affect modes of resistance to racism, for most non-white men from Tiger Bay, it was a case of literally fighting or threatening to fight when confronted with abusive language or behaviour. Gerald Ernest also volunteered for the air force and found himself confronted by racism from his first days at a training camp. Less educated than Actie and without the opportunity to become a pilot, he was sent to train as an aircraft fitter. As in Vera Johnson's case, the key to his survival was a refusal to accept racist treatment, but in much more conventionally masculine ways that involved instilling fear:

> When I was on that fitter engines course . . . I was out with one of the lads at night and we were going down to a dance and this fella passed on a bike and called out 'you black so and so, get out of the way' and that. So, Ginger, he knew who he was, and we then chased him down and when I got level with him I balled at him. He said, he never said anything of the kind. But that was a tutor and he gave me top marks when I went to his class. (Ernest, 2005)

The oral history suggests that men from Tiger Bay, like women from the area, were used to relating across colour and easily made friends among their white counterparts who, like Ginger in the above quotation, would stand by them in racist incidents. Gerald Ernest recounts how

> There were places where I wasn't welcome because I was coloured. Like, I went for a weekend with one of the lads, we went to Luton and we were walking across the street, we were going to the dance as usual. I was only dancing and this girl calls 'Eddie, Eddie Bird you're dealing with a nigger.' She called him and he went across. Next minute he slapped her across the face . . . I said, "Hey what you slap that girl for?" He said, 'After she said "what you doing with that black nigger, what you doing with him?"' And that's when he slapped her. (Ernest, 2005)

Gerald Ernest's resistance to racism built on his Tiger Bay tough guy image and his acknowledged proficiency in boxing. On one occasion he came into conflict over night working which he was sent to do when a white fitter refused and volunteered him instead:

> 'Black tyke,' he called me, the sergeant who was in charge of me. So I challenged him to come down the gym. I'll show you what a 'black tyke' can do, but he didn't come. Anyway they moved me to another flight and when I gets there they said, 'You're on nights this weekend.' I said, 'I can't do nights' and this sergeant turns around and says 'Look I've been across to India, I know how to handle you fellas, I've been abroad.' I said 'Have you? You ain't been abroad where I come from,' I said, 'Tiger Bay' and he just looked at me, he never said no more. So Tiger Bay had a bad name, we had a bad name and there was nothing wrong with the area. It's a name that's gone all over the world, Tiger Bay. (Ernest, 2005)

Yet the tough guy image had its limitations when it came to unveiled racism and institutionalized taboos against sexual relations across colour that were part of the normal everyday experience of people living in Tiger Bay:

> While I was at our fitters' course . . . there were two sides to the camp, a maintenance unit and the school of technological training, the side I was on. Now on the maintenance unit side there were all permanent members of the place and there was a lot of Jamaican boys there, and then in the station yard there's a sign 'No WAFs to go out with Jamaican airmen on the station'. I'm sorry I never ripped that sign off and sent it off to somebody, but I did tell my mother and she said, 'Oh don't take any notice'. But then I was going out with a WAF, an English girl, we used to go dancing and the lads used to pass next to her [and say] 'do with a black, woman'. She pointed them out one at a time and I sorted them out, only a word, they were that scared. And then they left her alone but then they posted her off the station and I found out she was posted on my account. So, then I tried myself to find her and they said you've proved she moved on account of your presence, we'll do something about it. Well, they posted me within 24 hours, I had to move. (Ernest, 2005)

When Gerald Ernest was discharged from the air force after the war he had no formal qualifications and had not benefited in any material way from his service life.

Tiger Bay as a haven free from racism

It was not only in the lived experience and collective memory of the people of Butetown that Tiger Bay functioned as a tolerant multi-ethnic, multiracial space in which sexual relations between people who were ethnically and racially different were accepted as normal. During the Second World War, Butetown became a space of resistance against the segregationist policies of the US army and air force based in the Cardiff area. For women, in particular, its borders offered a safe space for meeting new men and for many a future life as a GI bride. The borders that cut Butetown off from the rest of Cardiff were symbolically and materially reconstructed and enforced in US forces regulations and by the military police who would not allow soldiers or airmen, white or black, to go down the bay. Vera Johnson recalls how she and her sister eluded the authorities:

> My sister was a GI bride, she's still in America, she went there in 1946; her husband was a GI. And, uh, as I said, we use to have dances when my sister was courting her husband. I was dating Hank Jones, black as the ace of spades he was, Hank Jones. My mother invited him down for

tea, when my sister had already engaged her fella, they [the US military police] wouldn't allow the black Yanks down this area at all, or the white Yanks – it was out of bounds. And the bridge at the top [of Bute Street, the unofficial border of the community], they couldn't come under the bridge, but we use to get them down. We use to get a taxi and the taxi fella used to know us, like, you know. We'd sit them on the floor and just sit at the back, and they'd be on the floor of the taxi and we'd set them down, and my sister would have the door open, and they would run in. We had one little boy round here, he was the GI's mascot, and he would sit on their jeep, on top of the jeep and he'd show them which house the Americans were in and they'd come to your house, you know, are they any Americans there? Okay, this little guy must have watched us 'cause he'd get in the air raid shelters, get on the floor and be peeping like that and he'd show the men, the military police, where the Yanks went. This one day, we had my sister well schooled, Winnie, and she answered the door. She said 'Who's there?' – during the war you had to ask 'who's there' because you never opened your door unless you recognised the voice, because of the enemy. So they said, 'the Military Police, mam, we have reason to believe that you have American soldiers in your house.' And when he said, 'Can you open up and let us see', she shouted to him through the door, 'I'm sorry, I'm only ten and my mother's gone shopping and I can't open the door to anybody because you could be the enemy. There's no body here only myself and I can't open the door' and off he went [Vera laughs]. (Johnson, 2005)

Black American GIs not only found girlfriends and eventual wives in Tiger Bay, they repaid the hospitality that they received with gifts of food. John Jenkins (born Ronald Jenkins and known as Johnnie Boozer) recalled how he had befriended some black GIs on the train:

I met them on a train, I was working in Newport on a ship and the train came in and I saw these Yanks, 'cause I'd been over there, like, on ships. So I started talking to them. They weren't allowed down the Bay. They didn't want them mixing with Black people in this country, educate them too much . . .

We didn't worry much about rations. Well, from the time the Yanks came here, 'cause they used to call our house 'little America' . . . one or the other would come along and knock the door and you'd hear 'Laundry' and a thump on the floor and there'd be a kit bag with all kinds of stuff in it. One Christmas we had eleven turkeys and people couldn't even get chickens. (Jenkins, 2005)

Concluding reflections

In this chapter we have looked at how the multi-ethnic, multiracial, working-class docklands community of Butetown, previously known as Tiger Bay, was constructed in the popular imagination over 150 years as a place of Otherness, marked by gendered mixtures of hostile racist stereotyping and romanticized exoticism. Using extracts from oral histories, we have suggested that racism beyond the borders of Butetown both before and during the Second World War severely limited access to employment and to social mobility for both men and women (and this continues to be the case even today). Negative hegemonic constructions of Tiger Bay in the media, popular culture and in the statements of city fathers, set against the experience of everyday life 'Down the Bay', shaped insider narratives, identities and modes of resistance to racism outside the community in particular gendered ways. The forced bringing together of Butetown residents and white outsiders in time of war led to specific coping strategies in which women and men looked to conventional modes of working-class femininity and masculinity for resources with which to defend themselves against naked racism. These were combined with insider narratives of tolerance, self-sufficiency, toughness and, above all, an everyday experience of relating sexually and socially across difference. For the majority of women and men, who were confronted by racial, class and gender prejudice, moving up the social hierarchy proved impossible and their modes of resistance involved similar strategies of establishing invulnerability but with a gendered inflection. The everyday normality of relating across colour in Tiger Bay, together with a refusal to tolerate racial abuse might win over the white working-class people alongside with whom they came into contact. In moments of conflict, however, especially with those in authority, the only insider narrative on which they could successfully draw was of the uncompromising toughness of Tiger Bay as a place that it was dangerous to mess with. This was a narrative that found reinforcement in hegemonic versions of the nature of Tiger Bay. Cross-racial sexual mixing, when taken beyond the borders of Butetown, was subject to consistent formal and informal policing. Though successful in its immediate context, the 'tough guy' strategy of confronting racism as a mode of negotiating borders had severe limits and did not enable social mobility either during the Second World War or afterwards, nor did it work to transform racist structures. In the oral histories of Tiger

Bay, stories of discrimination and resistance to it resurface repeatedly among the positive tales of community life within the borders of the community. The embracing of tough and potentially threatening identities in the face of racialized white power also plays a role in maintaining the mystique of the area. Yet, it is the other insider narratives of ethnic and racial mixing and tolerance of difference that mark the deep sense of loss that comes through in the oral histories of Tiger Bay. The ways in which people from the bay tell their stories are marked not just by a sense of the loss of how things used to be, in which the narrative tropes of diversity and tolerance are paramount, but also by a restatement of the identity of being part of a community that was and is still subject to social exclusion but that will fight back. While old physical borders remain important to this sense of community, two waves of redevelopment have heightened the importance of Tiger Bay as an imagined community in which people from the area who now live beyond its borders also participate. Its reputation for racial and cultural diversity and tolerance has arguably become one of its chief assets.

Bibliography

Actie, John (2005). Butetown History and Arts Centre (BHAC) interview.

Colette, Mabel (2005). BHAC interview.

Collins, Sydney (1957). *Coloured Minorities in Britain*, London: Lutterworth Press.

Daniels, Fred (2005). BHAC interview.

Drake, St Clair (1954). *Value Systems, Social Structure and Race Relations in the British Isles*, Ph.D. thesis, University of Chicago.

—— (1955). 'The "colour problem" in Britain: a study in social definitions', *Sociological Review* (new series) 3, 97–217.

Evans, Neil (1980). 'The south Wales race riots of 1919', *Llafur: Journal of Welsh Labour History*, 3, 1, 5–29.

Ernest, Gerald (2005). BHAC interview.

Hall, Stuart, Charles Critcher, Tony Jefferson and John Clarke (1978). *Policing the Crisis*, London: Macmillan.

Jenkins, John (2005). BHAC interview.

Johnson, Vera (2005). BHAC interview.

Jordan, Glenn (1988). 'Images of Tiger Bay: did Howard Spring tell the truth?', *Llafur: Journal of Welsh Labour History*, 5, 1, 53–9.

Little, Kenneth (1942). 'Loudoun Square: a community survey I, II', *Sociological Review*, 34, 12–33 and 119–46.

——(1943). 'The psychological background of white–coloured contacts in Britain', *Sociological Review*, 35, 12–28.

——(1972 [1948]). *Negroes in Britain: A Study of Racial Relation in English* [sic] *Society*, London: Routledge and Kegan Paul.

Neil, Alec (2004). BHAC interview.

Sinclair, Billy (2004). BHAC interview.

Sinclair, Neil M. C. (1993). *The Tiger Bay Story*, Cardiff: Butetown History and Arts Centre.

Smith, Patti (2005). BHAC interview.

South Wales Echo (1970). Series of nine feature articles on Tiger Bay, letters to the editor and final assessment, 18 September–2 October.

IV

TEACHING GENDERED BORDERS

12

Locating the 'Border' in Gender: Creating Coherence in Border Pedagogy

JOCELYN C. AHLERS AND KIM KNOWLES-YÁNEZ

Introduction

The term 'border' can be, and often is, used to describe not only physical and political areas but also conceptual communities with ethnic, language and gender characteristics. In working towards the creation of a higher education course in border studies, we noted the use of the term to refer to a broad range of social phenomena, some with no connection to a geopolitical border, the most salient example in the context of this edited volume being gender. We found that we needed to develop a coherent pedagogy with a framework that captured the commonalities among these phenomena, in order adequately to convey to students the benefit of understanding this range of social constructs as 'borders'. To do so, we drew on the study of cognitive linguistics to capture the main facets of a prototypical border, and then showed how those are, often unconsciously, mapped on to non-geopolitical borders. When a researcher uses the term 'border' in discussing, for example, gender, class or ethnic difference, the use rings true to audiences because they, too, map the prototypical features of a physical border on to a variety of social phenomena. By making conscious the cognitive process which links borders to other social phenomena, we provide our students with a tool for analysing these social constructs and provide instructors in the programme with a mechanism for creating coherence as we consider the broad range of phenomena which fall under border studies.

For the purpose of this chapter, we focus on the understanding and presentation of gender vis-à-vis two apparently very different academic fields, the fields of linguistics and land-use planning, utilizing in each case a border prototype mechanism. After a brief discussion of processes within the history of our institution which led to the inception of the border studies programme, we each discuss ways in which applications of the prototype of border to gender aids us in presenting particular facets of our respective fields of study to our students.

The border studies programme

Liberal studies at California State University, San Marcos, was developed in response to two driving forces: the founding mission of the university and the course content dictated by California state-regulated kindergarten to 8th grade (K–8) teacher preparation. First, the university encourages the development of innovative interdisciplinary units; accordingly, the liberal studies department aims to support campus interdisciplinarity through its instruction, curriculum development and scholarship. Secondly, many students take the liberal studies major as a route towards preparing themselves for the California Subject Examinations for Teachers (CSET), which they must pass in order to enter the teaching profession; and California state teacher preparation regulations require that students be taught a diverse array of subjects. The liberal studies department thus necessarily includes academics from many disciplines, particularly those not represented elsewhere on campus, such as geography and linguistics. During the time in which the border studies curriculum was designed, the department contained a seemingly unlikely mix of faculty, including a medical anthropologist, a cultural geographer, an urban and regional planner, a political economist, two sociologists and two linguists.

Working within these parameters, the department, over the last ten years, has developed a well-articulated objective of emphasizing and developing the complementary aspects of its multidisciplinarity, recruiting and hiring faculty with the aim of creating cohesion. The principal overlap in the academic interests of its staff is activist research within communities; therefore, in its faculty recruiting process it has emphasized the importance of attracting teacher-scholars with a commitment to local communities and to community development as features of their instruction and scholarship. The university is located in the northern part of California's southernmost county, San Diego, a forty-five-minute drive away from the San Diego–Tijuana border, that is, the US–Mexico border. Today, then, many of us work with local communities bordering on and in close contact with other communities.

These commonalities led us to explore new ways in which to pursue both our research interests and the needs of our academic community. The department mission includes the following objectives: to supervise a four-year programme for future teachers; to promote interdisciplinary study on campus; and to promote community-based study. It was this overriding vision and our shared interest in working with communities in contact with other communities that led us in the autumn of 2002 to begin the creation of what we now call the border studies major.

We began planning the new major with a retreat in which we discussed what the word 'border' meant to each of us. Responses were diverse but fell into two broad groups: there were those for whom 'border' meant a geographical, physical border, conflated with the notion of a geopolitical border, and those for whom the term had broader connotations and included what we have chosen to call 'conceptual borders'. But we were all in agreement that we wanted to shape a new major which would provide graduates with the tools to work successfully at understanding not only communities in general but in particular the type of border community about which we knew so much through our collective research efforts and backgrounds.

The border studies major which developed out of these conversations is now one of three tracks available to students completing a liberal studies degree at San Marcos. It promotes interdisciplinary exploration of the communities and spaces that emerge in border regions worldwide, encouraging students systematically to examine the results of human interactions across both spatial and conceptual borders. By exploring the interrelationship of diverse groups across the boundaries that delimit them, it aims to provide an understanding of how communities take shape and operate. The new major prepares students for careers in the public sector, private sector, education and a wide range of other fields, or for postgraduate studies in urban and regional planning, demography, linguistics, area studies, public policy and other social sciences. It includes the following required courses:

World regional geography
Interdisciplinary perspectives in border studies

Border research methods
Diversity and discrimination in America
The US–Mexico border
Comparative border studies
Applied methodologies for border studies

Students are also required to choose from a series of other elective classes concerned with border issues.

While the core curriculum as outlined above provides students with a wide range of data and theoretical constructs with which to analyse borders, coherence between these broad offerings could best, we believed, be achieved through the use of an overarching pedagogical construct. The authors of this chapter accordingly initiated a series of conversations related to the teaching of the introductory border studies class, which led to the construct we describe here. Though our research areas may seem diverse – one of us is a linguist, the other a land-use and planning specialist – within the borders context they are complementary, for planning relates centrally to physical borders, while the focus of linguistic study is often conceptual borders, as we demonstrate below. We decided that we wanted carefully and systematically to introduce students to the idea of physical and conceptual borders and communities, using the information gained through the discussion of geopolitical borders to explore the border-producing effects of many social phenomena, including gender.

When the word 'border' is used – barring any context which might suggest otherwise – it calls to mind for most people the frame of international borders, and we are able to build on this common frame in class discussion. 'Borders', students agree, are in the most concrete sense physical and geographical in nature, and include examples such as the Pyrenees mountains which did not begin as the political border they are today, but as a physical entity hindering the movement of people. The Mississippi, the Alps, oceans, the Rio Grande, etcetera, are all physical, geographical boundaries which hinder human movement; linguistic boundaries are often situated in such spaces precisely because communities have stopped moving there. Because political borders are often formed in or around these blockages, a conflation of the understanding of purely physical boundaries and political ones often occurs. But the fact that borders between countries can change, as they have done recently in, for example, eastern Europe and parts of sub-Saharan Africa, makes it clear that these are, in fact, not immutable physical boundaries, but geopolitical constructs. One example of particular interest to our students is the fact that in 2007, in an attempt to build up and make less porous the border with Mexico, the US erred in a portion of its fence construction, and built 1.5 miles of the border between Mexico and the US state of New Mexico inside Mexico (see Caldwell, 2007). The error demonstrates the shifting arbitrariness of many physical boundaries constructed in political border spaces. Students' familiarity with the idea of a 'line in the sand' more or less arbitrarily dividing their country, state, or county from the neighbouring country, state or county, leads readily enough to an appreciation that the places where such divisions occur may repay study in and of themselves. This part of our curriculum – the geographical and political – is relatively straightforward to prepare and to present.

It has been more difficult, however, to explain the common application of the conventional meaning of 'border' within the construction of such concepts as that of 'gender', and to help students to understand 'gender' (along with class, 'race', etcetera) as a border-creating social construct. That is to say, gender is often used socially as a means of categorization; moreover, the categorization which takes place along gender lines has real-world consequences, in terms of social status, wages, opportunities and so on. In the literature on gender, the term 'border' is used frequently to describe people's gendered experiences. In particular, the notion of 'border crossing' is used to suggest for readers the feelings and consequences associated with breaking out of socially prescribed gendered roles. However, while the term is evocative, its use frequently lacks the sort of rigour that would allow students both to access a full appreciation of the implications of recognizing gender as a border-creating social construct, and to make deep connections in their understanding of the relationships among the many social phenomena referred to as 'borders'.

The introductory course for the major, Borders and regions: interdisciplinary perspectives, plays a vital role in developing such recognitions and transmitting to our students our vision for the major as a whole. This course introduces concepts, theories and issues central to the study of regions and borders, and provides students with a multi-issue analysis of communities in contact in complex international, national and regional settings. Students examine how the focus and methodologies of different disciplines contribute to the understanding and resolution of border and regional issues. Using the border/gender prototype described below, we are able to reinforce students' understanding of physical and political borders and stretch their critical thinking skills by asking them to apply this prototype to other conceptual borders such as those of ethnicity and class. This is a completely new concept to most of the students.

We start the process of encouraging the adoption of this critical thinking tool by having the students in the first or second class session collaborate on a collective description of physical borders. We ask them to describe the characteristics of physical borders and list them in detail on the board or in PowerPoint. This list/description is then referred to throughout the semester, particularly when we introduce the idea of conceptual borders. This iterative process allows students to make connections across different kinds of borders, and sharpens their critical thinking skills as they see in just how many ways the border prototype can be applied and how it can provide rigour in their thinking about divisive social constructs. Reference to this list also allows visiting faculty (who guest-lecture on the course in order to introduce students to a range of border-creating phenomena) to relate their field coherently to the information which has already been presented. To do this effectively, however, it is critical to understand the prototype invoked and evoked by the use of the term 'border', and to clarify the cognitive mechanism which allows this term to be applied coherently to such a broad range of phenomena.

Prototypes and pedagogy

The word 'border' calls to mind a cognitive prototype, which can be defined as the quintessential example or typical member around which a category is constructed (MacLaury, 1991: 55). Research on prototypes arose from Eleanor Rosch's work on category membership (Rosch, 1973, 1978) and her discovery that categories have internal structure. Members do not exist co-equally within a category; rather, categories have members which people consider to be better or worse exemplars of that category. Moreover, agreement about these judgements of centrality is remarkably consistent from person to person within a cultural group; this is frequently true in spite of real-world experiences which would suggest otherwise. For example, in the United States, category membership judgements regarding the relative centrality of various sorts of birds have been tested in a number of settings. Respondents generally agree that robins and sparrows are 'good' members of the category 'bird'. In tests in which respondents were asked to list good examples of birds, these central members of the category show up first, even for people in an urban setting who are probably exposed more often to, for example, pigeons than sparrows.

People also use prototypes to reason about the assumed attributes of category members. For example, when study subjects are presented with a scenario in which one kind of bird has a disease and asked whether that disease can be transmitted to another kind of bird, they are much more likely to assume that a robin (prototypical bird) can transmit the disease to a duck (non-prototypical bird) than vice versa (Rosch, 1975). Frequently, knowledge based on a prototype is unconscious and does not form part of the explicit reasoning and discussion about a particular practice or concept; thus it can be difficult overtly to challenge assumptions based on such category judgements, as the prototype is not necessarily a conscious construct.

It is important to note that a prototype is an exemplar of a category; not all members of the category contain all the features of the prototype, nor are they expected to. The category of 'game', for example, is one which has garnered a great deal of attention in the study of prototypes, precisely because it is not possible to develop a checklist of features of a 'game' which provides necessary and sufficient conditions for category membership; only an understanding of the category in terms of prototypes can explain the range of activities that are included in the category 'game'. While the category contains activities as diverse as hide-and-seek, ring-around-the-rosie, football, Monopoly and poker, some of those games are considered to be better examples of the category than others (when eliciting examples of games from college classes, Monopoly is consistently the first game mentioned by all classes). Those central members have the features that people consistently and centrally associate with a 'game': two or more players, an outcome involving a winner and a loser, rules and strategy and equipment. Monopoly and football clearly have all of these criteria. More marginal games such as hide-and-seek have fewer of them, and the least prototypical games, such as ring-around-the-rosie, have almost none. Yet, if the word 'game' is deployed in conversation, a hearer will assume that it is a prototypical game unless informed otherwise. This is an example of the kinds of reasoning that people do using prototypes.

Prototypes are particularly significant because they do not only include categories like 'game' and 'bird', but also social categories such as 'woman', 'man', 'African–American', 'white', 'rich', 'working class'. Each of these terms invokes its own prototype. As with the examples above, a prototype may not accurately describe many, or even most, members of the category, but people nevertheless consistently reason based on their understanding of the category, often even in the face of evidence which suggests that their prototype is inaccurate much of the time. Furthermore, when a social judgment is attached to the prototype, stereotypes develop, even in the face of consistent evidence that the stereotype does not match the vast majority of category members. Thus, prototypes are powerful cognitive constructs which play an essential role in structuring human experience.

Such prototypes are not only used in reasoning about category membership, but are also invoked in the phenomenon referred to as 'cognitive metaphor' (see G. Lakoff, 1993; Lakoff and Johnson, 1980). All human languages show evidence of cognitive metaphor on all levels, from the development of multiple related meanings of lexical items, as in the extended use of 'boiling' to speak not only of water but of angry emotions, to the creation of grammatical aspect markers like 'gonna' from the lexical verb 'going'. Such metaphors involve mapping information drawn from one, typically concrete, domain on to a more abstract domain, where a domain is an area of human experience with all of its attendant encyclopedic knowledge. Human beings use these mappings to reason about the more abstract domain in terms of a domain with which they have much more experience. For example, many languages consistently correlate the domain of verticality with the domain of amount, as in such utterances as 'Gas prices keep rising', or 'The stock market plummeted'. Cognitive linguists call this metaphor MORE IS UP (see Lakoff and Johnson, 1980, for a detailed discussion of this and other cognitive metaphors). The metaphorical linkage allows us to transfer knowledge from the more concrete domain (in this case, that of verticality) to the more abstract domain (that of amount). Thus, when hearing the statement 'The stock market plummeted', most hearers assume that the outcome is not a good one, based on their knowledge of the physical act of 'plummeting' as involving a rapid loss of height, often with disastrous consequences. This allows human beings to make use of previously held knowledge in dealing with new situations. Furthermore, people typically create social constructs which in some way match or support their metaphors. One example of this is the arrangement of most thermometers vertically so that an increase in temperature literally correlates with an increase in height; this arrangement is arbitrary but, because of the metaphor, it is coherent with how we conceptualize the world.

The term 'border' also frequently functions in diverse fields as a cognitive metaphor; people draw on their knowledge of the relatively concrete experience of borders to understand and reason about other kinds of experiences, for example, gender. In order fully to explore such practices, it is necessary first to lay out the central attributes of the domain of 'border'. The prototypical border has a number of features: it is a physical location; it is a border between two sovereign nations; it is typically a result of negotiation (and, in some cases, aggression); it is demarked by linguistic and/or ethnic differences (and is thus often a site of bilingualism); there are walls and guards present to maintain the border (barbed wire is often part of the prototype); it involves an empty space between the two 'real' places that are separated by the border; and it is peripheral to what is understood to be the 'main' national space. These assumptions are present in many discussions of borders in the public sphere; precisely because they are held in common by members of a culture, they do not need to be stated and can be taken for granted as given information in a conversation. That is to say, when the word 'border' is used, this prototype is invoked and can be relied on by both interlocutors in the interpretations of utterances within the context of the conversation.

The prototype plays a central role in our conceptual model of borders, which includes also our knowledge of what people do around borders, the purposes that borders serve and so on. One important part of this model is the notion of 'border crossing', a concept called upon frequently in the application of the term 'border' to other social phenomena. 'Border crossing' tends to include the following elements: decision-making on the part of the border crosser; movement from the familiar to the unfamiliar; a sense of uncertainty related to transition; the question of belonging; the question of whether the crossing is legal/open, or illegal/illicit; and, finally, the potential for contradiction between the imagined experience of border crossing and the reality as it unfolds. All of these features can easily be mapped on to experiences which do not involve international borders, and such a mapping aids in creating a more complete and detailed understanding of those experiences, as we show below.

Thus, 'border' takes on metaphorical meaning and is used as such in reasoning about experiences which are understood in terms of difference and otherness. Its features can be mapped on to our understanding of gender, for example, and a close reading of relevant academic literature suggests that they often are. Understanding the prototype and its functions is useful pedagogically because it helps the instructor of border studies to provide a coherent, overarching framework through which to explore border issues, both physical and conceptual, with students. It also makes explicit the assumptions that researchers make when talking about certain social phenomena in terms of borders, which in turn is pedagogically useful.

In the rest of this chapter, we demonstrate this utility more concretely by providing two case studies. In the first, Ahlers writes from the perspective of a linguist, focusing on gendered linguistic behaviour and genderlects, and their real-world consequences in the social marketplace. She also presents some of the strategies used in her Language and gender course to aid students as they explore these ideas. In some sub-fields of linguistics the term 'border' is used fairly regularly, but without rigour; in this case study she applies rigour to the use of the term. Her case study is presented first because gendered language underlies some of the interactions explored later in the second case study, in which Knowles-Yánez writes as a land use and planning specialist, developing various examples of how the border prototype sheds light on gender, communities and planning. Planners frequently discuss actual physical borders, but do not often invoke the idea of border as a metaphor: the term nonetheless proves useful in better understanding the relations between gender, land use and communities. These two case studies, then, prove good companions for one another and for our programme of study's focus on exploring both physical and conceptual borders, in that the first case, linguistics, is primarily conceptual in origin and the second, planning, is primarily physical in origin.

Case 1: language, gender and borders

As a linguist, I frequently face students who hold entrenched notions of good and bad linguistic behaviour. These judgements have been developed and institutionalized in no small part through educational practice, and are presented as objective judgements of the 'correct' and 'incorrect' use of language. Typically, this 'knowledge' is in direct contrast to a linguistic understanding of human language behaviour. For example, students are often taught explicitly that certain dialects of English are ignorant, and are evidence of a lack of intelligence or education or class. These social judgements are, in fact, judgements of the group of people speaking the language; viewed objectively, no dialect of any language is less logical or expressive than any other dialect. However, dialects which are associated with groups of people possessing power and prestige are commonly understood to be 'better' versions of a language than its other dialects.

Nowhere is the assumption that such social judgements are objective rather than subjective exposed more clearly than in understanding and teaching about gendered linguistic behaviour. While today's students have often been introduced to the notion that race and ethnicity are cultural constructs, and know from personal experience that it is possible to learn a language or a dialect of a language other than one's own, gender is the last holdout of biological determinism; the vast majority of my students are convinced that gendered behaviour, including gendered linguistic behaviour, is biologically based and, hence, immutable. Furthermore, they have been taught to value certain linguistic behaviours as more logical and correct; these behaviours are those which are typically associated with male speech in the United States. It is often difficult to bring them to approach the idea that these speech patterns are not inherently better suited to certain jobs or social positions but, rather, that their suitability for those positions is determined by who has held those positions in the past and by the way that members of those groups speak. Through being introduced to these ideas in classes focusing on language use and gender, students begin to acquire an understanding of language as a border-creating construct.

Genderlects (gendered dialects) have been extensively studied in the US and elsewhere (see Eckert and McConnell-Ginet, 2006; R. Lakoff, 1990; Tannen, 1991, 1992, 1994; West and Zimmerman, 1987), although that study has often focused on the speech of white, middle-class Americans. This research has most recently been grounded in the understanding of gender as performative rather than inherent (see West and Zimmerman, 1987; Butler, 2001). That is to say, gender is not an inherent attribute of human beings but a set of behaviours which can be mobilized at particular times and in particular places: it is a matter of *doing* rather than *being*. Conceptualizing gendered linguistic behaviours as tools available in the public production of gendered identity has been useful in clarifying the role culture plays in the creation of gender. Authors such as Robin Lakoff (1975) and Tannen (1992, 1994) have described many gendered linguistic behaviours of middle-class Anglo men and women in the US, and authors such as Holmes (1998) and Brown (1998) have problematized this discussion in interesting ways; I will summarize a few central points here.

Grice (1975) has argued that all human beings heed the following four maxims in conversation: 1. Maxim of Relevance (a conversational turn should be relevant to the ongoing discourse); 2. Maxim of Quantity (an interlocutor should say neither too much nor too little); 3. Maxim of Manner (a speaker should be clear in his or her speaking); 4. Maxim of Quality (a speaker should tell the truth). Later theorists have suggested that, while these maxims are of use in describing the expectations of interlocutors engaged in information exchange, much of human conversation is not, in fact, about exchanging facts, but about greasing the social wheels. In such cases, it is also useful to consider the notion of 'face' (one's social standing at any given time) and the ways in which human beings mitigate face threats in conversation (see Brown and Levinson, 1987). Cultures have many devices for mitigating such threats, but the question of who deploys which devices or behaviours, and when they do so, is complex, and, as I discuss below, gender plays a large role in this. These behaviours generally fall on a cline between those which are most 'positively polite' and those which are most 'negatively polite'. Positively polite behaviours are geared toward maximizing the connection between people. They often involve eye contact, a relatively close stance, direct questions and the offering of information. Negatively polite behaviours, on the other hand, are aimed towards the avoidance of imposition and the offering of options. Thus, negatively polite behaviour is associated with less direct eye contact, more distance between interlocutors and the avoidance of direct questions in favour of the creation of opportunities for conversational participants to offer information.

Each of these sets of behaviours can mitigate face threat in different ways, typically depending on cultural expectations in a given situation. Positively polite behaviours, by creating connections, make it clear that the participants in a discussion regard one another as close, trusted friends who are permitted, for example, to ask direct questions and give direct answers without the possibility of offering insult. Negatively polite behaviours, by creating options, mitigate the potential for face threat by allowing interlocutors to avoid the need, for example, to say 'no' to a direct request, possibly creating enmity or misunderstanding. When a person expects a particular set of behaviours, and their interlocutor engages in another set, misunderstandings often arise; these misunderstandings are rarely believed to be the result of mismatched communicative patterns but, rather, are attributed to the personalities of the speakers. Note that none of these behaviours is about information exchange per se, as described by Grice and summarized above. The same information may be conveyed through the use of either set of tools, or, more typically, through a combination of conversational devices, but conversationalists will regard their interlocutors as more or less socially or cognitively able depending on the relative match between their styles.

Societies more broadly have a tendency to value one style over the other, with the 'superior' style seen as being the most logical, polite and well bred; it is also typically the style associated with the group with the most political, social and financial power in a society. In the United States, that group is upper-middle to upper-class Anglo men, and the style usually associated with them is one which places an explicit premium on directness – on information exchange, with a minimum of emotional overtones. This focus on the message in a conversation is seen as typically masculine, while women are associated with a greater focus on what is called the 'metamessage', that is, the underlying meaning of a message, often conveyed through conversational implicature (see Grice, 1975). Women tend to be more focused on sending and receiving these metamessages, which can lead to miscommunication. This miscommunication is often then blamed on women in this culture, precisely because message-focused communication is valued. The cultural story that goes with this is that message-focused communication is valued because it is more logical, but it is clear from examinations of other cultures which function well through a focus on metamessage that logic is not so much the issue as social value.

The cultural judgements associated with gendered behaviour can be seen most clearly in their violation. While there is a strong positive association with linguistic behaviours which are direct and message oriented, and a concomitant negative association with indirect linguistic displays, women are heavily censured for engaging in direct communication under many circumstances.

While students readily recognize descriptions such as these (as evidenced by rueful laughter during our discussions), they often do not so easily see the entrenched nature or consequences of these behaviours within a particular social marketplace, nor do they see such consequences as mutable, precisely because of the assumed biological origins of genderlects. This blindness also applies to the kinds of social policing which enforces 'appropriate' linguistic behaviour, and which disregards the ways in which this enforcement empowers some while disempowering others. Framing a discussion of gendered linguistic behaviour, its origins and its consequences in terms of borders (in particular, of the bilingualism prototypically associated with borders) is extremely productive in opening the door to challenging students' understanding of genderlects and their naturalness. I briefly outline the cognitive links which can be made between the prototype of 'borders' and the social construct 'gender', and look more closely at some of the tools and exercises I use in class to help students create for themselves an understanding of genders as borders.

As stated above, one of the main features of the prototypical border is the idea that a border separates two distinct regions/countries/places/cultures. I would suggest that one reason why gender is so commonly understood to be a border is precisely because of the very clear parallels between the paired nature of places on either side of an international border and the prototypical pair of gendered identities: female and male. Furthermore, international borders are prototypically understood to be lines across which blending does not take place, and this implication is carried into reasoning about the realm of gender. I utilize several classroom practices to make these assumptions explicit and to problematize them. The readings in the first section of class are designed to show students that gender and sex are two different constructs, one social and the other biological. This is frequently a difficult notion for them to approach; in their experience, part of the understanding of gender is based on constraints on behaviour which are assumed to come from a person's morphological sex. An exercise that has proven effective in conveying to students the scalar nature of even physical attributes associated with gender is to have them leave their chairs and to arrange themselves in the classroom by height. It becomes immediately obvious that it is not possible to draw a neat line between men and women when they are thus arranged, though height is one of the differentiating attributes of men and women most frequently mentioned in my classes.

Furthermore, since I am working with students living in the San Diego–Tijuana border region, I am able to exploit their experiences with the border to problematize their assumption that gender is two sided, with a hard line between the sides. While a number of our students have had surprisingly little experience of crossing the border between the US and Mexico, many have an intimate knowledge of just how porous the border is and of how much cultural mingling has occurred and is occurring in this region. By utilizing the metaphor of the border to discuss gendered experience and behaviour, it is possible to make clear to students the ways in which gendered behaviour is scalar, rather than absolute, and in many ways to normalize non-prototypical gendered behaviour. This point can be made through comparison with the kinds of behavioural differences across borders which develop through differing practices of enculturation. While students have some sense of the ways in which culture affects behaviour (for example, differences in the emphasis on time in the United States and Mexico) and of the cultural judgements attendant upon those differences (again, vis-à-vis differences in the emphasis on time), they do not always understand how gendered behaviour develops in children through practice; a comparison to the acquisition of other culturally derived patterns of behaviour opens the door to understanding for many students. One effective tool in conveying this is to talk to students about cultural practices within their families, the value of those practices and misunderstandings and judgements they have dealt with from outsiders exposed to those practices. The strong feelings of attachment to such practice, in spite of external opposition, open the door to an explicit discussion of gendered behaviours as valued, but judged, social constructs.

In the current political climate in the United States, border crossing is a central topic and one which is much discussed and debated. Because of this, combined as it is for many with personal experiences of border crossings both political and cultural, it is possible to utilize the metaphor of border crossing easily in the classroom. Once we have established, as briefly described above and discussed further below, the idea that gendered behaviour is enculturated rather than innate, students frequently ask why we do not then change that behaviour when it is not to the benefit of those performing it. This is a perfect opportunity to begin the discussion of the social policing which is such a central part of the development and maintenance of, among other social behaviours, gender. This discussion draws on the points made in earlier classes about the intrinsic value of social practice. I can also utilize students' pre-existing understandings of the consequences of unauthorized border crossings at the international borders, and of the difficulties of assimilating behaviour to different cultural norms once a border has been crossed, as another tool in conveying to them the serious nature of the consequences that are brought to bear upon those who defy social expectations in the realm of gender. During this section of class, students complete readings which combine the border-creating effects of bilingualism and genderlects as a way of allowing them to view gender as border in 'the other'. I then provide opportunities for students to discuss times when language has been a barrier for them and, finally, instances when linguistic behaviours they can now identify as gendered have created borders in their lives.

One place where the social consequences of gendered linguistic behaviour play out clearly is in corporate America. For example, Yancy Martin has explored the ways in which gendered behaviour plays out in the workplace and the consequences of attempting to subvert expected norms. She relies on the construct of 'accountability' in order to explain the mechanism by which both men and women are channelled into appropriate behaviours. 'Accountability pressures prompt people to do gender appropriate to the situation, rejecting a claim that "free will" in the form of unfettered choice – "wanting to" – is the reason people practice gender at work' (Yancy Martin, 2003: 358). For example, women often find themselves in the position of offering ideas in the form of a suggestion, rather than as a statement or order. This is in keeping with the suggestion that women are much more attuned to, and likely to avoid, face threat in conversation. Giving orders, or stating a plan without requesting input, can be extremely face-threatening in conversation; such behaviour gives no options, is highly impositional and makes explicit the power relationships in the conversation. By contrast, women are socialized into behaviours which avoid such threats by offering a suggestion in the form of a question or option, leaving the conversational door open to input from an interlocutor. In the workplace, such behaviour can be interpreted as weak and indecisive. What makes this situation such a double bind for women is that, in order to behave in ways that are workplace appropriate, they must behave in ways that are considered inappropriate for a woman. This border crossing is heavily policed, and women who code-switch to speech behaviours associated with masculinity are heavily critiqued; terms such as 'ball buster' and 'bitch' are reserved for this sort of behaviour. This policing can be understood in terms of the consequences of crossing an international border illegally; while such behaviour may have some beneficial consequences, in the form of higher wages and a better standard of living, the threat of punishment, legal or social, is ever present. In the corporate world, punishment can take the form of a slower rise through the ranks with a concomitant lower pay, fewer choice assignments, mistrust on the part of co-workers and so on. However, speaking in ways that perform normative gender can have the exact same consequences, although for different reasons; the situation is untenable.

During this section of class, students are encouraged to analyse their own work experience in light of these facts. I ask them to observe their workplace as anthropologists and to explore the dynamics they observe. Typically, students find that they have a clearer understanding of the causes of dynamics they had noticed before taking the class. They also begin to question the functionality of the border that is being so heavily policed, and to suggest ways to disrupt or dismantle it (the phrase, 'that's not fair!' is frequently uttered during this part of class). In this way, the use of border as a construct leads to a challenge to the border-creating nature of gender as typically practised in the workplace.

It is particularly interesting in such discussions to point out to students those areas in which the 'same' behaviour is interpreted very differently based on the gender of the person performing it. Male gossip is one such behaviour. Yancy Martin (2003) points out that when women stop to speak to one another in the halls, such action is assumed to be gossip, and is discounted as a consequence; in fact, it is not only devalued, but is used as evidence of female unsuitability for certain kinds of work due to their distractible nature and focus on petty interests. However, when Yancy Martin observed exactly the same kinds of behaviour on the part of men in the office, including standing in the halls to discuss golf or weekend activities, such behaviour was interpreted both by observers and the speakers themselves as 'networking' and, as such, as a valuable workplace behaviour designed to lead to future success. Cameron (1998) noticed the same disparity, not in behaviour but in the interpretation of behaviour, in her paper about young men whose conversation included all the hallmarks of gossip: a focus on the personal attributes of people not in the room (including a long discussion about the fashion sensibilities of one colleague) and a conversational style which included many cooperative behaviours in turn-taking and storytelling. These features were overlooked by the young man who originally recorded and analysed the conversation. In discussing these articles, I encourage students to relate them to formal observations conducted at various sites around campus. By completing an exercise such as this, students become adept at observing day-to-day interactions and at making explicit the ways in which the gendered identities of speakers bias interpretations of hearers, creating a well-policed social border that is difficult to challenge or cross.

By explicitly utilizing the metaphor of the border, the hegemony of masculine speech patterns and the policing of that realm of speech through the use of social sanctions thus become clearer. Students are able to see that, in the same way that we interpret cultural behaviours differently depending upon the identity of the performer, we apply different sorts of assumptions to cultural practice depending on the gender of the performer. By bringing these underlying assumptions to light, they are more easily examined, questioned and problematized. Students who have in the past questioned the sorts of cultural biases that lead people to believe that their form of cultural practice is the only appropriate way to approach a situation can see more clearly how to apply that same line of questioning to gendered behaviours which were previously understood to be innate rather than acquired. Making this connection between borders and gender explicit also allows students to understand why it is appropriate to understand gender as 'bordered', and provides for a clear discussion of those aspects of gendered behaviour which are hidden by this bordering practice, as well as those which are emphasized.

The final project for this class is designed to reinforce the understanding of gendered linguistic practice as a border. Students working in groups design a project which requires the gathering and analysis of real-world linguistic data in light of what they have learned. Projects have included: an examination of classroom participation and teacher management of that participation; an analysis of the gendered presentation of self in MySpace pages; children's behaviour on grade-school playgrounds and the policing of games and space in that context and many others. For students, this is often the first time they have been required to see the world around them as a source of analysable data, and the border construct gives them a way to organize and access that data. What is perhaps most intriguing is the way in which students use the border construct as a springboard to a more refined understanding of gender as a scalar and complex phenomenon, rather than the dichotomous construct implied by the border model.

Finally, pedagogical practice itself is gendered in powerful ways; this fact provides an important meta-level to classroom practice in this course. Until fairly recently, men have dominated the teaching profession, and have maintained that dominance into the higher levels of education through the end of the last century. Because of this dominance, male discourse patterns have been established as the norm for classroom behaviour; this acceptance is due not to the inherent superiority of such patterns for the purposes of pedagogy but, rather, to the prevalence of men in the classroom. These behaviours include, for example, a focus on one correct interpretation of texts and data, on the giving of facts by an expert and receiving of facts by an unparticipatory audience, a focus on impersonal data rather than a connection to students' anecdotal life experience and so on. Thus, the focus is on prototypical Gricean communication, rather than on any concerns with the relative social standing or 'face' of participants.

Women bring very different social expectations, both of their students and of themselves, to the classroom as teachers and, therefore, are inclined to behave differently; for example, students' life experiences can be taken as real-world examples of more generalized data-sets and mismatches between 'the average' and personal experience can be used as a springboard for discussion. In the same way, students' interpretations of text become relevant to the discussion. Rather than demanding that students produce an accepted interpretation, female teachers, based on their socialized gendered behaviours, are more likely to require of students that they engage with the text on a personal level and to use that interpretation as a comparison point to a more generally accepted understanding of the text. Note that this matches the sorts of gendered behaviours discussed above in that, by doing this, female teachers mitigate the face-threat inherent in a classroom situation in which one person is the authority and other discussants have no standing; by opening discussion up to an inclusion of students' interpretations, they offer options and can suggest alternatives to interpretation in ways that de-emphasize the power differential in the classroom. The assignments and discussions that are central to this class are examples of this alternative pedagogical paradigm in practice.

Interestingly, students often police this border themselves, by showing less respect for the teaching abilities and knowledge of those who avoid authoritarian pedagogical practice; because of its association with feminist theory, such teaching is often dismissed as unduly 'feminist' (calling to mind the prototype of a bra-burning, man-hating woman), even if the teacher is a man. As shown in the assignments described above, I frequently utilize strategies informed by both kinds of conversational styles, and have noted many times the discomfort students have with being required to approach a text from their own perspective, rather than being told what they should be getting from it, as well as with working with data they have gathered themselves. But, at the end of one semester of teaching language and gender in this way, a number of students suddenly came to the realization that classroom behaviour is itself gendered and that their discomfort with an alternative pedagogical style was a reflection of their own socialization as gendered beings. By leading students to this understanding, the teacher affords them the opportunity of understanding themselves as border crossers, able to view their discomfort with the creation of a liminal classroom space as an opportunity to challenge their notions of 'appropriate' and 'immutable'. Thus, classroom praxis itself becomes a source of data for students to analyze.

Case 2: land-use planning, gender and borders

Land-use planning, gender and borders are discussed within the introductory border and regional studies class, which all majors are required to take. The classes described below take place at the very end of the semester, when students can be expected to be capable of applying conceptual tools acquired earlier on the course. In these classes, learning about gendered borders is approached through the study of planning-related case studies and readings on, 1. Hurricane Katrina; and 2. suburban lifestyles.

Land-use planning is the set of decisions which determine how land will be used in a community – how it will be carved up and parcelled out for various uses such as factories, housing, commercial centres, etcetera, by neighbourhood, city, or region. In the United States and in most developed countries, land use is highly regulated by zoning and other policies which dictate how particular pieces of land can be used. Planning agencies or departments commensurate with each geographic level of planning are tasked with employing the zoning and policies of that area. This kind of planning requires physical, on-the-ground, line-on-the-map borders, which are always decided by political means and only sometimes relate to genuine physical phenomena such as rivers or mountain ranges.

In most local communities in the United States, there are distinct physical/political borders between places like cities and counties. These divisions, which have legal designations and can be drawn out on a map or walked in the streets, enable the work of planning. Nowhere are these jurisdictional boundaries in higher relief than at international borders. For example, the region in which our university is located has been variously called the San Diego–Tijuana transnational area or border region, yet on the ground the planning and policies which have shaped San Diego and Tijuana have resulted in two contiguous cities which look very different from each other.

For a land-use planner, using a border prototype to teach students about gender provides for a dimension of learning and teaching that scholarly training in land-use planning might otherwise leave unacknowledged. In the world-view of the planner, borders are physical and political entities between countries and between the cities, counties and neighbourhoods for which we facilitate planning. Planners do not often invoke the idea of a border as a metaphor. However, as the border prototype can help us to see, this narrow view of land-use planning can leave much of what makes a community a place unexamined. The border prototype discussed above provides planning scholars with what we might otherwise miss in our principal focus on physical borders, communities and policy: a systematic framework for discussing the conceptual borders in our communities.

As would be expected, gendered relationships do affect general planning efforts. One of the attributes of the border prototype is that physical borders are the result of political negotiation. This is also true of community land-use plans, which are always being negotiated, written, adopted, renegotiated and rewritten, whether or not any given individual chooses to participate. This raises the question of who negotiates plans for any given community. Historically, it is not unusual for a male paradigm to drive human communities: see, for example, the linguistic exploration of genderlects and workplace sensibilities described above in this chapter. In the planning negotiations for a community, do men typically have a greater voice, as part of the dominant paradigm, and to the detriment of women's and children's participation and potential contributions? In order to explore this question, we turn to planning case studies.

Hurricanes Katrina and Rita stirred, uprooted and turned upside down the cauldron of race, gender and class along the Gulf Coast of the United States and in particular in New Orleans, Louisiana, in late August 2005. In order to appreciate this, students read *The Women of New Orleans and the Gulf Coast: Multiple Disadvantages and Key Assets for Recovery, Part 1. Poverty, Race, Gender, and Class*, by Barbara Gault et al. According to Gault, among the many heartbreaking legacies of the hurricanes are the differential impacts of the storm by gender:

> The women in the three metropolitan areas devastated by Hurricanes Katrina and Rita, like many women in the South, face multiple disadvantages, all of which must be understood in developing effective services and economic development strategies in the region. They are more likely to be poor and to lack health insurance and less likely to earn good wages than women elsewhere in the United States. They are also disproportionately African American and experience discrimination based on both race and sex. (Gault et al., 2005: 1)

As with all of the readings for the course, students answer in advance of class a 'reading response question' (RRQ) which is designed to spur them to think critically about the topic under discussion. In class, they are allowed to correct and add to their answer, in order to create multiple points of engagement with the material. For this particular reading, the RRQ asks them to describe the status of women's lives pre- and post-Katrina.

In class, we discuss (and to some extent, I lecture on) how New Orleans before Katrina contained neighbourhoods of entrenched female poverty and disempowerment. In many neighbourhoods, well before the storms blew through them, women faced different and greater barriers than men. When Katrina neared New Orleans, those who could fled the city by any means available. Those who could not flee stayed behind and suffered up close the flooding, horror and death witnessed on TV screens around the world. Eventually they become part of a second exodus from the city, as residents were dispersed all over the United States. They travelled from city to city, or were placed in US Federal Emergency Management Agency trailer parks in rural areas, and left to their own devices to reconstruct their lives. Families were scattered and had difficulty communicating, supporting and regrouping with each other. Women were forced out of their long-term familial and social support systems, and settled in sometimes randomly selected places. They left behind the physical boundaries of their gender, race and class in their New Orleans neighbourhoods, but assuredly the fact that they were female, impoverished and disempowered remained with them. They may have escaped the physical borders of their damaged neighbourhoods, but not the conceptual borders within which they existed. In fact, these conceptual borders of gender, race and class status became the dominant paradigm of their lives as they struggled to re-establish themselves amongst the limited employment and housing opportunities available to displaced lower-income workers, their situation further exacerbated by their outsider, gender and minority status (see Jones-DeWeever and Hartmann, 2006).

A second assignment designed to promote further understanding of the complex condition of women post-Katrina involved the use of director Spike Lee's documentary on the aftermath of Hurricane Katrina in New Orleans, *When the Levees Broke: A Requiem in Four Acts* (2006). One of the threads of learning which runs throughout the introductory border studies class is the use of oral history and narrative better to understand human interaction within border regions. Lee's documentary consists of a series of oral histories in which various residents, government officials and experts discuss the time period shortly before Katrina made landfall, the aftermath of the levees breaking in New Orleans and the ways in which residents' lives were affected. The sum total of the oral histories is a powerful narrative on race, class and gender in the United States. Many women are interviewed in the documentary and a complex portrait of their status emerges. We watch the documentary in class and I stop it at various points to allow students to discuss the questions it raises.

This viewing, along with an article on my own visit to New Orleans post-Katrina (Knowles-Yánez, 2007), then become launching points to discuss the way in which some women, as they returned to New Orleans, faced even more barriers created by their gender. The RRQ for my article requires students to consider the obstacles returning residents faced and come to class prepared to discuss them. In the Lower 9th Ward, one of the areas most devastated by the post-Katrina flooding, women who returned did so to virtually deserted neighbourhoods. Most of the area's previous inhabitants are now residents elsewhere, with little hope of returning to a place devoid of job prospects and without operable schools. Physically, the neighbourhoods have been decimated and there is very little habitable housing.

Most of the housing and retail stores, if not bulldozed and hauled away, are boarded up and empty. In fact, many land-use and community plans have been made for redeveloping the neighbourhoods and retail areas but, two years later, virtually nothing had actually been put into place due to lack of funding and a powerful bureaucratic gridlock.

When women do manage to return and start to rebuild, they do so in neighbourhoods where their old social support systems, including their extended families, are most often no longer in existence, due to the lack of habitable homes. The brave returners are thus often alone, and a woman alone is a vulnerable target and faces grave safety issues. In discussing the border prototype, we note that women typically do not have the same freedom of circulation as men: within the physical environment of their communities, women and men have differing needs. For example, women's safety concerns may not allow them to walk alone at night in areas seen as unsafe, though men may roam freely in the very same places. This greater freedom of circulation gives men access to a wider range of physical places and opportunities in their communities. In terms of land use, women must put themselves at greater risk in order to avail themselves of these same places and opportunities. When their neighbourhoods are ruinous and deserted, they face greater dangers simply by returning to them, issues of poverty, employment, housing and schools withstanding.

It seems that these women have entered the border prototype's characteristic empty space and become a kind of outcast group, even more 'peripheral to the national space', even more voiceless than before. Looking at this extreme example of how land use contributes to the isolating of women's voices provides an opportunity for students to consider how women in their own communities may be constrained behind barriers/borders of race and class and similarly left voiceless behind a gendered border, for these inequities can be found anywhere. Teasing apart the implications of gender, borders, disaster and community planning in the extreme and heart-wrenching example of the hurricanes of 2005 provides a platform from which to begin exploring these issues in a more general and personal way in students' own lives.

In the introductory border studies class, the Katrina–Rita discussion is followed by a general exploration of how land use and housing in the United States bear implications for understanding gendered borders and, particularly, women's lives. I encourage students to talk about their own kinds of housing, both now and what they grew up with. Here, existing planning literature can be helpful in that it includes some explorations of housing and gender, though, as Fainstein and Servon note, 'For most of the history of planning the subject of gender differences was invisible' (2005: 1). Reflecting on the spatial parameters of consumer shaped households in the United States, Dolores Hayden, for example, asks

> How does a conventional home serve the employed woman and her family? Badly. Whether it is in a suburban, exurban, or inner-city neighborhood, whether it is a split-level ranch house, a modern masterpiece of concrete and glass, or an old brick tenement, the house or apartment is almost invariably organized around the same set of spaces: kitchen, dining room, living room, bedrooms, garage, or parking area. These spaces require someone to undertake private cooking, cleaning, child-care, and usually private transportation if adults and children are to exist within it. Because of residential zoning practices, the typical dwelling will usually be physically removed from any shared community space – no commercial or communal daycare facilities, or laundry facilities, for example, are likely to be part of the dwelling's spatial domain. (Hayden, 2005: 50)

Again, students are asked to complete an RRQ which in this case asks them to compare and contrast their or their mother's lives with the portrait drawn by Hayden. In class, we find that students often respond strongly to Hayden's account of how women's identities are shaped by their housing, so that they are forced to become cooks, cleaners, child care experts, etcetera. This example of gendered borders is very salient for our students because it is what so many of them have grown up with. Multiple processes work to exclude women's voices from shaping the larger culture, in much the same way as the operations of border negotiations. Physical borders are demarcated by linguistic, class and/or ethnic differences, parallel to the culture of masculinity and femininity which demarks conceptual gender borders. In the mix of conceptual communities made up of people who speak different languages and are of different social classes and ethnicity, gender plays a very large role. For example, in the United States, the culture of femininity and masculinity usually results in the mother, not the father, being the one chosen to stay home to care for young children. This creates a group of women who lead relatively physically isolated lives in the suburbs as, during the daytime especially, they raise their children virtually alone and with little help.

Why, then, do people live in conventional suburban households? The most common answer, well understood by our students, is the perceived convenience and safety of the suburban lifestyle, an answer which neatly feeds approbation for continuation of the same kinds of suburban building policies currently common in the United States. Yet examining this prototype of the suburb reveals the concealed limitations it imposes on women's potential in much the same way as examining the prototype of the border reveals issues of safety, access, education and their unequal effects on men's and women's lives.

The border prototype includes walls and guards, with references to barbed wire. In terms of conceptual gender borders, this barbed wire is what works to keep women women and men men. The social price of not remaining a feminine woman or a masculine man is often too high to risk crossing the barbed wire of gender communities. Land-use planning often works to reinforce the barbed wire by 'trapping' women into specific roles in their community, where other roles might be more desirable. A woman's personal development might require access to a significant amount of interaction with other humans, in education and child care, for example, yet location in a suburb tends to isolate the individual from these development opportunities through its distance from a city's resources.

Indeed, the American suburb is an ideal setting for socialization into the culture of femininity. It shapes opportunities, or the lack thereof, for women. Suburban mothers who want or need to work part-time to help support their families, for example, find that they have to take on jobs for which they are overqualified, and in which they are uninterested, because so few posts are available in their area. College-educated women become lunch-hour monitors at their children's elementary schools, or take jobs at daycare centres, positions for which they are overqualified and which have no opportunities for advancement. Personal enrichment may occur, depending on the mother's state of mind, but at best such jobs are seen but as holding patterns and socialization opportunities, of little use on their résumés should they desire to return to the careers for which they were trained.

Thus the apparently innocuous suburb masks difficulties which disproportionately affect women. Unveiling the barriers it creates provides an excellent example of how teasing apart gendered borders helps us to understand better the practice and effects of land-use planning because it provides genuine insight into women's lives. Planning literature is moving in the direction of better understanding women's issues in different land-use settings. This movement, in turn, can also inform understanding of women in the particular geographic or conceptual spaces and borders of their lives, and provide in the classroom illuminating examples for students seeking to understand the world in terms of a gender border prototype. Overall, the border prototype is a useful tool for understanding more clearly the faceted nature of the social construction of the surrounding world.

Conclusions

A rigorous understanding of the interplay and meanings of physical and conceptual borders has come to play an important role in strengthening our nascent border studies programme. Indeed, the rigour with which we apply the border prototype to the construct of gender also carries over into our discussions and understandings of borders and communities of ethnicity, race and social class. In particular, we have found an application of the prototype of 'border' to the boundary-creating social construct of gender useful in two ways. First, it allows us to tie together a number of disparate social phenomena in a way that is useful pedagogically for engaging students in the complex of behaviours which take place around borders, and which are themselves the creators of borders. Furthermore, it explains clearly to students why it is that these behaviours are so frequently referred to as borders, by applying rigour to that use of the term and by explicating the features of these phenomena that the term highlights, as well as those aspects which are hidden. This technique provides for lively and meaningful classroom discussions, which are at the heart of what we are trying to accomplish with our students. As students engage in examination of their own notions of conceptual and physical communities via the gendered border prototype, they build a repertoire of tools with which to examine the world around them creatively and critically and prepare for the jobs and roles awaiting them in this era of globalization.

Bibliography

Brown, Penelope (1998). 'How and why are women more polite: some evidence from a Mayan community', in Jennifer Coates (ed.), *Language and Gender: A Reader*, Oxford: Blackwell.

Brown, Penelope and Steve Levinson (1987). *Politeness: Some Universals in Language Use*, Cambridge: Cambridge University Press.

Butler, Judith (2001). *Gender Trouble: Feminism and the Subversion of Identity*, New York: Routledge.

Caldwell, Alicia A. (2007). 'US border fence protrudes into Mexico', *The Washington Post*, 29 June, accessed on 10 August 2007 at *ttp://www.washingtonpost.com/wp-dyn/content/article/2007/06/29/AR200706 2901686.html*

Cameron, Deborah (1998). 'Performing gender identity: young men's talk and the construction of heterosexual masculinity', in Jennifer Coates (ed.), *Language and Gender: A Reader*, Oxford: Blackwell.

Eckert, Penelope and Sally McConnell-Ginet (2006). *Language and Gender*, Cambridge: Cambridge University Press.

Fainstein, Susan S. and Lisa J. Servon (2005). 'Introduction', in Susan S. Fainstein and Lisa J. Servon (eds), *Gender and Planning: A Reader*, New Brunswick, NJ: Rutgers University Press.

Gault, Barbara, Heidi Hartmann, Avis Jones-DeWeever, Misha Werschkul and Erica Williams (2005). *The Women of New Orleans and the Gulf Coast: Multiple Disadvantages and Key Assets for Recovery, Part 1. Poverty, Race, Gender, and Class*, Washington, DC: Institute for Women's Policy Research.

Grice, Paul (1975). 'Logic and conversation', in Peter Cole and Jerry Morgan (eds), *Syntax and Semantics III: Speech Acts*, New York: Academic Press.

Hayden, Dolores (2005). 'What would a nonsexist city look like?', in Susan S. Fainstein and Lisa J. Servon (eds), *Gender and Planning: A Reader*, New Brunswick, NJ: Rutgers University Press.

Holmes, Janet (1998). 'Women's talk: the question of sociolinguistic universals', in Jennifer Coates (ed.), *Language and Gender: A Reader*, Oxford: Blackwell.

Jones-Deweever, Avis A. and Heidi Hartmann (2006). 'Abandoned before the storms: the glaring disaster of gender, race, and class disparities in the Gulf', in Chester Hartman and Gregory D.

Squires (eds), *There is No Such Thing as a Natural Disaster: Race, Class, and Hurricane Katrina*, New York: Routledge.

Knowles-Yánez, Kimberley (2007). 'The disappearing neighborhood: an urban planner's tour of New Orleans', in Kristin A. Bates and Richelle S. Swan (eds), *Through the Eye of Katrina: Social Justice in the United States*, Durham, NC: Carolina Academic Press.

Lakoff, George (1993). 'The contemporary theory of metaphor', in Andrew Ortony (ed.), *Metaphor and Thought*, Cambridge: Cambridge University Press.

Lakoff, George and Mark Johnson (1980). *Metaphors We Live By*, Chicago: University of Chicago Press.

Lakoff, Robin (1975). *Language and Woman's Place*, New York: Harper and Row.

——(1990). *Talking Power: The Politics of Language*, New York: Basic Books.

Lee, Spike (2006). *When the Levees Broke: A Requiem in Four Acts*, Home Box Office.

MacLaury, Robert (1991). 'Prototypes revisited', *Annual Review of Anthropology*, 20, 55–74.

Rosch, Eleanor (1973). 'Natural categories', *Cognitive Psychology*, 4, 328–50.

——(1975). 'Family resemblances: studies in the internal structure of categories', *Cognitive Psychology*, 7, 573–605.

——(1978). 'Principles of categorization', in E. Rosch and B. B. Lloyd (eds), *Cognition and Categorization*, Hillsdale, NJ: Lawrence Erlbaum Associates, 27–48.

Tannen, Deborah (1991). *You Just Don't Understand: Women and Men in Conversation*, New York: Ballantine Books.

——(1992). *That's Not What I Meant: How Conversational Style Makes or Breaks Relationships*, New York: Ballantine.

——(1994). *Gender and Discourse*, New York: Oxford University Press.

West, Candace and Don Zimmerman (1987). 'Doing gender', *Gender and Society*, 1, 13–37.

Yancy Martin, Patricia (2003). '"Said and done" versus "saying and doing": gendering practices, practicing gender at work', *Gender and Society*, 17, 3, 342–66.

Index